D1571200

PAGAN PRIESTS

PAGAN PRIESTS

Religion and Power in the Ancient World

edited by

Mary Beard and
John North

Cornell University Press

Ithaca, New York

First published 1990 Cornell University Press

Librarians: Library of Congress Cataloging-in-Publication Data
in process.

International Standard Book Number 0-8014-2401-1
Library of Congress Catalog Card Number 89-42954

Printed in Great Britain

Contents

Acknowledgments

The editors and publisher wish to thank the following for permission to reproduce photographs: British Museum (2, 7-12, 14-19, 22 left, 29); Robin Cormack (26, 27); Egypt Exploration Society (13); Fitzwilliam Museum, Cambridge (3, 22 right, 28, 30); German Archaeological Institute, Rome (1, 5, 6, 31); Louvre (4); Erika Simon (21).

Thanks are also due to Richard Gordon and Keith Hopkins, for their readiness to offer comments and criticisms; to Terry Volk, for generous instruction in numismatic material; to Michael Crawford, for finding time in Rome to locate photographs; to the Geography Department of University College London, for preparing the maps; and to Patricia Woods and the secretarial staff of the Classics Faculty, University of Cambridge, for retyping half the book from one word-processing system to another.

Contributors

Mary Beard	Lecturer in Classics, University of Cambridge; Fellow of Newnham College
Robert Garland	Professor of Classics, Colgate University, New York
Richard Gordon	Senior Lecturer in European Studies, University of East Anglia
James Hooker	Reader in Greek and Latin, University College London
Amélie Kuhrt	Reader in Ancient History, University College London
John North	Senior Lecturer in Ancient History, University College London
Dorothy J. Thompson	Fellow of Girton College, Cambridge

Illustrations

Figures

Tables

Maps and diagrams

Abbreviations

Where possible, abbreviations follow standard conventions. The titles of Greek and Latin texts (if abbreviated) are cited according to the conventions of the *Oxford Classical Dictionary* (2nd edition, ed. N.G.L. Hammond), as are major works of reference on the Greek and Roman world. For titles of classical journals, the abbreviations are those of *L'année philologique*. For publications of papyri, we follow the abbreviations of J.F. Oates etc, *Checklist of editions of Greek papyri and ostraca* (3rd edition, BASP supp. 4, 1985). Near Eastern works are cited according to the conventions of *The Chicago Assyrian Dictionary*.

In addition, note the following:

BMC = *British Museum Catalogue of Coins of the Roman Empire* (London, 1923-)

I. Didyma = T. Wiegand, *Didyma* II, Die Inschriften (ed A. Rehm, Berlin, 1958)

I. Stratonikeia = M.C. Şahin, *Die Inschriften von Stratonikeia* (Bonn, 1981-)

IRT = J.M. Reynolds and J. B. Ward Perkins, *Inscriptions of Roman Tripolitania* (Rome and London, 1952)

Inscr. Cr = M. Guarducci, *Inscriptiones Creticae* (Rome, 1935-50)

Inscriptiones Italiae = *Inscriptiones Italiae* (Rome, 1931-)

LSA = F. Sokolowski, *Lois sacrées de l'Asie Mineure* (Paris, 1955)

LSG = F. Sokolowski, *Lois sacrées des cités grecques* (Paris 1969)

Meiggs, Lewis, *GHI* = R. Meiggs and D. Lewis, *A Selection of Greek Historical Inscriptions to the end of the fifth century BC* (Oxford, 1969)

PP = W. Peremans and E. Van't Dack, *Prosopographica Ptolemaica* (Louvain, 1950-)

RIC= H. Mattingly and E.A. Sydenham, *The Roman Imperial Coinage* (London, 1923-)

RRC = M.H. Crawford, *Roman Republican Coinage* (Cambridge, 1974)

Sammlung v Aulock = *Sylloge Nummorum Graecorum* (Germany: Sammlung von Aulock, 1957-)

TThZ = *Trierer theologische Zeitschrift*

Tod, *GHI* = M.N. Tod, *A Selection of Greek Historical Inscriptions* II (Oxford, 1948)

for
Robin Cormack
and
Helen Weston

Introduction

Mary Beard and John North

Pagan priests are surprisingly familiar in the modern world. Film and fiction offer images of ritual killing and magic; they tell stories of doom-laden prophecies and the seduction of virgin priestesses. There is, of course, a tendency to overemphasise the lurid; but the picture as a whole is by no means a modern invention. We know, for example, of several precise occasions on which the Roman authorities buried alive virgin priestesses, who they believed had broken their vow of chastity. This punishment was a horrible event; and indeed one writer of the second century AD tells us of the fearful reaction of the Roman crowd who watched it: 'All the people silently make way for the litter (carrying the priestess) and follow it without uttering a sound, in a terrible depression of spirit. No other spectacle is more appalling, nor does any other day bring more gloom to the city than this' (Plutarch, *Life of Numa* 10).

This book puts some of these lurid details in their historical context. It explores the activities and functions of priestly officials in various societies in the Mediterranean and the Near East – Babylon, Greece, Egypt and Rome – in the two thousand years before the rise of Christianity. Our aim has not been to produce a complete general theory of pagan priesthood, applicable to all these very different times and places; but we have tried to seek out common characteristics of priests in these ancient societies and so to gain a better understanding of the nature of pagan priesthood as a whole.

The reader will be struck first of all by the fact that pagan priests are quite unlike their modern Christian counterparts. The priestly officials discussed in this volume bear no significant resemblance to the comforting image of the wise Christian pastor, guiding his flock through the spiritual perils of the world: they did not play the part (at least officially) of moral leaders; they were not involved with a congregation which looked to them for advice and guidance. In political terms too ancient pagan priests seem distinctively different. Unlike the priests of Christianity and other modern world religions, who can communally wield power independently of (and sometimes in opposition to) the established political power in the state, pagan priests never (or only in exceptional circumstances) stood apart from the political order. There is hardly a sign of that – to us – familiar clash

1

between 'church' and 'state', between priestly interests and the
dominant political hierarchy.

More difficult to define are the positive common features of pagan
religious officials; but two important points concerning the division
and differentiation of religious tasks are clear enough at the outset.
First, even in the very simplest of the societies considered in this book,
religious duties were highly specialized: the function, for example, of
anointing the statue of the god was carefully distinguished from that of
bearing the god's image in procession; the task of producing oracular
responses was quite distinct from that of performing the rituals of war.
Religion and its various duties had a complex and highly differentiated
structure. The second point tends in the opposite direction. For,
although the religious tasks themselves were apparently closely
defined, they were not normally assigned to specialist full-time
practitioners. Most religious officials in the ancient world combined
priestly duties with other occupations. This was the case at all levels of
society: peasant farmers or blacksmiths, say, might play their part as
flute players or ritual water carriers; the major magistrates of the
state would also function as priests of the major deities. In this sense
priestly power was strikingly undifferentiated; it was embedded
within the social and political order.

In the rest of this introduction, we discuss particular problems our
contributors have faced in their attempt to generalize about the
category of priest in the individual societies with which they are
concerned: how far the word 'priest' itself is an appropriate starting
place for the analysis of ancient religious officials; how far ancient
priesthood can be understood in terms of any general modern theory of
priesthood; what particular functions in these societies – for example,
sacrifice or mediation between men and gods – can be identified as
distinctively *priestly* functions; what it is that distinguishes priests
from other kinds of religious officials. All these questions, from their
different angles, help us to focus more sharply on particular
characteristics widely, if not universally, shared among pagan priests.

Priesthood and the problems of language

In investigating priesthood in different ancient societies, our
contributors have had to assemble basic information from scattered
and heterogeneous sources. No surviving ancient writer provides a
general analysis of priesthood; nor is it likely that any such analysis
ever existed. And even those antiquarian texts that did, no doubt,
describe the details of ritual and priestly duty are preserved only in
fragments. Simply to reconstruct the duties of an office or the
qualifications for joining a particular group of religious officials
involves in most cases scouring a wide range of sources – not just

specifically historical texts, but also poetry, inscriptions, legal texts, political speeches and surviving fragments of papyri. The assembling of this information is already in itself a useful achievement.

Even in this preliminary task, the problem of language has been acute. Books about the ancient world present the priest as a universal figure, whether in early Egypt, Babylonian cities, archaic Greece or imperial Rome. This one element remains constant whatever the other titles or offices in the community – 'pharaohs', 'kings', 'archons' or 'emperors'. In fact, this seeming constancy is quite illusory; it results entirely from the habit of modern writers. They make careful distinctions in translation between different political offices; but when they come to an equally varied range of titles for religious offices they are content with the single word 'priest'. Two unargued assumptions underlie this general use of the term 'priest'. First of all it treats offices in many different periods and societies as if they were broadly equivalent; secondly it presupposes that these offices were specifically religious offices. But it is precisely these assumptions that need re-examination, if we are to gain any proper understanding of the nature of ancient priesthood. For different societies make different distinctions between types of official concerned with cult and religion, and they define what is religious and what are religious officials in their own particular ways. The risk is that the unargued decision to translate any given title by the word 'priest' not only involves imposing our own categories, but also may obscure from us the distinctive nature of that official's role in his own society.

All the contributions in this book raise one or another aspect of this set of problems. They try to define the nature of those traditionally called 'priests' in particular communities and in so doing they cumulatively raise the issue of whether there is any common core of similarity which would justify the use of the single English term 'priest'. This problem arises in its most acute form with the Mycenaean tablets of the thirteenth and twelfth centuries BC, where we have only a limited number of very difficult texts whose interpretation, even in the most general sense, is a matter of dispute. For it is clear that the decision to translate *karawiporo* (literally 'key bearer') as 'priestess' rather than, say, 'cult servant' (or even 'warder') makes a huge difference to our understanding of the situations and roles concerned: as a 'priestess' she seems dignified, important and 'religious'; as a 'warder', a low-grade functionary. In other cases, such as the Roman *sacerdos* or Greek *hiereus*, the difficulty may be concealed by the greater availability of information about the institution and its social context; but nevertheless the same problems of definition need to be faced.

The underlying point must be that priestly activity (as we would automatically or unthinkingly call it) in these pagan societies is undertaken by many more people than the obvious 'priests'; while those 'priests' also perform functions that we would not readily call 'priestly'. This is more than a simple problem of definition. It involves the whole function of priesthood and how that should be characterized or, indeed, recognized. In practice the contributors to this book have adopted different strategies in their identification of priestly activity in the societies concerned; but they have all sought to deal with this central problem.

Theories of priesthood

The diversity of approach in this book is partly to be explained by the fact that no adequate general theory of priesthood exists. Individual religions, of course, have their theories; but these only operate successfully within the system for which they were designed and from which they derive. At the broad cross-cultural level there is no agreed theory, still less a set of rival theories, which could provide a framework for understanding religious roles across a wide spectrum of ancient societies.

The most basic and broadest questions are raised in the work of Max Weber, who formulated a universal conception of priesthood, not restricted to any one society. In this he explicitly recognized that the defining features of priesthood were themselves a problem in view of 'the diverse and mixed manifestations of this phenomenon'. Weber's discussion of priesthood has been influential in many areas of religious history, but is problematic when applied to the ancient world.

Weber characterized priests essentially by means of establishing a contrast with other groups of religious officials – particularly magicians and prophets. Following the accepted views of the time (derived from Frazer and others) he saw the principal role of the magician as the *coercion* of the deity by formula and ritual; this he contrasted with the role of the priest who *entreats* the deity through prayer and sacrifice. He saw this contrast in terms of the development of a new concept of the divine: as the gods became all-powerful overlords rather than just supernatural powers subject to human manipulation, so activities of the human practitioners changed from magic to cult. It is within cult rather than magic that other features particularly associated with the ideal type of priesthood developed: association with a fixed cultic centre, the possession of doctrine or vocational qualifications, the operation of priests as functionaries of some social group rather than as individuals, isolated and 'self-employed'.

In drawing a contrast between prophets and priests Weber laid the greatest stress on the personal call or charisma of the prophet. While the priest derives his authority from the traditional office which he holds, the prophet, like the magician, exerts his power simply by virtue of his personal gifts. The prophet, relying on support from the laity, characteristically attacks the traditional order of which the priests are the guardians and transmitters. A struggle for power ensues in which either the prophet succeeds in establishing his new order or the priests (by reaching a compromise with the prophetic claims or by successfully reasserting the validity of the traditional code) emerge again as dominant. In a sense this recurrent conflict between priest and prophet is seen by Weber as a cause of religious and (consequently) social change, with the prophet serving as a breakthrough to a higher stage of religious development

Unfortunately this powerful scheme provided little help with the particular problems we have faced in discussing the priesthoods of the pagan world of Near Eastern and Graeco-Roman antiquity. The distinction between magicians and priests in particular is an unproductive one: first because it is based on largely discredited nineteenth-century theories of magic as a precursor to real religion; secondly because the distinction between coercive and non-coercive relations with the gods does not help us to classify the different kinds of religious officials we meet in the ancient world. In fact, most of them enjoy both, supposedly alternative, types of relations with the gods. The distinction between prophet and priest is a more helpful one; yet it is a distinction which has found a place only at the very margins of our subject where the pagan world with which we are basically concerned meets prophetic Christianity. Ancient pagan priesthoods exist within and outside the poles set by Weber's magician and Weber's prophet.

Weber was (and remains) unusual in offering a theoretical interpretation of the category of priesthood as a whole; his scheme may be inappropriate to the problem of pagan priesthood in the ancient world, but he was at least attempting cross-cultural generalization against which the role of individual functionaries in different societies might be assessed. More recent anthropological studies have tended to concern themselves with the priests and the cult officials of particular societies – and societies, by and large, where religious practitioners are easily identifiable and easily differentiated from their political counterparts. However important these studies have been – in investigating, for example, the social status of Buddhist temple priests or their changing relations with Indian government authorities – they do not raise the particular problems of identification that the contributors to this volume have had to face.

Anthropological studies of individual societies do occasionally show passing recognition of the underlying problems of the definition of priesthood and priestly authority; but even here the implications of that recognition are not followed through. A clear example of this is provided in Evans-Pritchard's famous series of studies of the religion

and society of the Nuer, a tribe of the southern Sudan. In *Nuer
Religion*, one of the later studies in the series, he discusses the figure of
the *kuaar twac*, whom he calls the 'Leopard-Skin *Priest*' (*twac* =
'leopard skin'). He admits, in the course of this discussion, that in his
previous work on the social life of the Nuer he had followed the colonial
government of the Sudan in designating these characters 'Leopard-
Skin *Chiefs*', and he justifies at some length his change of practice: his
earlier usage had been chosen to avoid needless incompatibility with
local government records and also to reflect the political significance of
the *kuaar twac* in Nuer Society; the later usage was adopted as more
appropriate for a study of Nuer *religion* and a more accurate
description of a functionary who lacked any real authority and who
enjoyed a political role only through the exercise of religious functions.
He spends some time discussing the issue of nomenclature, yet it never
apparently occurred to him that our exclusive categories of 'priest' or
'chief' are simply not appropriate in the politico-religious world of the
Nuer. He persists in seeing the issue in terms of a straightforward
choice between the title of 'priest' or 'chief', although his own
treatment of the functions of the *kuaar twac* implies that neither
description is really adequate. This particular combination of acute
observation and lack of interest in the overall problem of priesthood
itself suggests the absence of a framework of cross-cultural discussion
of the nature and role of priestly activity.

Our contributors have explored many of these general issues, and
particularly the overlap between religious and political power in their
various ancient societies. They have tried, on the one hand, to draw out
the implications of a system in which priestly power was embedded
within the political order; and on the other, to identify what functions
might still be regarded as distinctively priestly, outside the attractive,
but inapplicable, scheme offered by Weber. In doing this they have
broken new ground.

The Graeco-Roman city-state: priesthood, politics and mediation

The first three chapters in this book are concerned with the relatively
familiar world of the Graeco-Roman city state – the cases of
fifth-century Athens and the Roman Republic. Here, despite the
patchiness of the ancient evidence, we have a fairly clear
understanding of the historical and social context within which the
priests operated. This makes it possible to analyse the interrelationship of religious and political power in these societies and at
the same time has highlighted the need for a 'defining principle' to
isolate specifically priestly activity within the complex amalgam of
public life in the classical city. One particular line of approach is

discussed in these first papers and recurs later in the book: that is, to propose the function of *mediating between men and gods* as one characteristic and defining function of ancient pagan priesthood.

The religious life of the classical city-state – of Athens or Rome, for example – would strike the modern observer as unfamiliar and alien. Most difficult to intuit would be the lack of any clear formal division between religion and politics. Of course, even in modern western society that division can sometimes be fluid: in Britain, for example, bishops sit in the House of Lords and comment on matters of politics, and in the USA issues such as prayers in schools can become part of a presidential electoral platform. Yet most of us, most of the time, know (and agree) where Church ends and State begins. This is quite unlike the classical city-state, where the overlap between the spheres of religion and politics is evident both in institutions and office-holding and, in a rather more complex way, in the activity and authority of priests and politicians.

This fusion raises rather more complex issues when we come to think about the processes of religious decision-making and the nature of religious and political life. In fifth-century, democratic Athens the assembly of adult male citizens took all major religious decisions in the same way as secular decisions. In Rome the great public figures – Pompey, Caesar, Cicero, Antony – acted in our terms both as priests and politicians; and the senate, the major council of state, had to meet on consecrated ground. These are not accidental lapses or confusions in the system. They are indications, quite simply, that the city authorities dealt with gods as well as with men; that religion was not a separate department from politics.

The position of Julius Caesar in Rome – both his gaining of religious office and his activity within that office – illustrates the complexity well. Caesar became *pontifex maximus* (conventionally, if wrongly, translated 'chief priest') in 63 BC. He won this post – like any major office of the Roman state – as the result of a public election and he gained from his 'religious' success substantial political advantage in public life. But it is hard to be sure what is cause and what effect: his political career was aided by his attainment of major religious office; but then, conversely, his attainment of the office of *pontifex maximus* was itself aided by his political prominence. Later, during the 40s BC Caesar took action to reform the Roman calendar, traditionally within the competence of the pontifical college. On the one hand, his authority for this action must have derived from his, by now, political dominance at Rome; but on the other, his competence in these religious matters depended on his position as *pontifex maximus*. Probably no Roman would have thought to disentangle religious from political elements here; but for us it is largely because priestly authority is so embedded in political and social authority that the definition of priesthood is so problematic.

There are two obvious tactics for the modern observer faced with this complex fusion of religion and politics. The first is to accept it as it is presented and not attempt to disentangle what seem to us the quite separate elements of priestly and political authority; to emphasise, in other words, that the priestly function in the ancient city state was an element inextricably embedded in political life. In part, this is an appropriate method of approach and it is, in part, what our contributors have done. But on its own it is not sufficient. After all, however much religion and politics may be seen to have overlapped, they were not, in fact, identical spheres of operation: there were some aspects of political authority that were not conceivably priestly and some aspects of religious authority that were not simply an element of political life. Moreover, not every type of religious official – the man who cleared the temple gutters or the woman who carried the sacred water – could reasonably be called a priest. The second tactic then is to consider the question: what is it that priests *do* within a society that makes them priests? The answer to this question can then help to identify the individuals or groups which should be regarded as priestly; it can locate, in other words, the function of priesthood within the social and political organization of the city state.

More than one of the contributors have taken the function of mediating between gods and men as the defining characteristic of priesthood. This has the advantage of excluding from consideration mere religious functionaries – the cleaners and porters – and also removing from the picture those aspects of political life that have no real bearing on man's relations with the divine – taxation, for example, or voting practice. It enables us to see priestly functions as spreading well beyond those officials whom we would call 'priests', but not so diffused through the whole of society that the term 'priesthood' loses any specific force. At Rome, for example, we can see the group of priests known as augurs carrying out a mediating function – in marking out the ground, for example, from which it was permitted to watch for signs from the gods. But the major magistrates fulfilled a similar function – in actually watching for heavenly signs from the space marked out by the augurs; and, for some other categories of signs, it was the senate, not the priests, which regularly had the responsibility for judging which should be taken as true messages from the divine.

Mediation, however, involves its own problems of definition. It is clear enough that those concerned with the messages sent by the gods to men should be seen as mediators between humans and the divine; and that this function involved a relatively restricted group of people at Rome or in any city state. But one might also think of mediation in terms of conducting rituals, particularly animal sacrifice, that serve to link the spheres of gods and men. In this case mediation lacks any analytic precision: for while in Rome, for example, some priests and magistrates conducted sacrifices on behalf of the state, so also did fathers on behalf of their families, and even individuals on their own behalf. Indeed if we were to accept that mediation in this sense was the function of priesthood, we would be in the unhelpful (if not absurd) position of calling every Roman adult male a priest.

Mediation, as a term of analysis (especially when it is relatively restrictively defined), enables us to focus on priestly functions, whether fulfilled in contexts *we* would think of as religious, or whether apparently located in the political sphere; and so it has been used by several of our contributors. 'Mediation' on its own is not sufficient definitively to pinpoint 'priesthood' within the social and political structure of the ancient city; but it is useful as one tactic among several in isolating the priestly function.

Outside the city-state: priest and temple

The next three chapters in the book deal with societies – Hellenistic Egypt, sixth-century BC Babylon, Mycenaean Greece – which form no such homogeneous type as the city state; their social and religious organization is less well documented and their overall characteristics are, in any case, less well understood. It is not that we lack simple information on these societies – after all, literally millions of cuneiform documents survive from Mesopotamia, preserving letters, contracts and laws; it is rather that we lack any contemporary synoptic account of these societies to provide a context for the operation of priests. It follows that our analysis of priesthood must be conducted in a rather different way from that of the Graeco-Roman city state. No coherent survey can be offered of the position of priests or the priestly function within the overall social and political context of the society concerned.

Two particular methods of approach have been adopted. First, in the case of Mycenaean Greece, where we rely for almost all our information on a relatively restricted number of clay tablets, it is possible only to analyse the language of the documents; to look for those men and women who are stated to be active in relation to the gods; and to try to assess from the bare written evidence their religious, political and social position. Few definite conclusions emerge; but the very sparsity of the material highlights some of the major definitional problems that underlie most of the other contributions in this book. How, for example, can one define a priest within a vast range of different religious officials? How can one represent to our modern western understanding the complex ancient categories of religious functionary? Mycenaean Greece, in a sense, represents a limiting case for this crucial nexus of problems.

The second method of approach has been to concentrate on a single incident (or a series of incidents) where there is, by chance no doubt, some historical context for understanding the relationship between priestly authority and other forms of social and political power. It may not be possible to offer any broad synoptic view of the function of priesthood in these societies; but we can, at least, focus on individual occasions when the historical record (however inadequately, however briefly) allows us to construct some kind of narrative in which priests play a role. It is only such narratives that allow us to observe the activity of particular priests in relation to representatives of other forms of authority in the state – monarchs, royal or city officials, foreign rulers – and so to gain some notion of the extent and limits of priestly power. For both Babylon and Hellenistic Egypt, starting from a relatively narrow problem (for example, supposed priestly opposition to a particular monarch), our contributors have been able to propose certain more general conclusions about the nature of priestly power and its place in the organization of the state.

Despite the inadequacy of our information, the definitional problems surrounding priesthood seem at first sight easier to handle for the Near East and Egypt than for the Graeco-Roman city state. For the institution of the temple – a bounded area, devoted to gods or goddesses, with an elaborate hierarchy of officials – seems to offer at least a precise location for religious authority in the state. Unlike the Graeco-Roman city, where priestly operation was geographically diffused (as in every other sense), the cities of the Near East and Eygpt appear to have concentrated religious power in a specifically religious centre. If you want to find the priests, we may suppose, you should look in the temple. In fact the definition of priesthood in these societies proves not so simple as it might appear. The temples themselves were rather more complicated institutions than the apparently straightfor-ward notion of a separate religious centre immediately suggests. They incorporated a wider range of activities – for example, crafts, music-making and agricultural work – than we would automatically classify as religious; and they were integrated into the political and social life of their communities particularly as major landowners. It follows from this that among the many functionaries attached to the temple-complexes – the goldsmith, the singer, the oil presser – it is very hard to determine which should be seen as specifically religious and then, of these, which should be designated 'priests'; even harder to decide what the consequences of that designation might be. This has particular implications for the political analysis of temple-based societies. It has long been an established view that in the temples of Babylon, for example, there was a powerful and independent priesthood which could and did intervene in politics as the voice of religion. This can now be seen (as Kuhrt's paper suggests) as little more than a modern construction, based on Christianizing assumptions about the nature of the temples and of the priestly officials within them. A more plausible interpretation might be to see once again a complex interaction of religious and political authority, much as in the Graeco-Roman city state. The existence of a defined temple hierarchy certainly suggests additional criteria for the definition of priestly authority; but it does not necessarily imply that religious and priestly authority was sharply separate from political authority.

The Roman Empire: priest as sacrificer and the origins of Christian priesthood

The three last chapters take as their theme priesthood in the Roman Empire over the first two centuries or so of the Christian era. Here we might seem to be back in the more familiar world of Graeco-Roman antiquity; and in some senses we are. But the problem now is one of sheer size and diversity – for we are dealing not just with the innumerable local religious traditions in the vast expanse of Rome's conquered territory, but with their changing relations one with another. The Roman historians, of course, give us a context in which to understand religious development in the capital city itself, but they provide little help with any wider perspectives that concern the religions of the Empire as a whole – Druidism in Britain and Gaul, the traditional city cults of the Greek part of the Empire, the cult of Isis in Egypt and countless more. Even for Judaism and Christianity, where we have, of course, much richer material available, we are still faced with a problem when we try to define their relationship to other religious forms in the Empire. As Richard Gordon emphasises at the beginning of Chapter 8, there is no single subject (or even subjects) in the religions of the Roman Empire; there is only a vast profusion of different topics and sporadic, undigested information. Paradoxically the Roman Empire presents as difficult a problem in discussing the nature of priesthood as the much more remote and ill-documented societies of the Near East that we have just considered.

The approach to priesthood (and priesthoods) in the Roman Empire proposed in these last three essays is to focus, at least as a starting point, on the act of animal sacrifice and on its practitioners. This is not to treat sacrificers simply, and unsatisfactorily, as mediators between gods and men; but rather to explore the classic image of the ancient priest as a man or woman publicly engaged in sacrifice – it is to recognize, in other words, that, however complex and multifaceted the nature of priesthood was in the ancient world, it was commonly represented by the picture of a celebrant at sacrifice. This method of approach to the priestly function is no more comprehensive or definitive than the others we have outlined; but it is particularly useful in so far as it throws important light on a major development in priesthood during the early years of the Roman Empire. For it came to be the emperor, and only the emperor, who was ever represented on public official monuments as the celebrant of a sacrifice, and as such it was the emperor who monopolized also the public image of priesthood. It was not, needless to say, that the emperor was literally the only person to conduct sacrifice in the Roman Empire – hundreds and thousands of ordinary men and women must have performed the ritual; rather that he provided the paraded image of the sacrificer and the paraded example of priestly power to all other religious officials in the Empire. We can see this development partly in the context of the fusion between religion and politics, so typical of the ancient world: as the emperor appropriated to himself the major political functions in the state, so necessarily he took over the major priestly function.

The official state religion, as represented by the emperor, was by no means the only form of religious activity in the Roman Empire. Of particular interest, from the point of view of priesthood, was the variety of alternative religions – such as Mithraism or the cult of Isis – that became popular among certain groups at Rome and throughout the Roman world during the first two centuries AD. Most of these cults had much earlier roots and were in part the development of particular local cults in the empire; the cult of Isis, for example, had been traditional in the religion of Egypt. But the religious and political significance of these cults in Roman imperial society did not depend solely (or even largely) on their traditional, local origins, but on their function as alternatives to the official religion of the Roman Empire. In several crucial respects they set themselves apart from that state religion – in their practice of ritual initiation and of congregational worship, in their claims to salvation and in their, at first sight, very different kind of priesthood.

Priesthood in many of these new cults seems much more familiar to us than the priesthood of the Graeco-Roman city state – or of the Near Eastern temple societies. One description of a priest of Isis in Apuleius' novel *The Golden Ass* (written *c.* AD 160/170) immediately strikes a chord. The hero, an Isiac initiate who wishes himself to become a priest in the cult, is speaking:

> I frequently spoke of (becoming a priest) to the High Priest, begging him to intitiate me into the mysteries of the holy night. He was a grave man, remarkable for the strict observance of his religious duties, and checked my restlessness, as parents calm down children who are making unreasonable demands, but so gently and kindly that I was not in the least discouraged. He explained that the day on which a postulant might be initiated was always indicated by signs from the Goddess herself, and that it was she who chose the officiating priest and announced how the incidental expenses of the ceremony were to be paid. In his view I ought

to wait with attentive patience and avoid the extremes of overeagerness and obstinacy; being neither unresponsive when called nor importunate while awaiting my call. (*Golden Ass* 11, 21)

This introduces the idea not only of a priestly calling, but also of priestly kindliness and almost paternal care for those in his spiritual charge. Both of these elements are part of the traditional image of the Christian priest.

It has often been argued that many of the characteristic features of Christian worship and Christian priesthood are to be associated with these alternative cults in the Roman Empire, such as the cult of Isis. Christianity differed from these other alternative cults in the important (and dangerous) respect that it demanded *exclusive* commitment from its adherents; but it still seems to share with them a common tendency towards doctrines of morality and salvation, common ritual elements in, for example, initiation or baptism, and perhaps, a common opportunity for growth in the same range of social and political pressures. It can plausibly be argued that the immediately apparent similarity between Christian and Isiac priests is not fortuitous; it is, in fact, a reflection of the underlying similarity between the two cults.

In the last chapter in the book Gordon argues against any such view of the rise of Christianity and of the Christian type of priesthood. He bases his argument, once more, on the ritual of animal sacrifice and its practitioners. Apart from Christianity, all the alternative cults accepted the central position of the sacrificial act. Although they might try to alter its significance, change its ritual forms or even parody it, sacrifice remained the crucial vehicle of religious meaning; and the priests remained primarily perceived as the practitioners of sacrifice. Only Christianity entirely broke away from the dominance of animal sacrifice; and so only Christianity was able to define priesthood in an entirely new way – as is illustrated by the new set of priestly titles (for example, 'presbyter' or 'deacon') entirely different from those traditional in the Graeco-Roman world. If Gordon is right, we must see the Christian priest as even further set apart from his pagan predecessors than we might have imagined.

*

This book originated as a series of seminars at the Institute of Classical Studies, London, given under the title 'Priests and Power'. Our aim in this series was tentative and exploratory. It was obvious that ancient pagan priesthood was a diverse and wide-ranging category; we hoped that, by drawing together various examples of priests from different societies, we might be able to detect common

features shared by such religious officials and work our way towards
some general conclusions on the nature of pagan priesthood as a whole.
We were far from sure that we could make the subject cohere; but at
any rate it seemed worth the attempt. We certainly had no developed
theory of priesthood that we were concerned to test or justify –
although the title of the series itself suggests that we were already
thinking precisely in terms of locating priestly authority in relation to
other forms of power in the state.

This book demonstrates, we hope, the success of our project. We have
produced no single definition of pagan priesthood – an impossible goal,
given the wide range of different types of functionaries, in very
different societies separated by thousands of miles and as many years.
But we have shown common and distinctive characteristics shared by
priestly officials in many of the societies we have considered and we
have been able to suggest common methods of approach to the analysis
of the priestly function. Underlying all the essays in the book, in fact, is
a sense that the definition of specifically religious officials in the
ancient world is problematic and that the function of priesthood is
deeply embedded in public and political life.

It would, of course, have been possible to produce a very different
series of seminars and so also a different book. In particular we could
have given much fuller consideration to Jewish and Christian
priesthood – an absolutely essential element, if we had chosen to write
a book on the priests of the ancient world as a whole. That, however,
remains a project for the future; this is a book about pagan priests.

PART I

The Graeco-Roman City-State

1

Priesthood in the Roman Republic

This first chapter is concerned with the central problems of the definition and location of priesthood and priestly authority in the society of Republican Rome. The period involved is a long one: the Republic began (so legend told) in 509 BC, when the last of the early kings of Rome, Tarquin the Proud, was expelled from the city; and it ended almost five centuries later in the civil wars that ushered in the reign of the emperor Augustus and a new kind of monarchy. Much changed during these centuries: Rome expanded from its postion as a small city-state to that of the dominating power throughout the whole Mediter-ranean; the governing class of the city was transformed from a narrow, hereditary oligarchy to an élite that was open to the claims of, at least, all citizens of wealth. Yet the institutional framework of the city remained sufficiently constant to justify seeing the period, in some significant respects, as a single unit. From the Roman perspective the absence of kingship was probably the most important factor in defining the Republican form of government. But there were other positive elements of continuity: the three basic institutions of a central advisory council (the senate), a series of annually elected magistrates and a popular assembly (or assemblies) were present – admittedly in slightly different forms – throughout the period. The system we can witness most clearly at the end of the Republic was a recognizable development from that which had emerged from the downfall of monarchy 500 years before.

Rome was never a democracy in the modern sense of the word – still less in the radical sense associated with the society of Classical Athens. The wealthy élite always dominated political action and decision-making. Yet there were elements in the governmental system of Republican Rome which, if not democratic, at least acted to diffuse political power. Not only were the élite dependent for their position as magistrates on the votes of the popular assemblies, but office-holding was so spread amongst the élite as a whole that no one person or group could gain overweening power. Election to each of the series of magisterial offices was (normally) for one year only; in each office no man held power independently, but with a colleague or colleague of equal rank and power. The Republican political system constantly fragmented the power of the élite – until, in the first century BC, Julius Caesar and then Augustus established their position as dominant above their peers.

The last fifty years of the Republic are perhaps the best documented of all ancient classical societies and form a necessary focus for any study of Republican priesthood. The chapter that follows draws particularly on the writing of Cicero (106-43 BC), whose suriviving letters and speeches throw much light on the day-to-day political activities of the Roman élite and their dealings, as priests and magistrates, with the gods. It is extraordinary material and provides for the latest phase of the Republic an incomparably rich picture of religious operations at Rome. But even so, much vital information on priesthood is lacking: most notably, the ritual involvement of priests, their words and actions at the religious festivals of the city. In part, at least, the political emphasis of this chapter is a consequence of the particular preoccupations of the available source material.

This introductory study of priesthood in one comparatively well-documented ancient society raises many of the questions that will recur throughout the book. How do priests relate to the political structure of the state? How is the wide diffusion of priestly authority (often through apparently 'non-priestly' bodies) to be understood? How does the language of ancient priesthood correspond to our own? In this case, is it appropriate or useful to accept the conventional translation of the Latin *sacerdos* as 'priest'? Some clear answers to these questions emerge, which provide a useful framework for our understanding of the problems of priesthood in other, rather more shadowy, ancient societies.

Priesthood in the Roman Republic*
Mary Beard

The diversity of Roman priesthoods

Roman Republican priesthoods are marked by their diversity, by differences in organization, in method of recruitment, in type of priestly duty. Even excluding recognizably 'foreign' imports (such as the Etruscan *haruspices* or the Eastern priests of Cybele or Isis), the range of those groups traditionally entitled 'priesthoods' seems to defy generalization.[1]

Consider the list contained in Table 1, which provides an outline of the major characteristics of the various Republican priesthoods. A cursory glance at this skeletal information immediately reveals substantial differences between the various groups of priests. Most priests, for example, were male; but some (the Vestal Virgins and the obscure Salian Virgins) were female. Most priesthoods were constituted as a group; but some (the *flamines* and *rex sacrorum*) had a particular role as individuals within the Roman religious system. The form of priestly title also varied. Some titles (such as *pontifices*, literally 'bridge-builders') were specific, distinctive appellations; others (such as the *XVviri sacris faciundis*, 'The Priesthood of Fifteen') were of unspecific, generic type.

Further investigation reveals yet deeper divisions between the different types of priest. The qualifications for priestly office, for example, varied from priesthood to priesthood, and changed with time. In the earliest period of Rome's history all priestly offices, it is normally (and reasonably) conjectured, were restricted to patrician families. This restriction was gradually broken down, so that, by the third century BC, plebeians were admitted to most priesthoods; the

---

* Thanks are due to Peter Brunt, Richard Gordon and Keith Hopkins, whose comments have (I hope) improved the original version of this paper.

[1] The term 'foreign' is always liable to be misleading in a religion (such as Rome's) which constantly absorbed new elements from the outside. However, in order not to overstate the case for diversity, I have consistently excluded from this paper those priests treated by contemporary ancient sources as in essence 'non-Roman'. So, for example, I have not considered the priestesses of Ceres (though, in some senses, public priests of Rome) because of their paraded Greek origin; see Cicero, *Balb.* 24, 55. Nor have I included the 'Latin' priesthoods, such as the *Laurentes Lavinates* (Wissowa, *RK²*, 520).

Table 1. A simplified guide to Roman Republican priests

Title	Number	Status & known qualifications (all male & freeborn, unless stated)	Duration of office	Method of selection	Date of foundation	Major duties	Other special features
Augures (Augurs)	Originally ? 3; increased gradually. 9 in 300; 15 under Sulla; 16 under Caesar.	Originally patricians. Also plebeians from 300.	For life, even if condemned & exiled.	Originally cooption; from 104, part popular election, interrupted under Sulla.	Pre-Republican	Ascertaining approval/disapproval of gods for political & military action. Advising senate & magistrates. Defining sacred space on earth.	
Flamen Dialis	One	Patrician. Parents married by confarreatio.	For life – but resigned on death of wife or on committing major ritual fault.	Chosen by Pontifex Maximus.	Pre-Republican	Cult of Jupiter. Participation in ritual, e.g. Vinalia, confarreatio (traditional marriage ceremony).	Conduct hedged by taboos – so that normal senatorial career was almost impossible. As other flamines, wore special priestly hat (apex).
(Flaminica Dialis)	One	Wife of flamen	For life (or until death of flamen).		Pre-Republican	Assisted flamen with ritual. Regular sacrifice of ram to Jupiter.	Some taboos apply to wife as well. Distinctive dress.
Flamen Martialis	One	As flamen Dialis	For life – but resigned on committing major ritual fault	As flamen Dialis	Pre-Republican	Cult of Mars. Sacrifice at the festival of October horse.	
Flamen Quirinalis	One	As flamen Dialis	As flamen Martialis	As flamen Dialis	Pre-Republican	Cult of Quirinus. Sacrifices to Consus & at Robigalia, Larentalia.	
Minor flamines (flamens)	12	Plebeians	?	?	Pre-Republican	Cult of individual deities.	Only 10 out of 12 known: flamen Carmentalis, Cerialis, Falacer, Floralis, Furrinalis, Palatualis, Pomonalis, Portunalis, Volcanalis, Volturnalis. Lower status than 'major' flamens, above.
Fetiales	20	Originally patricians. ? later also plebeians.	Normally for life.	Cooption	Pre-Republican	Religious aspects of Rome's relations with outside world. Treaties, rituals on declaration of war.	
Fratres Arvales (Arval Brethren)	12	?	For life, even if condemned & exiled.	Cooption	Pre-Republican	Cult of Dea Dia, at cult centre in grove a few miles outside Rome.	Perhaps extinct in late Republic; revived by Augustus.

Priesthood	Number	Membership	Tenure	Selection	Date	Functions	Notes
Luperci	2 groups (Fabiani & Quinctiales). Total unknown.	By late Republic, included ex-slaves.	??temporary	?cooption	Pre-Republican	Ritual of Lupercalia.	
Pontifices (Pontiffs)	Originally unknown; gradually increased, 9 in 300; 15 under Sulla; 16 under Caesar.	Originally patricians. Also plebeians from 300.	Normally for life.	As for *augures*	Pre-Republican	Ritual duties, including Carmentalia, Fordicidia, Argei, celebrations of Consus. Wide ranging religious/administrative role (e.g. tomb law). Advice to senate on religion.	'Head' of college known as *Pontifex Maximus* (from 3rd century chosen by form of popular election). Powerful personal religious competence.
Potitii & Pinarii		Members of 2 families			Pre-Republican	Before 312, charge of cult of Hercules at Ara Maxima.	
Quindecimviri sacris faciundis	Originally 2; 10 in 367; 15 by 51; 16 under Caesar.	Originally patricians. Also plebeian from 367.	Normally for life.	As for *augures*	Pre-Republican	General charge of oracular Sibylline books. Supervision of foreign cults at Rome.	
Rex Sacrorum	One	Patrician. Parents married by *confarreatio*.	Normally for life	Chosen by *Pontifex Maximus*	Start of the Republic (trad. 509)	Believed to have taken over religious functions of king, at fall of monarchy. Ritual of Agonalia & Regifugium.	Prohibited from political career.
Saliae Virgines (Salian Virgins)	?	Women. Probably low, ? not freeborn, status.	?	Hired	?	Annual sacrifice with *Pontifex Maximus*.	
Salii	2 groups of 12, Palatini & Collini.	Patricians, with mother & father living at time of selection.	For life, but resignation common on obtaining major magistracy or priesthood.	Cooption	Pre-Republican	Ritual song and dance through city in March and October (start & end of war season).	
Septemviri epulones	Originally 3; 7 under ? Sulla; 10 under Caesar.	Patricians and plebeians.	Normally for life.	As for *augures*	196	Took over from *pontifices* organization of ritual feasts for gods.	
Sodales Titii	?	?	?	?	Pre-Republican	Some augural function.	
Virgines Vestales (Vestal Virgins)	Originally ? 2; later ? 4. 6 through the historical period	Virgin girls entering priesthood between 6 and 10, with both parents still living. No bodily defect. ?? Originally patricians.	Could leave priesthood after 30 years	Lot, from candidates selected by *Pontifex Maximus*.	Pre-Republican	Guarding of sacred hearth of city. Cult of Vesta – and other ritual involvement (Vestalia, Fordicidia, rites of Consus)	Penalty of death if found to be unchaste. Full-time attendance on ritual duties, resident in Atrium Vestae next to temple of Vesta. Distinctive dress. Many social and legal privileges.

Mary Beard

Fig. 1. Part of the processional frieze from the enclosure wall of the Augustan Altar of Peace (Ara Pacis) in Rome (13-9 BC). On the right stand two *flamines*, identifiable by their distinctive headdresses.

formal qualifications required of potential *pontifices*, for example, or augurs or *XVviri* were simply freebirth, Roman citizenship and an absence of bodily defects.[2] Patrician status, however, remained a requirement right through the Republic for the major *flamines, rex sacrorum* and the *salii*.[3] And for some priesthoods there were additional criteria: the Vestal Virgins, for example, could enter their office only between the ages of six and ten and it was required that both their parents should be alive when they did so.[4]

Different methods of recruitment were employed by different priestly groups. Leaving aside such intractable problems as who it was who 'hired' the Salian Virgins and by what process, we can distinguish three major methods of entry into priesthoods. For the office of *flamen, rex* or Vestal, the most appropriate candidate was chosen by the *pontifex maximus* (the head of the pontifical college) from those who were suitably qualified. The criteria for his choice are generally lost to us, though they are occasionally reported as being (to say the least)

---

[2] Despite the low legal qualifications, in practice the major priests were always drawn from the Roman élite. Note, for example, Cicero's emphasis (*Dom*. 1, 1) on Roman priests as one and the same as the political leaders of the Roman state. At least by the late Republic, however, some of the less prominent priesthoods (such as the *luperci* – Cicero, *Att*. 12, 5, 1) were associated with a lower rank of the Roman social hierarchy.

[3] The patrician status of these priests is stressed, for example, by Cicero, *Dom*. 14, 38.

[4] See, for example, Aulus Gellius, *NA* 1, 12, 1-2.

Fig. 2. Head of a Vestal Virgin, second century AD. The hairstyle is characteristic of Vestals and probably reflects the so-called 'six-locks' (*sex crines*). This was a style that the Vestals had to adopt throughout the tenure of their priesthood, and was otherwise worn only by brides on the day of their marriage.

idiosyncratic – as when P. Licinius Crassus (*pontifex maximus* 212-183 BC) chose C. Valerius Flaccus for the office of *flamen Dialis*, in an attempt to turn him away from his youthful, wayward lifestyle.[5] Most other priestly groups recruited new members either by cooption or, in the late Republic, by direct popular election. The process of cooption left the decision entirely to the priests themselves, who filled any vacancy in their group by independently selecting a replacement from amongst the Roman citizen body, provided that (according to the traditional rules) he was not a personal enemy of any existing member of the priesthood.[6] In the last century BC, however, following the *lex Domitia* of 104 BC, *pontifices*, augurs, *XVviri* and *VIIviri* were chosen, in part, by a process of popular election. The priests themselves produced a shortlist of candidates which was submitted to an electoral assembly made up of seventeen out of the thirty-five Roman tribes. The

[5] Traditionally, in the choice of Vestal Virgins, the *pontifex maximus* himself selected a pool of twenty suitable candidates; the final decision was then made by lot – see Aulus Gellius, *NA* 1, 12, 10-12. For *flamines* and *rex*, it seems that a list of candidates was prepared by the pontifical college as a whole, from which the *pontifex maximus* alone made the final selection – see Livy 27, 8, 4-10 (on C. Valerius Flaccus); 40, 42, 8-11.

[6] For the traditional absence of personal enmity within the priestly colleges, see Cicero, *Fam.* 3, 10, 9.

candidate thus elected was then formally coopted by the priests.[7]

Duration of priestly office also varied. The norm seems to have been that a priesthood was held for life, unless the man or woman committed a serious error in the performance of a religious ritual or was legally condemned and exiled.[8] But there were exceptions. The Salian Virgins as hired priestesses presumably held office for a short time only and were perhaps chosen afresh each year.[9] The *flamen Dialis* was forced to give up his office if his wife died.[10] The Vestals were permitted to resign their priesthood after thirty years if they wished and the *salii* likewise were allowed (but not forced) to give up their office if they obtained a major magistracy.[11] By contrast the augurs and Arval Brethren, unlike all other priests, remained in office until death, even if they had been condemned and exiled.[12]

The duties, rights and obligations connected with these different priestly offices incorporated even greater variations. Two points of contrast are particularly striking. The first concerns the relationship of priestly and political office. Most priesthoods were easily combined with a political career; and indeed it was traditionally assumed at Rome that the same men would undertake the major magistracies and priesthoods of the state.[13] In one case, however, that of the *rex sacrorum*, political office was expressly forbidden for the holder of a priesthood,[14] and in other cases the obligations of a priestly office made a concurrent political career practically impossible. The *flamen Dialis* was particularly hindered in this way, for his priesthood (as is clear from Table 1) brought with it a large number of taboos and restrictions

---

[7] On the change of procedure in 104, see, for example, Cicero, *Leg. agr.* 2, 7, 18; Suetonius, *Ner.* 2, 1. The electoral assembly of seventeen tribes was modelled on that used for the selection of *pontifex maximus*, who had been chosen by this form of direct popular election since at least the third century BC. The whole process of nomination, election and cooption to the priestly colleges after the Domitian reform is clearly explained by J. Linderski in 'The aedileship of Favonius, Curio the Younger and Cicero's election to the Augurate', *HSCPh* 76 (1972), 91-2.

[8] See, for example, Livy 26, 23, 8 – the abdication of a *flamen Dialis* who had made an error in handling the entrails of a sacrificial animal.

[9] Our only information about these women is provided by Festus, *Gloss. lat.* p. 439.

[10] See Aulus Gellius, *NA* 10, 15, 22.

[11] For the resignation of Vestals, see Aulus Gellius, *NA* 7, 7, 4; Plutarch, *Num.* 10, 2. For the *salii*, see Valerius Maximus 1, 1, 9; note also the *fasti* of the *salii* under the principate (e.g., *CIL* VI, 1978; 1980), which clearly indicate the resignation of priests who have assumed major magisterial office.

[12] Augurs: Plutarch, *Quaest. Rom.* 99; Pliny, *Ep.* 4, 8, 1. Arval Brethren: Pliny, *HN* 18, 2, 6. Note, however, that the municipal Lex Urso – closely modelled on the law of the city of Rome – envisages circumstances in which local augurs gave up their office; see Riccobono, *FIRA* 1, 21, ch. 67.

[13] This overlap is emphasised by Cicero, *Dom.* 1, 1.

[14] The prohibition on office is explicitly stated by Dionysius of Halicarnassus, *Ant. Rom.* 4, 74, 4; it is implicitly revealed by an episode in Livy (40, 42, 8), which concerns the attempt of a *pontifex maximus* to secure the resignation of a *duumvir navalis*, as a preliminary to his appointment as *rex*.

on his behaviour. How, for example, could he fulfil the military obligations traditionally expected of a Roman magistrate, when the taboos of his priesthood prevented him from even *seeing* a force under arms?[15]

The second major point of contrast in the duties of different priestly groups lies in the onerousness of their religious obligations. In some cases the priestly tasks were light. The *luperci*, for example, participated in just one annual festival; and the *salii* likewise had ritual duties only at two periods of the year, in March and November.[16] By contrast the duties of the *pontifices* were arduous. Not only did they take part in numerous festivals spread throughout the year (see Table 1), but they also had a wide variety of religious administrative duties, ranging from regulation of the calendar to the control of burial law and advising the senate on the handling of religious problems.[17] Yet even with this level of obligations the *pontifices* – both as a group and as individuals – remained essentially 'part-time' priests. The Vestal Virgins, on the other hand, were full-time professionals. Not only did they have a wide range of, sometimes time-consuming, ritual duties; but they also had a permanent occupation in guarding the sacred hearth of the city and they lived with their work, fully supported by the state, in a special residence next to the temple of Vesta in the forum.[18]

Many further differences could be listed, but they would add little new at this point to the overall picture. The diversity of Roman priesthood, as I have laid it out, is striking and (to say the least) unusual within the boundaries of a single traditional society. It encourages a fuller investigation not only of individual priestly offices, but also of the nature of priesthood and of priestly function at Rome in broader terms.

Approaches to Roman priesthood

The most perceptive work on Roman priesthood was produced in the nineteenth century by the German scholars Georg Wissowa, Joachim

---

[15] For a detailed list of the taboos surrounding the *flamen Dialis*, see Aulus Gellius, *NA* 10, 15.

[16] The religious obligations of these two priesthoods are clearly summarized in Scullard, *Festivals and Ceremonies*, 76-8 (*luperci*); 195 (*salii*).

[17] Full details of the duties of the *pontifices* are laid out in Wissowa, *RK²*, 513-18 and in Bouché Leclerq, *Les pontifes*, 267-318. The obligations on any individual pontiff are not, however, as large as they might at first sight seem; for many of the pontifical duties no doubt required the participation of only one or two members of the college. Cicero, *Har. resp.* 6, 13 implies a quorum of three for certain decisions.

[18] A convenient summary of the ritual duties of the Vestal Virgins is provided by J.P.V.D. Balsdon, *Roman Women: their history and habits* (London, 1962), 235-43 – although his *interpretation* of their cult role is misleading. For further discussion and a full bibliography, see Beard, 'Vestal Virgins'.

Marquardt and Theodor Mommsen. Wissowa confronted directly the problem of the status of priests within the Roman religious system and advanced the important negative argument that they did not act as representatives of the gods on earth and were not defined as mediators between gods and men.[19] Marquardt, with a slightly different emphasis, laid stress on the role of the priests as specialists, as expert counsellors subordinate to the senate.[20] With a different emphasis again, Mommsen – from the standpoint of a constitutional lawyer – considered the relationship between priest and magistrate in the Roman Republic and stressed the separateness of the two functions (even when the offices were held by one and the same individual).[21] Unfortunately none of these discussions gave sufficient emphasis to the sheer diversity of priestly office at Rome; none took fully into account the range of ancient evidence on the Roman priesthood. But all these nineteenth-century scholars identified important aspects of Roman priesthood overlooked or misunderstood by many later writers.[22]

An exception is to be found in the work of John Scheid, who has recently taken up and developed Mommsen's treatment of Roman priesthoods. Scheid has attempted a synoptic description of priestly and magisterial power – arguing that these two functions were mutually interdependent in the Roman political order and, at the same time, profoundly separate: priests, that is, represented the sphere of the sacred which was, at least potentially, an autonomous sphere within Roman public life and ideology. In my view, Scheid's approach does not yet represent a sufficiently radical new solution to the problem of Roman priesthood; in particular, it leaves the category of 'priest' (itself the centre of difficulty, as will become clear in what follows) largely intact. Yet, even so, it stands apart from most other modern work in its breadth and insight.[23]

---

[19] Wissowa, *RK*[2], 479-80.

[20] J. Marquardt, *Römische Staatsverwaltung* 3 (2nd ed., Leipzig, 1885), 219-20.

[21] See, especially, Mommsen's treatment of the *pontifex maximus* and the pontifical college, *Staatsrecht*[3] 2, 18-73. For further discussion of particular points, Bleicken, 'Oberpontifex and Pontifikalkollegium' and 'Kollisionen zwischen Sacrum und Publikum'.

[22] But note Szemler, *Priests of the Roman Republic*; though there is very little original here, the book is occasionally useful as a summary of the important earlier work, as well as a list of known priests.

[23] See Scheid 'Prêtre' and *Religion et piété*, 36-57; 66-74 (an expanded version of his earlier *La religione a Roma* (Rome, 1983)). For fuller discussion both of the importance and of the remaining problems in Scheid's approach, see J.A. North, 'Religion and politics, from Republic to Principate', *JRS* 76 (1986), 257-8. Note also, in relation to individual priesthoods, Scheid's recent masterly attempt (in 'Le flamine de Jupiter') to understand the *flamen Dialis* and Vestals as, in different ways, 'doubles' of their deities.

Scheid is, in part, influenced by the work of G. Dumézil – which itself should be exempt from the generally negative judgment I have expressed on studies of Roman priesthood. Much of Dumézil's argument (in, for example, *Archaic Roman Religion*) has a bearing on individual priests and priestly organization; but his overall aim to understand Roman

Four major trends may be identified in other recent studies on Roman priesthood, at least in those works which go beyond a mere listing of the duties and privileges of individual offices. The first, in contrast to the views of Marquardt, regards Roman priests as essentially religious 'amateurs': insofar as they did not undergo any period of noviciate and were not normally exclusively religious officials, they are classified paradoxically as 'laymen', unpriestly priests.[24] The second attempts to establish a hierarchy within the priestly organizations at Rome: in particular, it invests the *pontifices* (as the 'heads' of Roman religion) with power and control over the religious and priestly system as a whole.[25] The third entirely politicizes Roman priesthoods and implies that their only importance lay in the competition generated around election and cooption; that is, priestly office provided the Roman élite with another access to glory (and another focus for factional rivalry), alongside the competition for strictly magisterial office.[26] The fourth trend attempts to provide a chronological ordering of the full range of Roman priesthood and so, implicitly, to explain its diversity. This approach rests on the assumption that different priestly types represent different stages in the development of Roman priesthood – the 'primitive' taboo-laden *flamen Dialis*, for example, belonging to an early stratum, the more 'forward-looking' *pontifices* being later in origin. Once the proper ordering is established, it is supposed that the apparent confusion of priestly types is removed.[27]

None of these approaches is satisfactory, and all compare unfavourably with the more sophisticated nineteenth-century studies. My particular objections to the first three will emerge explicitly or implicitly in the course of this chapter. The last requires brief consideration at this point; for if it were correct, it would offer a simple explanation of the diversity on which I have laid so much emphasis. In fact, to explain this diversity by appeal to a chronological order is to miss one crucial point: the striking feature about the Roman priestly organization is not just its diversity, but the very early date at which that diversity was established. All the priesthoods listed in Table 1 (with the exception of the *VIIviri* and perhaps some minor *flamines*)

---

religious institutions within a common Indo-European framework tends to obscure many central problems of the nature, characteristics and definition of priesthood.

[24] See, for example, Scullard, *Festivals and Ceremonies*, 28.

[25] So, M. Le Glay, *La religion romaine* (Paris, 1971), 32-3.

[26] This view clearly underlies L.R. Taylor, *Party Politics in the Age of Caesar* (Berkeley etc., 1949), 90-7; and (more subtly) E. Rawson, 'Religion and politics in the late second century BC at Rome', *Phoenix* 28 (1974), 207-12 and Richard, 'Quelques grands pontifes plébéiens'.

[27] An extreme version of this approach is found in the chronological development of the Roman priesthood postulated by K. Latte, *RRG*, 195-7.

were established, as far as we can tell, before the Republic began, in the Regal Age of Rome (traditionally 753-510). Some were no doubt founded before others; we cannot know. But it seems unhelpful to explain the diversity that remained within a working religious system for over 400 years by reference to origins that are almost entirely lost from our sight.[28]

Towards a new approach

Two principal difficulties lie in the way of anyone wishing to generate a new approach to Roman Republican priesthood: first the sheer complexity of the subject; secondly the lack of precise evidence on the role played by the different priests in Roman ritual and ceremony.

A proper study of Roman priesthood must attempt to locate the priestly function as accurately as possible within the religious system as a whole; it involves, ideally, consideration of the full range of contacts between gods and men in Republican Rome. Yet at the same time that breadth of coverage may make it hard to retain a specifically priestly focus. Those who set out to write on the Roman priesthood may find that they are writing on nothing less than Roman religion in general. The example of Bouché Leclerq is instructive here. He wrote in the 1870s a lengthy study entitled *Les pontifes de l'ancienne Rome*, whose contents prove, on examination, to be somewhat surprising; for the book is, in fact, a narrative history of Roman religion into which the *pontifices* have, from time to time, been inserted, as if it were due to them that the character of Roman religion developed as it did.[29] This apparent failing was, I am sure, no simple oversight on the part of Bouché Leclerq; it was rather an understandable consequence of the difficulties encountered in attempting to isolate the study of Roman priesthood from the study of the Roman religious system as a whole. Within the narrow compass of this paper, I have made every effort to keep a strictly priestly focus. But many of my remarks are necessarily related to my own overview of the character of Roman religion, which I have not the space fully to explain here.[30]

The lack of precision that can be reached on the ritual practice of the various priests presents a different problem. It might at first sight seem that the obvious starting point for a study of Roman priesthood would consist in a careful analysis of the exact role played by the

---

[28] This chronological approach has already been criticized by Dumézil, *Archaic Roman Religion*, 102-12 and Scheid, *Religion et piété*, 39. Though somewhat differently founded, my objections tend in the same direction.

[29] Bouché-Leclerq, *Les pontifes, passim*.

[30] This overview is outlined in Beard and Crawford, *Rome in the Late Republic*, 25-39. See also M. Beard in *CAH²* 9 (forthcoming) and the discussion of general approach in M. Beard, J.A. North and S. Price, *Roman Religion* (Cambridge, forthcoming).

priests in public religious ceremonies. From an analysis of the ritual actions they carried out, of the words they used in the performance of ritual and of the position they occupied in relation to other (non-priestly) participants in religious festivals, we might at least start to locate the role of the priest within the 'topography' of the Roman religious system. Unfortunately this attractive analytical strategy is out of the question; for, although our ancient sources often record the presence of a particular priest at a particular festival, they rarely provide any more information on his or her role than that; they rarely make it clear exactly what the priest said or did. Consider, for example, the patrician marriage ceremony of *confarreatio*. We know that both the *flamen Dialis* and *pontifex maximus* were present at this ritual, and scholars have often conjectured that the priests performed the required sacrifice or dictated the ritual formulae to the bride and groom. Such conjectures, however, are based on nothing more than a plausible guess and can provide no firm basis for detailed discussion of the priestly role. They may simply have been present as formal witnesses of the ceremony.[31]

This chapter attempts to circumvent both difficulties by approaching Roman priests from two, rather different, angles. First, it will consider the function of 'mediation' between gods and men in Rome. This function is assumed to be the defining characteristic of organized priesthood in many societies, although that was firmly denied in the case of Rome by Wissowa. Can Wissowa's view be more fully justified? Where in Rome was the prime focus of mediation between gods and men?

Secondly, I shall analyse in detail the differences between two of the major priestly colleges: the *pontifices* and *augures*. So far I have presented only a superficial sketch of the variety and diversity of Roman priests. The question remains: How deep did this diversity go? How far were the different priestly groups perceived to occupy a different position in relation to the gods? How far did they play different roles within the full range of contacts between humans and the divine? In the case of the *pontifices* and *augures* (priestly colleges on which we are more than usually well informed) it will appear that the differences are not merely immediately striking, but also fundamental.

Drawing on these two major areas of analysis, I shall finally consider in more general terms the category of 'priesthood' and the nature of religious authority at Rome. This will involve both a modern and an

---

[31] The only text specifically to document the presence of the priests is Servius, *Commentary on Virgil*, G 1, 31. The discussion of P.E. Corbett, *The Roman Law of Marriage* (Oxford, 1930), 71-8 clearly highlights the uncertainties that surround the details of the ceremony.

ancient perspective: on the one hand, I shall investigate the ancients'
usage and understanding of the Latin terms *sacerdos* (conventionally
translated as 'priest') and *sacerdotium* ('priesthood'); on the other, I
shall offer a modern analytical framework for understanding the
diversity of the Roman priesthood and the wide diffusion of religious
power at Rome.

Mediation between gods and men: the role of the senate

The term 'mediation' can be used in a wide variety of religious
contexts. Following the broadest definition, we might argue that any
individual who offers sacrifice or says a prayer to the gods is himself
mediating between the human world and the world of the divine. In a
narrower sense, mediation can be taken to apply to many, more
specialized, forms of religious activity – such as the operation of the
divinely inspired prophet (who provides a direct vehicle for the word of
god to be communicated to man), or administrative control over the
forms of human worship, as exercised by an organized priesthood over
(for example) the formulae of prayers. None of these applications are
'wrong'; but if mediation is to provide a useful way into an
understanding of priestly function, we need to be more specific.

In this chapter I have taken mediation to be primarily an
institutional function and one which defines, delimits and controls
human approaches to the divine and the communication of gods to
men. To think in terms of a concrete, physical analogy, the focus of
religious mediation in any society may be understood as the channel
through which messages pass between the sphere of the gods on the
one side and the sphere of men on the other; and the principal
mediating institution is the one which (more than any other) has
control over that channel of communication. Religious 'mediation' in
this sense overlaps in part with the wider notion of religious
'authority', but is rather more narrowly defined: whereas religious
authority can be understood in a *passive* sense (as, for example, when
it is embedded in a book or set of sacred texts), mediation is an *active*
force, involving direct contact with the sphere of the gods.[32]

This definition is not final nor incontestable. In our present enquiry,
however, it has the advantage of avoiding too individualistic an
approach. For to consider mediation as a function fulfilled by every
individual in prayer (even if fulfilled more strikingly by some than by
others) is simply to mask the more distinctive and controlling aspects

---

[32] Any attempt to define very precisely the semantic range of these two words is probably
counter-productive; and, in any case, much of what I say in this chapter will be focussed on
the area of overlap between the two terms, the area (perhaps) of '*active* religious authority'.
Nevertheless there is a broad distinction to be made. For a Roman example of religious
authority vested in books, note the oracular Sibylline books.

of mediation normally associated with the priestly function.

The principal focus of mediation in Republican Rome was the senate. It was not the only such focus; as I shall show, assemblies of the people, magistrates and some priestly groups also fulfilled the function of mediating between gods and men. But the senate took the major role here: that is, if mediation is rightly regarded as the defining function of priesthood, it was largely (and, at first sight, paradoxically) carried out in Rome not by those men we know as 'priests', but by a body traditionally thought of in simply 'political' terms.

This startling claim requires some justification. Four examples of senatorial power will, I hope, confirm the general point.

The most obvious instance of senatorial control over human approaches to the gods lies in their power of decision in the introduction of new state-cults. It was the senate which ordained in 205 BC that the cult of Magna Mater should be brought to Rome;[33] and, conversely, it was the senate which proscribed 'foreign' cults in the city of Rome in 213 BC and again in 186 took action to restrict Bacchic cults in Italy.[34] Of course, in matters such as this the senate could take advice from the various bodies of priests; but the final decision was never delegated and lay firmly in the hands of the senate.[35] The senate here enjoyed the power of mediating between men and gods insofar as it controlled the forms of worship offered by men to the gods.

The position was similar with the recognition and handling of prodigies. The procedure in this case is clearly documented by Livy. At the beginning of the year, one of the consuls reported to the senate on the prodigies observed during the preceding year and the senators then voted on whether each one was to be recognized as a public sign of divine origin. If the senate recognized a sign in this way, then it either ordered some immediate action of expiation or it referred the matter to one of the priestly colleges. In this case, the priests would later report back to the senate – and the senate, no doubt on the basis of this report, would take the final decision on appropriate action. In short the senate was seen to have the power of deciding what constituted a sign sent by the gods and it controlled human responses to such signs.[36]

[33] Livy 29, 10, 4-8. The later reception of the cult in Rome was also arranged by the senate: Livy 29, 14, 5-14.

[34] 213: Livy 25, 1, 11-12. 186: Livy 39, 8-19; *ILS* 18 = Degrassi, *ILLRP* 511. On the incident of the Bacchanalia more generally, see J.A. North, 'Religious toleration in Republican Rome', *PCPhS* 25 (1979), 85-103 – with documentation of other instances of senatorial religious control (e.g. prohibition on human sacrifice in 97 BC, Pliny, *HN* 30, 1, 12; action against the cult of Isis in 50 BC, Valerius Maximus 1, 3, 4).

[35] The precedence is made clear in Livy's account of the introduction of Magna Mater (n. 33 above): an oracle recommending the installation of the cult at Rome was produced by the *Xviri*; the senate took the executive decision which led to its installation.

[36] See, for example, Livy 22, 1, 8-20; 40, 19, 1-5. The whole procedure for the handling of prodigies is discussed by R. Bloch, *Les prodiges dans l'antiquité classique* (Paris, 1963), 112-29.

The senate also had the power to resolve 'problems' that arose in men's relations with the gods and to re-establish proper relations between the divine and human sphere, if they were temporarily disrupted. Several incidents described by Cicero illustrate this point. The clearest record concerns the actions taken in 61 BC, after the night-time ceremonies of the Bona Dea (Good Goddess), which were rigidly restricted to women alone, had been invaded by a man; he was not firmly identified, but believed by many to have been P. Clodius Pulcher, later to become a notorious tribune. The senate here took the initiative: it first of all instructed the Vestal Virgins (who had already repeated the ceremony) and the college of *pontifices* to investigate the matter; it later issued a decree that the consuls should promulgate a bill to institute a formal trial of the man under suspicion.[37] In the case of such an obvious rupture of the correct forms of human approaches to the gods, it was the senate that directed and coordinated human reactions.

Similar senatorial power is evident in the debate which surrounded the consecration by the same P. Clodius of a shrine of Liberty on the site of Cicero's house during the orator's exile. When Cicero returned, he contested the validity of Clodius' action and claimed that the ground had no special religious status. The senate took charge of the problem and referred the matter to the college of pontiffs for investigation and adjudication. The priests however produced no binding decision; that lay with the senate who finally ruled (in accordance with priestly opinion) that the consecration had been invalid and that Cicero could reoccupy the site.[38] Once more the senate is seen to have control in defining the correct relations between gods and men – in this, deciding on the different claims of gods and men to a particular piece of land.

The fourth example of senatorial power in religion is of a rather different type, but provides striking (negative) confirmation of the position of the senate as focus of communication between men and gods. The sittings of the Republican senate were never, as far as we know, subject to hindrance or interruption on religious grounds, by the declaration of ill omens or the like.[39] This contrasts markedly with the

[37] The senatorial initiative is made clear by Cicero, *Att.* 1, 13, 3.

[38] The precise course of events was as follows: (1) the matter was referred to the pontifical college by the senate (Cicero, *Har. Resp.* 6, 11); (2) the pontifical college produced a *responsum*, defining the terms for the senatorial decision (Cicero, *Att.* 4, 2, 4); (3) the senate issued the final decision (*Har. Resp.* 7, 13; *Att.* 4, 2, 4). Note also that even in the speech delivered to the pontifical college during their deliberations Cicero lays stress on the power of the senate in the matter; see, for example, *Dom.* 58, 147.

[39] The only possible example of such interruption occurred after the murder of Caesar, in the confused months of 43 BC – Cicero, *Fam.* 10, 12, 3. But this incident was of a different type from that classically associated with hindrance of business in the assembly (see n. 40 below): no clash of will was involved; the *pullarii* (keepers of the sacred chickens) simply reported a mistake in the auspices taken before the senatorial meeting and the magistrate concerned agreed and suspended the meeting. On the surprising absence of religious

meetings of electoral and legislative assemblies of the people, which could be at any moment (and sometimes were) disbanded by the announcement of contrary omens.[40] At first sight this difference appears puzzling; for the political stakes of proceedings in the senate were often just as high as those in the assemblies, and the political benefits to be gained from postponing business there would no doubt have been just as great. The difference becomes understandable, however, if one thinks in broader religious terms. The underlying 'message' in the declaration of contrary omens was that (albeit perhaps conveniently for the individual politician who made the declaration) the particular assembly was in an improper relationship with the divine and so could not be allowed to proceed.[41] The absence of such interruption from the business of the senate makes precisely the opposite point. It suggests that the senate, as the body which formed the focus of communication between gods and men, *could not* be seen as in an improper relationship with the gods; it could not logically be interrupted by an ill omen.

The senate was the principal, but not the only, focus of mediation between gods and men in Republican Rome; active religious authority was not restricted to one institution of the Roman élite. I shall show in the next section how some priests played a mediating role in the relations of the Romans with their gods; here it is sufficient simply to draw attention to some mediating functions of popular assemblies and magistrates.

The people in assembly were perceived to have some power of decision over public dedications to the gods. On occasion, at least, the question of whether a dedication had been authorized by the people had weight in deciding whether it was a legitimate part of man's approaches to the divine; although it is by no means clear on such occasions how the authority of the popular assembly related to that of the senate or priestly colleges. One famous example of this power of the people concerned a public dedication of an altar (*ara*), shrine (*aedicula*) and sacred couch (*pulvinar*) by the Vestal Virgin Licinia in 123 BC. On the decision of the senate, one of the *praetors* of the year (Sex. Julius Caesar) referred the question to the pontifical college. The college replied that, since the dedication had been made without the order of the people (*iniussu populi*), it did not seem to be valid; and this view was confirmed by the senate, which ordered the destruction of the

---

hindrance from meetings of the senate, see also Liebeschuetz, *Continuity and Change*, 15.

[40] Note the following classic cases: Cicero, *Att*. 4, 3, 3-5; Plutarch, *Cato Min*. 42. Such incidents were not, however, as frequent as many historians (preoccupied with the 'decline' of Roman religion in the late Republic) have often supposed. See the sane remarks of Liebeschuetz, *Continuity and Change*, 7-29 and J. North, pp. 52-4 below.

[41] The logic of this process is laid out in greater detail in Beard and Crawford, *Rome in the Late Republic*, 31-3.

monument.[42] Once again it seems that the final decision lay with the
senate; but the authority of the people (or, in this case, the lack of it)
was also an element in determining the religious status of the
dedication.

The mediating role of the major magistracies of Rome was more
important and clearer. In particular, it was the responsibility of the
presiding magistrate to ensure, before each assembly, that the gods
approved of the holding of the meeting. During the night before the
assembly, in the place in which it was due to meet, the magistrate 'took
the auspices': he watched for a sign from the gods that they were in
favour of the proceedings. If this sign came, the meeting went ahead.[43]
Of course, as I have already mentioned, this religious approval might
be disrupted before or during the meeting by a magistrate or augur
sighting a contrary omen; but the underlying principle remains that
the presiding magistrate had an institutional role in ensuring the
proper relationship between the political activity of the assembly and
the will of the gods.

No other focus of mediation, however, neither the people nor the
yearly succession of magistrates, challenged the central position of the
senate. The direct contact of the magistrates with the gods in ensuring
divine approval for political activity in the assembly was undoubtedly
of great importance. Yet individual magistrates lacked the authoritative religious control of the senate and also its permanent status:
holding office for just one year at a time, they found a permanence of
religious authority only through their shared membership of the
senate. In this context Wissowa's view that Roman priests were not
essentially religious mediators may be granted acceptance and
extended in a more positive direction; for the senate, not the 'priests',
largely fulfilled that mediating function commonly regarded as
distinctively priestly.

Priests: pontifices and augures

The problem of the so-called 'priests' still remains. It is not sufficient to
evade the issue by a simple act of redefinition; by designating the
senate as the principal 'priestly body' and so ignoring the 'priests'. We
still need to investigate more fully the function of those groups
traditionally designated 'priests' and, in particular, their relationship
to the senate; for only thus will we understand the full context and
precise extent of senatorial religious control.

[42] Cicero, *Dom.* 53, 136; a similar example (a dedication by C. Cassius) is discussed at
Dom. 51, 130-1 and 53, 136.
[43] A clear description of this procedure is given by A.H.J. Greenidge, *Roman Public Life*
(London, 1911), 162-7 – esp. 165-6; and, more fully, by Mommsen, *Staatsrecht*[3] 1, 76-116 –
esp. 96-106.

Fig. 3. Gold coin issued under Julius Caesar, whose name can be read on the obverse of the coin (left). On the reverse (right) are represented various priestly symbols: the curved staff (*lituus*) and jug of the augurs; and the axe (*culullus*) of the *pontifices*. The female head on the obverse may represent the Goddess Vesta. (RRC 466, 46 BC.)

I have chosen to concentrate on two of the major priestly colleges of Republican Rome, the *pontifices* and *augures*. There are two main reasons for this. First, both of these priesthoods are comparatively well documented and allow detailed investigation. Secondly, although in many respects closely similar in organization, they can be shown to have occupied fundamentally different positions in relation to the gods.

The pontiffs and augurs are often treated together because of the similarity of their historical development. Their earliest membership, its number and organization, is almost entirely lost from our sight.[44] But from the late fourth century BC both colleges were legislated for and expanded together: they were both made subject to the Lex Ogulnia in 300 BC, which raised the number of each college to 9 and ensured that 5 priests in each should be drawn from plebeian families; both colleges were then raised to 15 by Sulla and 16 by Caesar.[45] In

---

[44] It is often said that both colleges originally consisted in three members – Wissowa, *RK²*, 503, repeated by Szemler, *Priests of the Roman Republic*, 27, n.7 and Hoffman Lewis, *Official Priests*, 9-10). There is no clear evidence, however, that this was even a consistent supposition in the ancient world; see, for example, Cicero, *Rep.* 2, 14, 26 – an original college of three augurs raised to five under Numa, with the foundation of a pontifical college of five at the same time.

[45] Livy's discussion of the Lex Ogulnia (Livy 10, 6 – 9, 2) is probably mistaken to suggest that the pontifical college was raised only to a membership of eight; it is certainly in contradiction with the next full list of the college we possess (*MRR* 1, 282). Throughout his discussion Livy seems confused by the numerical calculations and his low total may indicate that he failed to include the *pontifex maximus*. The character of the mixed patrician-plebeian pontifical college in the late Republic is exemplified by the membership list preserved in Cicero's *Har. Resp.* (6, 12) – fully discussed by L.R. Taylor, 'Caesar's colleagues in the pontifical college', *AJPh* 63 (1942), 385-412. For the increase under Sulla, see Livy, *Per.* 89; and under Caesar, Dio 42, 51, 4.

104 BC, along with the colleges of *XVviri* and *VIIviri*, the principle of partial popular election to their number was introduced, to be revoked by Sulla and then finally restored in 63 BC.[46] From at least the middle Republic these two priesthoods could sometimes be treated as a pair.

More striking are the differences between the two colleges in their relations with the gods. As I shall show, the *pontifices* were perceived to have no direct access to or communication with the divine; and their mediating power (such as it was) consisted in mediation between the centre of Roman religion in the form, principally, of the senate and the individual citizens, as they lived their lives. The augurs, by contrast, were perceived to have a direct line of communication with the divine – although they were in many respects subordinate to the senate, the principal focus of mediation.

This distinction between the two colleges is one confirmed in the writing of Cicero. Although the definitions I have just offered of the different roles of the two colleges are both modernizing and oversimplifying, they are, in fact, closely compatible with two Ciceronian formulae; for he refers to the *pontifices* as 'interpreters of observances' (*interpretes religionum*),[47] while calling the augurs 'interpreters and messengers of Jupiter Optimus Maximus' (*interpretes internuntiique Iovis Optimi Maximi*).[48] The difference between *religiones* ('observances') and Jupiter Optimus Maximus, the god himself, is crucial; as is also the addition of *internuntii* ('messengers' – almost, in our terms, 'mediators') in the context of the augurs. Within this language is inscribed the view that the *augures* had a direct link with the divine not possessed by the *pontifices*. But fuller discussion is needed.

The most evocative piece of ancient writing concerned with the pontifical college is Cicero's speech *De Domo* (*On his house*), delivered before the *pontifices* when they were considering the issue of the consecration of the building and whether it still rightfully belonged to Cicero. From Cicero's flattery of the college and from the qualities he chose to stress, we may gain a vivid first impression of one image of the *pontifices* within élite Roman society of the first century BC. Cicero lays great emphasis on the knowledge and expertise (*sapientia* and *scientia*) of the priests. It is immediately clear that (although no specific training was required to enter the priesthood) once a man had become a *pontifex* his status was that of religious expert: he *knew* things about religion that other men did not know and gained from that knowledge considerable authority (*auctoritas*). This is a theme harped on throughout the text and it seriously undermines any

---

[46] See above, n.7. For the restoration of popular election in 63 BC, see Dio 37, 37, 1.
[47] *Dom.* 1, 2.
[48] *Phil.* 13, 5, 12; note also the similar expression (*internuntii*) at *Leg.* 2, 8, 20.

suggestion that the *pontifices* are to be understood as religious laymen or amateurs.[49]

The activities of the *pontifices* spread widely, far beyond the particular competence (in adjudicating consecrations) stressed in the speech *De Domo*. Of the different duties indicated in Table 1, three (and in particular two) principal types of pontifical activity stand out: their specialist role in the performance of ritual and (more importantly) their control over the religious behaviour of individuals and their advisory function in relation to the senate. On the first of these, owing to our general uncertainty on the exact conduct of Roman rituals, it is possible to do little more than repeat the point that emerged from Cicero's *De Domo*; that the *pontifices* had a *specialist* role, in this case performing actions in particular festivals that no one else could normally legitimately perform.[50] On the other two topics more may be said and some significant conclusions drawn.

The control of the *pontifices* over the religious behaviour of individuals touched many areas. A large part of their concern seems to have been the regulation of burial practice and tomb-law. They were responsible for establishing (both in general and in particular) who was bound to perform regular rites for the dead at the tomb and they determined what constituted proper sanctified burial.[51] Cicero quotes, for example, the decision of P. Mucius Scaevola (*pontifex maximus* 130–c. 115) that, in the case of a man who had died on board ship and whose body had been thrown into the sea, his family could regard this as proper burial (since the bones did not lie above the earth) – so long as the usual sacrifice of a sow was performed and three days holiday kept.[52] The pontiffs likewise had the power to authorize the exhumation and transfer of human remains. In fact, an inscription of the mid-second century AD records the request to the *pontifices* of one Arrius Alphius that he should be allowed to transfer the remains of his wife and son from a clay to a marble sarcophagus. The request was passed from one member of the college to the *promagister* (a senior member acting on behalf of (*pro*) the head of the college, who was

---

[49] See, for example, *sapientia* and its cognates – *Dom*. 1, 1; 1, 2; *scire* 12, 33; *disciplina* 46, 121; *scientia* 54, 138. Note also Cicero's hesitancy in his discussion of Pinarius Natta, a living contradiction, as *pontifex* without knowledge – 45, 117-8.

[50] For documentation of the ritual role of the *pontifices*, see, for example, Dio 43, 24, 4 (October Horse); Dionysius of Halicarnassus, *Ant. Rom*. 1, 38, 3 (*Argei*); Degrassi, *Inscriptiones Italiae* XIII, 122-23 (*Fasti Praenestini*) (*Armilustrium*); Ovid, *Fast*. 2, 21-2 (*Lupercalia*).

[51] See, for example, Cicero's *Leg*. 2, 18, 45 (an idealized account, but essentially based on contemporary Roman practice) with Bouché-Leclerq, *Les pontifes*, 148-58. For the general principles of Roman tomb-law, see J.A. Crook, *Law and Life of Rome* (London, 1967), 133-8; F. De Visscher, *Le droit des tombeaux romains* (Milan, 1963).

[52] *Leg*. 2, 22, 57.

always by this date the emperor) and it was swiftly granted.[53]

The *pontifices* were also concerned with the religious status of the living members of the community. Most obviously they controlled the behaviour of individuals on days of religious festivals: they forbade, for example, the cutting of hay or the thinning out of trees, while allowing other necessary tasks that it would be dangerous or damaging to leave undone; on days sacred to the spirits of the dead (*feriae denicales*) they specifically prohibited the irrigating of fields and the yoking of mules.[54] In more general terms they regulated the religious life of families; they supervised, for example, the process of adoption, which involved the transference of a man from the private religious orbit of one family to that of another.[55]

By contrast, the role of the *pontifices* in relation to the senate was essentially advisory. We have already seen from a senatorial perspective that in public religious decision-making the priestly colleges played a subordinate role to the senate; let us now briefly reconsider this role from the perspective of the pontifical college. The pontiffs represented a repository of religious knowledge on which the senate could call; they were consulted on matters that fell within senatorial control but where (because of their complexity or difficulty) specialist religious advice was required. So, for example, in the case of Cicero's house, it was the *pontifices* who conducted the investigation of the full circumstances and weighed the evidence against the precise religious rules for consecration.[56] They also issued a judgment on the case, which was authoritative – insofar as it represented the opinion of religious experts – but was not binding or final; the final decision lay with the senate.[57] We might loosely think of the pontifical college as a subcommittee of the senate: most *pontifices* were also senators;[58] as a group they relieved their parent committee of certain specialist areas

---

[53] *CIL* VI, 2120 + 32398a = *ILS* 8380. Other inscriptions documenting the pontiffs' role in tomb law include *CIL* VI, 2963; 10675; 22120; *CIL* IX, 1729 = *ILS* 8382; 8386; 8383; 8110.

[54] See specifically Servius, *Commentary on Virgil*, *G* 1, 270; Columella, *Rust.* 2, 21, 5 (and note the other observances detailed in the rest of the chapter). For a general discussion of the pontiffs' determination of the religious character of days in the calendar and the appropriate behaviour on each, see Bouché-Leclerq, *Les pontifes*, 113-32.

[55] Adoption was regulated and authorized by the *comitia curiata* or *calata*, convened by the *pontifex maximus* (see Aulus Gellius, *NA* 15, 27, 1-3; Tacitus, *Hist.* 1, 15). Full details are given by Bouché-Leclerq, *Les pontifes*, 205-7, with a more general statement of the relationship of private law to sacral concerns in F. Schulz, *History of Roman Legal Science* (Oxford, 1946), 6-8 and 19-22.

[56] The background of religious *rules* is stressed by Cicero, *Dom.* 49, 127–55, 141 (with an indication of the complexity in R.G. Nisbet (ed.), *M. Tulli Ciceronis de domo sua ad pontifices oratio* (Oxford, 1939), App. 6, 209-12.

[57] See n.38 above – especially Cicero, *Har. Resp.* 7, 13; *Att.* 4, 2, 4.

[58] But not *all* were (at least yet) senators. See, Cicero, *Har. Resp*; *Att.* 4, 2, 4 (with Scheid, 'Prêtre', 248-58).

of discussion; they produced recommendations not likely to be overturned by that parent committee; they never, however, usurped the formal authority and control of the parent committee, in whose hands the power of decision was perceived to lie.

This twofold focus of pontifical activity – control over the religious behaviour of individuals and an advisory function in relation to the senate – offers the key to an understanding of the position of the *pontifices* within the Roman religious system. The pontifical college stood between the senate and the individual Roman citizen; it looked both inwards towards the centre of Roman religious mediation and outwards, fulfilling different functions according to its different perspectives. On the one hand, in relation to the individual citizen, the *pontifices* acted as representatives of the central religious power; they played the part of intermediaries, determining the religious conduct of private citizens on behalf of the state. On the other, in relation to the senate, they provided a pool of religious expertise, at the service of the central religious power.

The pontifical college played no particular part in the mediation between men and gods. Their mediating function operated between two human poles: the human centre of religious authority in the senate and the private citizens of Rome. The importance of this function should not be underestimated. In practical terms, from the point of view of the individual Roman, the *pontifices* must have seemed strikingly powerful; for it was they who determined men's day-to-day religious conduct and controlled areas of importance to the individual, such as burial and the religion of the family. In terms of more general religious structure also this mediating function was crucial; for, as Cicero implicitly recognized in his *De Legibus* (*On Laws*), a religious system, such as Rome's, whose centre lies in the institutional and public sphere, must find some means of linking that centre to what is non-institutional and private. The *pontifices* provided precisely that link, a bridge between the central power of the senate and the individual citizens as they lived their lives.[59]

The role of the college of *augures* can be sharply contrasted with the *pontifices*. Most important, the augurs did fulfil a directly mediating role between men and gods. They, and they alone, for example, had the power to create a *templum* on earth; that is, they could 'inaugurate' a piece of land and so place it in a special relationship with the gods – as a 'temple' in our sense of the word or, more strictly, a place from which

---

[59] For Cicero's perception, see *Leg.* 2, 8, 20 and 2, 12, 30 – note especially the link between 'qui sacris publice praesint' and 'religio privata'. It is this particular aspect of the pontifical role that, in my view, accounted for the prominence of the *pontifex maximus* and the keen competition for that office among the Roman élite; they did not compete for empty honours – the office was perceived to be powerful.

a magistrate could watch for signs from the gods.[60] They also, and again they alone, had the power *authoritatively* to interrupt an assembly once it had started by declaring ill omens; that is, they had the power to demonstrate that an assembly was not proceeding in accordance with the will of the gods.[61] Moreover, this direct power of mediation was retained by the augurs individually throughout their lives, no matter what their circumstances. As has already been mentioned, these priests alone of all the major colleges retained their priestly office even if condemned and exiled.[62]

There were, however, other aspects to the role of the augurs. They also fulfilled a function similar to the *pontifices* as a specialist sub-committee of the senate. In particular they gave advice to the senate when problems had arisen with the auspices and the relationship of magistrates to the gods. So, for example, in 215 BC, after Marcellus had been elected consul to assume office at once, the augurs were summoned by the senate to give their opinion on the clap of thunder which had occurred just as Marcellus was entering upon his office. They stated that there had been a defect in his election (such that indicated that the election had not been carried out with full divine approval). The senate, receiving this report, concluded that the gods did not endorse the election of two consuls of plebeian status and so replaced Marcellus (who obligingly resigned) with the patrician Q. Fabius Maximus.[63] Just as with the relations of the pontifical college to the senate, the augurs pronounced their specialist opinion, while the senate issued the final decision and took the consequent action.

The augurs differed markedly from the *pontifices* in their relations with the gods: unlike the *pontifices*, part of their religious role did involve direct access to the divine and a mediating function between men and gods. Yet, in their relations with the senate, they were more similar than different; for both colleges played the part of specialist advisers to the senate, which remained itself the organ of decision-making and control.

[60] The establishment of a *templum* on earth had the effect of putting a piece of ground into direct relationship with a heavenly *templum*; it linked the heavens and the earth. See Varro, *Ling.* 7, 8-10. *Templum* in this sense is much wider than our 'temple' and includes for example the Roman senate house (*curia*) and the *rostra* (Cicero, *In Vatinium* 10, 24). See the full discussion of P. Catalano, 'Aspetti spaziali del sistema giuridico-religioso romano. Mundus, templum, urbs, ager, Latium, Italia', *ANRW* II, 16. 1, 440-553 (esp. 467-79) and Linderski, 'Augural Law'.

[61] See Cicero, *Leg.* 2, 12, 31; *Phil.* 2, 32, 80 – 33, 84 (with Mommsen, *Staatsrecht*[3] 1, 109 and J.D. Denniston (ed.), *M. Tulli Ciceronis in M. Antonium orationes Philippicae prima et secunda* (Oxford, 1926), 180-2).

[62] See n.12 above.

[63] Livy 23, 31, 13-14. The same process no doubt lies behind the incidents described in Livy 8, 23, 13-17; 45, 12, 10.

The category of 'priest'

So far I have made a number of observations concerning Roman priests, religious authority at Rome and the focus of mediation between men and gods. I have shown that the senate functioned as the principal centre of mediation in the Republican city; and I have demonstrated that two of the major colleges of priests – the *pontifices* and *augures* – were perceived to differ sharply in their relationship with the gods, while occupying a very similar position (as specialist advisers) in respect of the senate. No doubt, if detailed investigation could be undertaken of other priestly groups at Rome, yet further differences would emerge.[64] More important, however, than extending the subject of study is to attempt to build on the observations made so far and to ask what picture they together present of priests, priesthood and priestly function in Republican Rome.

Our own everyday, rough-and-ready, category of 'priest' is not applicable to what we find in Rome. So much is obvious. The idea of priesthood that most English speakers have formed out of the traditions of post-Reformation Western Christianity incorporates training, sanctity and normally full-time remunerated employment. We expect also clear distinguishing features and external marks of sanctity which set the priest apart from his secular compatriots; after all, most of us, in most day-to-day contexts, recognize priests from their 'funny' clothes, collars turned back to front or long skirts worn, paradoxically, by men. Neither the senate nor the major priests of Republican Rome can be accommodated to this model.[65]

The same problem occurs even in more technical discourse; if we introduce, as I have, the notion of religious mediation as a useful identifying feature of established priesthoods, we still find it difficult to relate this easily to the ancient evidence. How then can we understand the Roman priestly function, in terms that do not just admit

---

[64] In the absence of detailed information on the duties and competence of many of the priesthoods, a profitable area of enquiry lies in the different Roman views of the aetiology and history of the different priestly groups. Some, for example, were perceived to have their origin before the major priestly foundations of the second king of Rome, Numa – notably the augurs (Livy 1, 18, 6), the Arval Brethren (Aulus Gellius, *NA* 7, 7, 5-8), the Potitii and Pinarii (Livy 1, 7, 12-15); some had a foundation legend which linked them directly with the world of the divine – the *salii*, for example, were supposedly founded to guard a shield that had fallen to earth from heaven (Dionysius of Halicarnassus, *Ant. Rom.* 2, 71, 1-2); others had a debated origin – the Vestal Virgins for example, attributed to both Romulus and Numa (Plutarch, *Rom.* 22, 1). See M. Beard, 'Acca Larentia gains a son', *Festschrift J. Reynolds* (forthcoming).

[65] The Vestal Virgins accord most closely with our own perceptions of priesthood – see Beard, 'Vestal Virgins'; also perhaps the *flamines*, particularly the *flamen Dialis* who was under an obligation to wear his distinctive hat (*apex* or *albogalerus*) at all times out of doors – see Festus, *Gloss. Lat.* p.9; Servius, *Commentary on Virgil, Aen.* 2, 683; Aulus Gellius, *NA* 10, 15, 17. See further, Scheid, 'Le flamine de Jupiter'.

bafflement or simply characterize it as 'different from our own'?

I shall conclude this chapter by offering some preliminary answers
to this question, investigating three topics in particular. I shall first
explore the fragmentation of priestly authority at Rome, looking more
carefully at the division of responsibility between the senate and
priestly colleges, and at the relationship of the different groups of
priests one to another. Secondly I shall consider the category of
priesthood in Roman terms and the use of the word *sacerdos*,
suggesting that this category was problematic even for the Romans
themselves and was only gradually being differentiated as an
independent element in the religious and political system towards the
end of the Republic. Finally I shall highlight the changes in priestly
function that occurred with Augustus and the advent of the principate.
By looking ahead, it will be possible to put the distinctive features of
Republican priesthood into sharper focus.

Fragmentation of priestly authority

I have delineated a religious system in which the senate was
distinguished by its power in mediation betweeen men and gods, but
was not perceived as specially endowed with religious knowledge. The
priests, on the other hand, if we take the pontiffs and augurs as
representative, were distinguished by their knowledge and specialist
expertise, but in relation to the senate were not perceived as powerful.
This seems at first sight paradoxical; for knowledge we expect to be
closely associated with power.[66]

The paradox can best be understood by analogy with the overall
structure of Roman Republican paganism. Ancient civic paganism was
a religion of no fixed centre, a religion whose centre was (in Derridean
terms) constantly *deferred*. It consisted not so much in a defined and
closed body of doctrine, but in a series of interpretations and
reinterpretations – satellites around an elusive and intangible core.[67]
The structure of religious authority followed much the same pattern.
The senate was, as has been shown, the centre of religious power, yet
that power was, like the centre of the religious system as a whole,
elusive and intangible. It was power without knowledge and power
without clearly defined executive force. Consider, for example, the
decrees of the senate, the *senatus consulta* which embodied its
religious (and other) decisions. These were not law and had no

---

[66] This association has been recently explored by, in particular, M. Foucault. See, e.g.
Power/knowledge (Brighton, 1980); see also, drawing on Foucault, but in an area cognate
with that under discussion, L. Lindstrom, 'Doctor, lawyer, wise-man, priest: big-men and
knowledge in Melanesia', *Man* 19 (1984), 291-309.

[67] On the idea of *deferral*, see J. Derrida, *Writing and Difference* (London, 1976).

statutory force; however authoritative, however rarely challenged, they were in theory obeyed simply by common consent and agreement, which could always be withdrawn.[68] This was religious power quite unlike (say) the binding decisions of a Catholic pope; it was elusive and unfixed. And around this elusive centre the priestly groups, as satellites deploying their religious knowledge and expertise in advice to the senate, could provide the focus for reinterpretation and restatement.

The question remains how it was that priests, as repositories of religious knowledge and specialism, did not also gain religious power. Here the crucial factor was the diversity and variety of the priestly structure at Rome, highlighted at the beginning of this chapter. Priestly knowledge was so minutely divided between different priestly groups, that the very limited area of expertise accorded to each priesthood effectively prevented that expertise providing an independent access to power. A comparison may be drawn here with the structure of the Roman magistracy. At the head of the regular series of magistrates stood the consul who had wide executive power over almost every area of Roman life. This power was limited, however, by time: each pair of consuls held office for only twelve months; none were magistrates long enough to gain in the office a permanent basis of power. Roman priests, by contrast, generally occupied their priesthood for life; the power of the individual priest and of each priesthood as an institution was limited by their very narrow range of specialism.

The division of responsibility between senate and priestly groups in Republican Rome ensured that religious authority was diffused as widely as possible among the Roman élite. All senators, by their membership of the senate, were incorporated into the central focus of medation between men and gods and the prime organ of religious control. Many too would have belonged to one priesthood or another, and so would have possessed one small part of religious knowledge and expertise. No one individual nor one institution could claim overriding independent religious authority.

Sacerdotes

I have laid emphasis at various points in this paper on the diversity of

---

[68] It is hard to get the correct emphasis here between the traditional view that the senate was the *consilium* of the magistrates (and, as such, only an advisory body) and the more recent stress on the *de facto* normative, if not strictly legislative, power of the senate. See H.F. Jolowicz and B. Nicholas, *Historical Introduction to the Study of Roman Law*) 3rd ed., Cambridge, 1972), 30-45 (especially 30 and 44-5) and C. Nicolet, *Rome et la conquête du monde méditerranéen* 1 (Paris, 1977), 'Les structures de l'Italie romaine', 357-92 (esp. 380-4). From my own point of view, the most important factor is that *senatus consulta* were not law. (I am grateful here to Peter Brunt, whose comments on the first version of this seminar enabled me to put the position of the senate in a Derridean perspective.)

the Roman priesthoods, on their different forms of organization and their different relations with the divine. While admitting a common element of specialism in their function, I have implicitly denied that the wide range of those officials traditionally entitled 'priests' should be seen as a single subject for analysis. Yet, it might be objected, the Latin words *sacerdos* ('priest') and *sacerdotium* ('priesthood') encourage us to think that for the Roman themselves there was a common core of priestliness and a recognizable category of priesthood which did embrace all those elements which seem to us so diverse. At first sight this objection may appear persuasive. But further investigation of Roman categories of priesthood and the use of the words *sacerdos* and *sacerdotium* reveals a much more complex situation than is immediately imagined; the category of priesthood is not only problematic for the modern observer, it was problematic also for the Roman themselves. Some illustrations will make this clearer.

First, the various priesthoods listed in Table 1 were not grouped or hierarchized by the Romans in any consistent way. We tend to think of a central category of priests in the four *amplissima collegia* ('most distinguished colleges') – *pontifices*, *augures*, *XVviri* and *VIIviri*; and this category was sometimes adopted during the Republic by the Romans themselves, when (for example) they legislated on the procedure for entry into these four priesthoods together, as a group.[69] Yet this was not the only or even the standard grouping. Cicero, for example, uses a classification which comprises a group of three priesthoods – *pontifices*, *augures* and *XVviri*.[70] And Polybius offers a quite different set. After discussing the Salii, he writes that this priesthood was one of the three colleges (*systemata*) that carried out the most important sacrifices in Rome.[71] It is not at all clear which were the other two organizations that Polybius had in mind; it is clear, however, that Polybius was operating with a rival schema from that of Cicero or from that standard in modern discussions.[72] The evidence suggests that in the late Republic attempts were made to classify (or even impose order on) the various types of religious functionary, but that, as yet, no orthodoxy had been achieved.

[69] See n.7 above (*Lex Domitia*, 104 BC) – although no ancient author explicitly names the colleges associated with this law, there can be little doubt that it applied to the four 'major' priesthoods. Otherwise all clear references to the *amplissima collegia* are imperial – see, for example, Dio 53, 1, 5; Augustus, *Res Gestae* 9, 1.

[70] Such a classification of three is implied by *Har. Resp.* 9, 18 (adding also the *haruspices*, cf. Valerius Maximus 1, 1, 1); *Leg.* 2, 12, *Nat. D.* 3, 2, 5 (including the *haruspices* with the *XVviri*). Note also the titles of books 2 to 4 of Varro's *Antiquitates Rerum Divinarum*: *De pontificibus, De auguribus, De XVviris sacrorum*.

[71] Polybius 21, 13, 10-11.

[72] F.W. Walbank, *A Historical Commentary on Polybius* 3 (Oxford, 1979) ad loc., 107 reviews various suggestions on the identity of the other two priesthoods. A cynic might, of course, argue that Polybius attributed great importance to the Salii simply because his patron Scipio was a member of that priesthood.

Roman problems of classification are highlighted also by a comparison of Cicero's handling of priesthood in *De Legibus* and Plato's treatment of the subject in his *Laws*, the work whose theme and form provided the model for Cicero's dialogue.[73] The Greek author deals with priesthood quite simply, treating it as a single category and generalizing about it as such. He discusses priestly selection as a whole (arguing for the use of lot), length of priestly office (ideally one year) and the most appropriate age for priests (over 60). The contrast with Cicero's treatment is striking. Although he starts from the generalizing, abstract term *sacerdotium*, generalizations, in fact, appear rarely. He presents, instead, a series of individual discussions of individual functionaries (the *pontifices*, the *augures* and so forth), ending with a lengthy (almost rambling) treatment of the role of the *pontifices* in Roman tomb and burial law. It seems a reasonable deduction that the multifarious variety of the Roman priestly groups (in contrast to those of Greece) presented Cicero with serious difficulties in generalizing in Hellenizing terms, which he did not fully overcome.

From the Greek point of view also, the terminology for discussing Roman priests was not easily established. In Greece too religious authority was widely diffused;[74] but the Greek term *hiereus* ('priest') at least evoked one well defined category of religious official, within a standard cult framework. The *hiereus* was the functionary of one particular deity (the 'priest of Apollo', for example, or that of Athena) and was traditionally attached to one particular sanctuary of that deity, not acting as the priest of Athena in general, but as the priest of Athena Parthenos on the Acropolis.[75] The term *hiereus* is not, however, consistently used by Greek writers in their discussions of those Roman officials we traditionally know as 'priests'. Although our English translations would make *hiereus* ('priest') appear the obvious word for a Greek to adopt in referring to *pontifices*, *augures* and so forth (all also 'priests' in our terms), it was more common practice, at least for writers of the late Republic and earliest period of the Principate, to transliterate the Roman priestly title or give an explanatory gloss. So, for example, when Polybius mentions the office of Scipio as Salian priest, he transliterates the title as *salios*; and instead of saying that the *salii* were one of the three most prominent priesthoods (*hierosunai*) of Rome, he glosses with the phrase, 'one of the three colleges whose duty it is to perform the principal sacrifices'.[76] Likewise Dionysius of

---

[73] Cicero, *Leg.* 2, 8, 19 – 9, 22 and 12, 29 – 27, 68; Plato, *Laws* 759a – 760a; similarly Aristotle, *Politics* 1322b; 1331b.

[74] See R. Garland on Athenian religious authority, pp. 75-81 below.

[75] See the excellent summary by W. Burkert, *Greek Religion: archaic and classical* (Oxford, 1985), 95-8.

[76] Polybius, 21, 13, 10-11.

Halicarnassos, when discussing the functions and possible Greek titles for the *pontifices*, does not talk of them as *hiereis*, but suggests the following variants: *hierodidaskaloi* ('teachers of the sacred'), *hieronomoi* ('legislators of the sacred') *hierophylakes* ('guardians of the sacred') and *hierophantai* ('revealers of the sacred'); while for augurs he uses *oionomanteis* ('prophets from birds'), *oionopoloi* ('those concerned with birds') and *oinoskopoi* ('watchers of birds').[77] This practice, at first sight strange, may best be understood as a feature of the awareness on the part of Greek writers that Roman priests were not equivalents of their own *hiereis* and were, in fact, no single category at all.

The word *sacerdos*, with its abstract *sacerdotium*, still, however, seems to suggest that there was a sense in which the Romans did perceive their various, diverse religious officials as falling within a common category – however different from our own conception of priesthood. After all, both *sacerdos* and *sacerdotium* are words well attested in Republican literature; and by the early imperial period almost all the different officials listed in Table 1 have been referred to or defined by some Roman author as *sacerdotes*.[78] This observation is accurate, but conceals a more striking point. Not only is the word *sacerdos* (and its derivatives) comparatively rare in Republican Latin; but it most commonly denotes not the Roman officials we know as priests but foreign (normally Hellenizing or Eastern) religious functionaries. In Cicero's *Verrines*, for example, by far the commonest use of the word is in the context of the Greek shrines rifled by Verres in Sicily;[79] and in surviving Republican inscriptions the word is almost exclusively used outside the Roman context as the title of (often female) priests of individual deities, on the Greek pattern.[80] It seems at least plausible to imagine that with the word *sacerdos* we are dealing with a term that was originally an 'external category' for the Romans – one which classified phenomena of the *outside world*. Only later did it provide a means of classifying also Rome's domestic institutions and officials.

The category of priesthood in Republican Rome is an elusive one. The various points just raised, however, each concerning difficulties or uncertainties about the nature of Roman priesthood in the Republic, seem to me explicable in the context of the wider process of structural differentiation in the last two centuries BC and the gradual

---

[77] Dionysius of Halicarnassus, *Ant. Rom.* 2, 73 (*pontifices*); 2, 64, 4; 3, 69, 3; 3, 71, 2 (augurs). See in general H.J. Mason, *Greek Terms for Roman Institutions: a lexicon and analysis* (American Studies in Papyrology, 13, Toronto, 1974), 115-17.

[78] So, for example, Cicero, *Dom.* 57, 144, *Font.* 21, 47 (Vestal Virgins); Pliny, *HN* 18, 2, 6 (Arval Brethren); Cicero, *Dom.* 54, 139, Varro, *Ling.* 6, 21 (pontiffs).

[79] For example, *Verr.* 4, 45, 99; 45, 100; 61, 137; 5, 8, 21.

[80] See, for example, *ILS* 3344; 3351; *CIL* IX, 2569; 3087; X, 5191 = Degrassi, *ILLRP* 62; 66; 273; 65; 63.

development by which 'religion' (or 'religious authority') became defined for the first time as an independent category.[81] The traditional religious system of Rome of the early or middle Republic fragmented religious authority; it comprised a large number of different officials whose responsibilities might easily seem (as is evident from Table 1) to have very little in common. Through the late Republic, however, there was a growing tendency on the part of the Romans themselves to classify and categorize their own experience and institutions. In part this was a predictable tendency within an increasingly complex society and needed no outside stimulus; but in part also Rome's increasing contact with the Greek world, and with intellectualizing systems of categorization developed there, encouraged the Romans to reflect on their own society in Hellenizing terms. As this tendency to classification met the traditionally fragmented and diverse system of Roman religious authority, gradually there emerged a category of 'priesthood' – workable and plausible up to a point, to the extent that the men and women thus categorized shared an official concern with the gods. But, in any terms more precise than this, the nature of the category remained – even for the most sophisticated Roman commentators – uncertain and, moreover, partly at odds with the deep structure of Roman religious authority. From this underlying contradiction stemmed the difficulties outlined in this section – the uncertainty of the grouping and hierarchizing of priesthoods, the avoidance of the apparently obvious Greek equivalent and the tentative use of the word *sacerdos*.

Augustus as pontifex maximus

Throughout this chapter I have stressed in various ways the close interrelationship between (to use modern categories) the 'religious' and the 'political' dimension of the Roman state. I have shown, for example, that the senate (traditionally regarded as a 'political' institution) played a crucial role in the mediation between men and gods in Republican Rome; and I have argued that the complex diffusion of priestly responsibility must be understood not only in the relationship of one priesthood to another, but also in the relationship of the senate to the priestly organization as a whole. Indeed, in more general terms, it has become clear that wide diffusion of religious responsibility was closely cognate to the diffusion of political responsibility within the Republican governing aristocracy of (at least notional) equals.

It goes almost without saying that the changes in the political

---

[81] See K. Hopkins, *Conquerors and Slaves* (Cambridge, 1978), 74-96; Beard and Crawford, *Rome in the Late Republic*, 70-1.

structure of Rome at the advent of the Principate will have heralded crucial changes in the structure of religious authority and the position of the priestly groups. I wish here to highlight just one aspect of these changes, an aspect not only important in itself, but one which will by contrast serve to re-emphasise the distinctiveness of the Republican priestly structure.

In 12 BC Augustus became *pontifex maximus*, head of the pontifical college.[82] Ever after, throughout the pagan empire, all emperors followed his example: the office of *pontifex maximus* became part of the imperial office and marked the emperor out as 'head of the state religion'.[83] In addition, following no Republican precedent, but like every other emperor after him, Augustus became a member of all the major priestly colleges.[84] For the first time priestly knowledge had been brought together with executive power; and the emperor, as focus of political authority, became also a focus of priestly authority – with a hierarchy of major and minor priests radiating outwards from his centre. The pattern of fragmentation of religious authority and of its constant deferral was gone for ever.

This was a new world. Official religious authority had for the first time a single human face. Official religious power was clearly defined and located: the utterances of the emperor constituted 'religious policy'.[85] Consider for a moment how impossible it would be, even for the most ruthless modernizer, to talk of a 'religious policy' during the Roman Republic, emanating from the diffused structure of authority that I have described. That impossibility symbolizes the gap between the Republic and the Empire. 'Religious policy' depends in its genesis and efficacy on everything that the Republican structure of religious authority was not.[86]

---

[82] Augustus, *Res Gestae* 10, 2.

[83] The first emperor to repudiate the title *pontifex maximus* was Gratian, some time between AD 379 and 383. See A. Cameron, 'Gratian's repudiation of the pontifical robe', *JRS* 58 (1968), 96-102.

[84] Augustus, *Res Gestae* 7, 3.

[85] Although anachronistic such an expression as 'religious policy' has a point. To a large extent the emperor could determine and change the legitimate, official means of approach to the gods and forms of worship. Out of many possible examples, note Pliny's consultation of Trajan over the persecution of Christians (*Ep.* 10, 96 and 97) and the far reaching 'reforms' of Elagabalus: the establishment of a temple of (Sol) Heliogabalus to which were transferred the emblem of Magna Mater, Vesta's fire, the Palladium, the shields of the *salii* (SHA, *Heliogab.* 3, 4). Throughout this section I have used the word 'official' advisedly. I do not mean to suggest that that emperor monopolized all forms of religious authority; simply that the *state religion* now had a single focus of human power.

[86] See further Scheid, *Religion et piété*, 66-74 and R. Gordon, pp. 79-84 below.

2

Diviners and Divination at Rome

This chapter is concerned, like the first, with the society of Republican Rome; but it investigates in greater detail just one element of religious practice – divination – and its practitioners.

Divination is a central element in traditional religious systems, providing access to the divine will or knowledge of future events through the interpretation of all kinds of oracles, signs, dreams and portents. We tend from a modern Western perspective to consider such practices as marginal to 'religion', and so tend to categorize ancient divination rather as we would today categorize popular astrology or the reading of tea-leaves. But in other societies it is clear not only that divination is of central importance in man's relations with the gods; but also that it is perceived as a 'science' – that is, accepted as one of a range of methods of understanding the world, all with an equal claim to be called 'rational'. It is this latter aspect, of divination as a *form of knowledge*, that has been the focus of much recent anthropological work on oracles and predictions; it has been argued that in traditional societies the principles of divination mirror, or even perhaps determine, the ways in which knowledge is organized and classified more generally, outside the (at first sight) narrow sphere of religious prediction.

This chapter is concerned more with the practitioners than with the practice of divination. It seeks to determine who in Roman society was perceived as skilled in ascertaining the will of the gods and how the possession of such skill related to other axes of power in Rome. In doing this, it reveals in one area of religious practice the same kind of diffusion of religious power that was seen in the last chapter to be characteristic of religious authority in Republican Rome more generally. But by taking also a longer perspective, stretching back to the early regal period, and on to the Principate, it shows how the image and function of the practitioners of divination were differently defined and perceived in different political systems: the role of diviners within the Republican system of government was necessarily different from their role under the monarchy.

A full understanding of priesthood depends on an understanding of both how the priest functions and how he is perceived within his community. This chapter, much more than the last one, introduces the problem of the image of priesthood and demonstrates strikingly how one group of diviners, the Etruscan haruspices, was perceived quite differently in Rome and in Etruria: the same activity by the same men was seen in very different terms in the two different societies between which they operated. It is not always a question of discovering simply what priests did, but also how their activity was seen and paraded.

Diviners and Divination at Rome
John North

Divination forms a very prominent part of the historical tradition that has come down to us from the Roman Republican period. The surviving books of Livy's history of the middle Republic, covering the years 219 – 167 BC, offer the richest material for reconstructing the year-by-year activities of various kinds of priests and officials concerned with divination; but it is all too easy to read Livy for his military or political narrative and skip over the (for modern readers) curious and unappealing records of prodigies, signs, consultations and rituals. Nor is it easy to disentangle from these reports any coherent picture of the relative importance of different groups of officials, who in one way or another played their parts in consulting the gods before any major action in Rome or abroad. Three groups of diviners regularly feature in these narratives as important elements in Roman activities, in peace or in war:

(1) The college of augurs, whose special concern was with the taking of the auspices before public action of any kind.

(2) The interpreters of prodigies, either the Etruscan diviners (*haruspices*) or the keepers, called *XVviri sacris faciundis*, of the Sibylline books, a set of oracular poems in Greek allegedly going back to the time of the kings.

(3) The readers of the entrails (they were also called *haruspices*) who practised their special art (extispicy) at most acts of public sacrifice in Rome or outside.

These three types of divinatory performers and the procedures they employed were strikingly different from one another and need to be looked at separately before any attempt can be made to generalize about them.[1] Some negative points, however, can be seen at once. There was no single identifiable authority in charge of all this religious

---

[1] For a basic introduction to the Roman diviners see Dumézil, *Archaic Roman Religion*, 594-610; a more detailed account is in the standard hand-book Wissowa, *RK²*, 523-49; cf. Latte, *RRG*, 396-8. On the individual groups see further: Radke, 'Quindecimviri'; Thulin, *Disziplin*, and MacBain, *Prodigy* (on the *haruspices*); J. Linderski has recently collected and analysed much of the material on the *augures* and their activity in *ANRW* 2.16.3.2146-2312, with rich bibliography.

activity, nor any identifiable institution which subsumed it all; modern accounts often use 'State Religion' as a general term, but that should only be regarded as an indication of a particular (alleged) area of Roman life, not as an institution of the Roman system. Divinatory rituals were widely disseminated amongst all the religious, political and military activities of the Romans, not concentrated in any single place. The situation is a microcosm of the location of religious activity in Rome generally; divination was some part of all religious activity, but had no special location of its own; in the same way, religious ritual in general formed part of every other activity in the city, though it lacked any autonomous power-structure of its own. There was no 'Church' to the Roman 'State' – just the Republic (*res publica*).

This picture of diffusion is confirmed when we turn to the persons who participated in these rituals. I have mentioned three groups of 'diviners', but the members of the three groups were not exclusively engaged in religious activities, nor were all their religious activities connected with divination (unless, perversely, we define divination in an extraordinarily broad way), nor were they the only officials involved in public acts of divination; in fact, the taking of the auspices was primarily the duty of magistrates, not priests, and so were the sacrifices that gave rise to extispicy. Priestly colleges commented on prodigies only if the senate asked them to, and the senate was the place where all the major decisions about religious matters were taken.[2] The various groups of priests provided the senate with a pool of expertise, on whose advice they normally acted; but, so far as we know, there was nothing that obliged the senate to take priestly advice on any particular occasion. If Cicero is to be believed, the augurs in 57 BC publicly expressed the view that Caesar's laws of 59 BC were flawed (*vitiosae*); they did this at a *contio* (that is a meeting called by a magistrate), but not in response to a formal request for a ruling from the senate; they made it clear that, had they been asked, they would have given this as their formal ruling; but the senate had not asked them before the *contio*, and did not ask them afterwards either; and so the Julian laws continued to be laws. The senate had good political reasons for this inaction and evidently had the authority to let prudential considerations stand in the way of consulting the priests on a point of religious law, even though they knew well what the answer

---

[2] For a typical example of the procedure for dealing with prodigies, see Livy 22,1,8-20 (217 BC); 14-16, in particular, make it clear how central is the Senate's role – making some decisions themselves, choosing to consult the priests about some others, but still taking the action themselves. On prodigies in general, Bloch, *Les prodiges*, 112-57; their evolution in the late Republic, J.A. North, 'Religion and politics, from Republic to Principate', *JRS* 76 (1986), 255-7.

would be if they did ask.[3]

The ritual performances themselves involved still more agents, lower-class specialists who were expert in the techniques of sacrificing (*victimarii, popae*) or of reading the auspices (*pullarii*). The reading of the *exta* at sacrifices was done by *haruspices*, who had the same title as the group who advised the senate on prodigies; it seems likely, though unprovable, that these were lower-class (though perhaps citizen) *haruspices*, much less dignified than those the senate would have seen fit to consult. In fact, the status of the senate's *haruspices* (we never hear the names of individuals) is also very much an area of uncertainty for us.[4] It seems a fair enough generalization to say that the dignified senior places were occupied by nobles and that the skilled specialists came from lower-class groups. So, again, we find ourselves with a complex diffusion of roles – dignified priests, magistrates, other ritual agents, the senate and even the popular assemblies all come into the picture at some point, all have some influence over interpretation and outcome. Our texts themselves sometimes seem confused over who had the final authority. It would be very difficult to make a simple statement as to where 'divination' was, or who had the power to control it. The question needs to be asked: why should that have been so?

Before any answer can be attempted, it will be necessary to examine more closely the three categories of divinatory activity distinguished above; and also to step back from this whole body of evidence and see how it relates to the society of Republican Rome in a broader context. The taking of auspices provided a standard set of procedures by which the human community could ascertain the will of the gods. The augurs did not in general carry out these rituals themselves, but they were the recognized experts in the principles and law of the science; as such, they acknowledged various techniques for the practice of augury, which was originally based on the interpretation of the flight of birds; by the first century BC, and probably for some time earlier, the auspices were normally taken by consulting sacred fowl, who were taken to have given a favourable answer to an enquiry if they took their food, an unfavourable one if they refused it. First-century sources offer a good deal of contemptuous comment on this particular technique.[5] Whatever the method used, the structure of the

---

[3] The *contio* over the *leges Iuliae* is reported by Cicero, *Dom.* 40; it was called and organized by Cicero's great enemy Clodius. Cicero habitually distorts the significance of Clodius' activities, so his interpretation should not be trusted; but it cannot be doubted that the events he describes in this passage actually occurred, whatever may have been Clodius' actual motives.

[4] The little we know about the identity of Republican *haruspices* was collected by Thulin, *Disziplin*, 3.150 and recently up-dated by Torelli, *Elogia*, 122; see E. Rawson, 'Caesar, Etruria and the Disciplina Etrusca', *JRS* 68 (1978), 140-6, for full discussion of the problems.

[5] See the discussion in Cicero, *Div.* 70-4.

consultation was the same: the auspices were taken by a magistrate at a prescribed moment in the exercise of his office – before the senate met, before electoral or legislative assemblies, before crossing the sacred boundary (the *pomerium*) of the city, before a battle and so on; the proper performance of the ritual was a precondition of a valid magisterial action in any of these spheres. The god was essentially asked to recognize the action about to take place; not that he was expected to guarantee the outcome, but at least to give some favourable indication before the action began.

In the case of the prodigies, the communication clearly began from the gods, not from a human enquirer; the prodigy, if accepted by the senate (which here as elsewhere had the right to decide such things), indicated that the relationship of Rome with the gods had been somehow disrupted and therefore required restorative action. We have a great deal of information from Livy about the lists of prodigies that were accepted and dealt with by the senate.[6] We know what events were counted as prodigies (the birth of monsters, buildings and statues being struck by lightning, the raining from the sky of blood, stones or milk); we know what the senate initially decided about them and what action should be taken; all this in respect of many years in the third and second centuries BC, though the amount of detail recorded varies from year to year, even from prodigy to prodigy. Despite this wealth of material, it is still difficult to be sure how the priests and senate decided to choose particular ceremonies, what techniques they employed to isolate the danger and to specify the appropriate religious responses. All the evidence, taken together, does suggest one very general conclusion: in the overwhelming majority of the instances where Livy records the details, the concern of the priestly responses and the senate's decree was not with the interpretation of the prodigies, nor with the elucidation of the dangers they implied, still less with specific prophecies about the future, but rather with the establishment of the appropriate ceremonial to avert the dangers of which the prodigies were a warning. The responses of the Sibylline books recorded in Livy consist almost entirely of ritual prescriptions;[7] so, mostly, do those of the *haruspices*, at least in the middle Republican period down to the middle of the second century BC.[8] It can and should

[6] MacBain, *Prodigy*, 82-112, provides a useful index of prodigies with references to the ancient sources and an indication of the priests involved in dealing with them.

[7] As rightly emphasised by Radke, 'Quindecimviri', 1115-28; on the Sibylline books, Diels, *Sibyllinische Blätter*; Wissowa, *RK²*, 536-47; Gagé, *Apollon* (with copious speculation); Latte, *RRG*, 160-1.

[8] For lists and discussion MacBain, *Prodigy*, 121-6. He argues that prophetic interpretation was at all dates characteristic of the *haruspices* as opposed to the *XVviri*; but evidence about this side of their activities is very flimsy between the early third century and the late second, that is including the well-documented years 219-167 BC, as his own lists show. See pp. 60-1 below for discussion of the problems raised by haruspical activity in Rome.

be argued that in these ritual prescriptions there is in any case an implied element of prophetic content. The prodigy acts as a warning of disaster, but the warning does not need to be spelled out in great detail, because what matters is not what would happen if the proper rituals were omitted, but knowing how to avert the threatened disaster by the proper rituals. That, not interpretation, was the skill that mattered.

The third category, the reading of the entrails, was the one that had come to prominence by Cicero's time, as the other augural techniques had partly been discredited, partly become the victims of an incidental process of change.[9] One category of the auspices, still important as late as the second century BC, was the military auspices, taken by the commander before battle; by the first century BC these no longer took place at all, not because of any decision or change of religious ideas, but simply because the men who fought the battles were no longer doing so during their year of office as consuls, but during the following year as pro-consuls, still qualified to command, but no longer to take the auspices.[10] Military divination still took place, but was now closely connected with the ritual of sacrifice before action. The successful completion of the sacrificial ritual was called *litatio*; this implied that the various stages of the ritual had been gone through without mistake or mishap and that the *haruspex* had examined the entrails and found them satisfactory. Not infrequently something was found to be wrong with the *exta* (bits of organs missing; the lobes of the liver disintegrating when the victim was opened up, etc.), which meant that the victim had been rejected by the god or goddess to whom it had been offered.[11] In that case, the correct procedure was to take a new victim and start again from the beginning. If the victim was eventually accepted this was called *perlitatio*; failure to reach *perlitatio* was, of course, a disastrously bad indication.[12] Extispicy could also be used to ask more complicated questions and hence to produce more specific answers. It is not clear whether the *haruspices* had two distinct sets of procedures for these different types of occasion.[13]

This preliminary survey has served to show that it is not a simple matter to detect the prophets and diviners in the Roman system. They are not a single defined group, paraded on special occasions. Rather we have to take account of a multiplicity of priests and procedures, all

[9] On the practice of extispicy at Rome: G. Blecher, *De extispicio capita tria* (Religionsgeschichtliche Versuche und Vorarbeiten 2.4, Giessen, 1905); Latte, *RRG*, 386-92; Schilling, *Rites*, 183-90.

[10] Cicero, *Div.* 2,76; Mommsen, *Staatsrecht* 1³.101; *PW* s.v. *auspicium* 1.2583 (Wissowa).

[11] See e.g. Livy 8,9,1; Cicero, *Div.* 1,118-19, cf. 2,35-6, for discussion of the extreme case in which a victim was found lacking a heart.

[12] Livy 27,23,4; 41,15,4; Plautus, *Poenulus* 489.

[13] Schilling, *Rites*, 183-90 discusses the distinction and its significance.

Fig. 4. The inspection of the entrails of the animal at a sacrifice. The relief (the so-called 'Louvre extispicy', first century AD) illustrates the variety of personnel involved in the ritual of sacrifice – from the half-naked attendant with an axe (probably a slave who had performed the killing) to the fully-clothed figure on the left apparently supervising the inspection (perhaps the *haruspex* himself).

concerned with assessing the risks of possible actions and the need for possible rituals. This examination of their activities starts in the first section from an examination of the Roman idea of divination as we meet it in the late Republican sources; the next section assesses some possible interpretations of the function of divining in the Republican system; in the third and last section, it will be suggested that there is a correspondence between the character of the divinatory system as it is presented to us and the Republican socio-political context in which it operated.

The concept of divination

The first question to be considered is the status of the concept 'divination' itself. There might seem to be no difficulty here, since the word is a Latin one, employed to describe the very situation under discussion; so there can hardly be any of the problems that so often arise in transferring our own religious terminology to another society. This term at least is playing on home ground. However, there are still some curious disjunctions, in particular between the way Cicero's *De Divinatione*[14] (the dialogue on the subject that he wrote in 45 BC, in the period of Julius Caesar's dictatorship) talks about divination and the historical divinatory activity that has just been described.

In part, the problem arises from Cicero's dealing with the conceptions of Greek philosophy: he is using the term *divinatio* as a translation of the Greek word *mantikê*; the Latin word, at least as an abstract noun, has no history before Cicero's use of it; as a verb, the word is found in the second-century playwrights Plautus and Terence, though they use it rather sparingly.[15] What Cicero is doing in his dialogue is to give a version, carefully adapted to a Roman audience, of a specifically Greek philosophical debate. It is not his main concern to give an account of Roman religion, least of all an account of its historical development. He is concerned with conducting a debate on a particular predetermined theme: is it possible for a diviner on the basis of his skill or his gifts to have knowledge about the future? For the purpose of illustrating this debate, Cicero brings in all the practices mentioned above; but that does not necessarily imply that he was using a traditional category. He may simply have been re-arranging and re-classifying incidents known to him, in a way that suited the exigencies of a Greek philosophical problem. Here as elsewhere, it is necessary to be aware that Cicero and his contemporaries were not static reporters of a dead past, but actively engaged in the process of rethinking and rearranging traditional modes of thought and even traditional vocabulary.[16] We should see them as analysts of great creativity in a period of rapid religious change; that is why it is so dangerous that we have to rely on them for basic information about the past history of their religion, as well as for reconstructions of their own religious situation. In a case like the present one, the fact that Cicero wrote a dialogue on divination should not be taken to imply that earlier generations of Romans would have recognized such a category.

One striking aspect of the dialogue is Cicero's dependence for his examples on the public divinatory activities of the Romans – the doings of *haruspices*, of Sibylline prophecies – not so much on incidents in private life. This could, of course, be explained in various ways:

[14] For recent debate on the overall purpose of Cicero's dialogue, which presents the case for (Book 1) and against (Book 2) belief in divination, see J. Linderski, *PP* 36 (1982), 12-38; Momigliano, 'Theological efforts'; Beard, 'Cicero and divination'.

[15] Plautus, *Miles* 1257; Terence, *Hecyra* 696; other evidence about the words in *TLL* 5.1613-14; 1618-19.

[16] This is well emphasised by Momigliano, 'Theological efforts', 199-204.

perhaps he regarded public life as the area in which examples of successful prophecy could best be verified and hence as providing the best evidence to prove what he wanted to prove; or perhaps he simply drew his examples from the range of activities with which he was most familiar – appropriately enough, since he was an augur himself; or perhaps he regarded private divination as a less than respectable area for discussion; or perhaps historical cases were simply the easiest to find – a serious consideration in view of the speed at which he was working.[17] In any case, it is not clear how the public divinatory system we have been discussing related to the wider conception of divination in Rome. Should the public system be seen as the major element on which our general judgments can be based or should it be seen as a rather formalized, sterilized version of a rich prophetic tradition that existed, unknown to us, in private life? If there ever was such a rich tradition, we have virtually no evidence about it. There are occasional mentions, mostly implying élite disapproval, of lower-class diviners; and we should not forget that in later centuries divination, together with magic, was to become the focus of much official hostility and intolerance, and to be seen as a major threat to the established order of imperial times.[18]

One important, and much misinterpreted, passage from the elder Cato's book on agriculture (second century BC) suggests that divination could after all be seen as a threatening force already under the Republic; the fact that we know so little about this might therefore be the result of our lack of information, not a reflection of the actual state of affairs at the time. Cato is writing about the role of the *vilicus*, that is the overseer, often a slave or freedman, in charge of a rich man's estate; in the middle of a list of prescriptions he says:

Aruspicem, augurem, hariolum, Chaldaeum nequem consuluisse velet.

Let him [the vilicus] not consult any *haruspex*, augur, *hariolus* or astrologer. (Cato, *De Agricultura* 7,4)

The first two characters on Cato's list sound like the respectable personages we have been discussing so far, but since he regards them as available, at least potentially, for consultation by a mere *vilicus*, they must have been rather the poor man's substitute, presumably the

---

[17] For Cicero's literary productivity in these years, when Caesar's dictatorship had denied him any political role, see E. Rawson, *Cicero* (London, 1975), 230-47; on the nature of his philosophical project, Beard, 'Cicero and divination', 36-40.

[18] Expressions of hostility towards diviners: Ennius, *Telamo* 319 (with H.D. Jocelyn, *The Tragedies of Ennius* (Cambridge, 1967), 396-8; Plautus, *Amphitruo* 1132. On the different atmosphere under the emperors: Liebeschuetz, *Continuity and Change*, 122-6; R. Lane Fox, *Pagans and Christians* (London, 1986), 212-13.

haruspex as a reader of entrails, the augur as a reader of bird-signs; the *hariolus* (the word is not uncommon in early Latin) was sometimes represented, unlike the others, as prophesying in a state of possession, wild and raving;[19] the *Chaldaeus*, the astrologer, was of course the most obviously foreign import into Cato's list. One significant implication of the passage is that all these different specialists must have been available for private consultations, or it would scarcely have been worth issuing the warning against them. That in itself suggests the existence of a richer divinatory tradition than might be supposed.

The passage has frequently beeen quoted to demonstrate Cato's contempt for diviners in general:[20] it is taken to mean that the *vilicus* should not waste his time on such rubbish as the various listed diviners would offer him. The context of the remark, however, shows that that is not at all the point of Cato's injunction. The recommendations on dealings with your *vilicus* may cover a good deal of ground, but they have a precise unifying theme: the absolute necessity that the *vilicus* should be kept in his proper place and not be allowed to impinge on his master's control of the whole enterprise:

> He must not assume that he knows more than the master. He must consider the master's friends as his own friends. He must pay heed to anyone to whom he has been told to listen. He must not carry out religious rites without the master's order, except on the occasion of the Compitalia at the cross-roads, or at the hearth. He must extend credit to no one but must collect the loans made by the master. He must have two or three households, not more, from which he borrows and to which he lends. He must make up accounts often with the master. He must not hire for more than a day any one day-labourer or servant or caretaker. He must not seek to make any purchases without the knowledge of the master, nor seek to keep anything hidden from the master. He must not have hangers-on. Let him not consult any *haruspex*, or augur, or *hariolus* or astrologer ...

In this context, what Cato's readers must have understood was that the consultation of the diviners was potentially too dangerous to be left to an underling: not that the *vilicus* would be wasting his time with the diviners, far from it, but that he would be threatening his master's domination, just as much as if he were hiring and firing, buying or borrowing out of the master's control. This would of course be consistent either with Cato's believing or with his not believing in these forms of divination himself. Nor can this passage tell us what kind of questions would have been asked by the *vilicus* or what kind of

---

[19] *PW* s.v. *hariolus*, Supp. 3.886ff. (Thiele)
[20] e.g. by W. Warde Fowler, *The Religious Experience of the Roman People* (London, 1911), 296-8; it is interesting to see how dated, compared to much else in the work, is this whole discussion of 'quack' diviners.

answers he might have expected. But this general interpretation of
Cato's warning suggests a theme to which we shall return later on: the
connection between the exercising of power and the right of access to
divination.

When Cicero is defining what he means by *divinatio*, the essential
element is prediction or prophecy. We have already seen that this
creates an apparent conflict with much of our other evidence, because
the bulk of our texts are far from suggesting that prophecy was the
central objective of Roman divination. It would be an oversimplification, however, to say that prophecy was not *one* of the
objectives of Roman divination. We know of many occasions in the
hundred years or so from the 140s to 44 BC on which the *haruspices* in
particular did produce predictions in the straightforward sense. For
the most part, they were very stylized and unspecific, foretelling civil
dissensions, riots, defeats and the like.[21] The one we know in most
detail is the interpretation they produced in 56 BC, which forms the
text discussed in Cicero's speech to the senate about the *haruspices'*
response (*de haruspicum responso*); but that alone would be enough to
show that producing predictions, on the basis of their interpretations
of prodigies, was very much the *haruspices'* business at least by that
date.[22] Something similar could be said about the Sibylline books as
well; many of the first-century prophecies we hear about are of
disputed genuineness,[23] though of course bogus oracles are just as good
evidence as 'real' ones of contemporary expectations. But even if we
look back to earlier periods, say late third/early second century BC, it
can be shown that there were official and unofficial texts in existence,
or known about, which contained at least some prophetic element.[24]

It is important at this point not to be drawn into historical
reconstructions of the kind that writers on Roman religion so often find
irresistible. It could be argued either (a) that since there was an
element of prophetic utterance in Rome in the late Republic, we have
no reason not to postulate its existence in earlier periods as well; or (b)
that since there is no evidence about the existence of a prophetic

[21] Macbain, *Prodigy*, 122-5, gives lists and discussion. Much of the information comes
from a late imperial author, Julius Obsequens, of whom we know little except that he takes
his information methodically from Livy, whose history is lost for these years.

[22] The response quoted apparently *verbatim* in various passages of the *Har. Resp.* was
collated into a text and discussed briefly in Thulin, *Disziplin*, 3.78; J.O. Lenaghan, *A
Commentary on Cicero's Oration DE HARUSPICUM RESPONSO* (The Hague, 1969) provides
useful material and bibliography, but is not penetrating on religious issues.

[23] For instance a famous prophecy circulated in 44 BC (perhaps, and perhaps not, at
Caesar's own instigation) that the Parthian Empire could never be conquered except by a
king; Suetonius, *Iul.* 79,3; Cicero, *Div.* 2,110; Dio Cass. 44,15,3; see S. Weinstock, *Divus
Julius* (Oxford, 1971), 340-1.

[24] The carmina Marciana, e.g., which seem eventually to have been included in the
Sibylline collection, were clearly prophetic in character; see especially Livy 25,12, who
quotes from them; for other texts, Wissowa, *RK*^{2}, 536 n.6.

tradition in early Rome, we should see prophecy as a new development probably under foreign influence of the late Republic. Either hypothesis would be possible, but premature: there are still serious conceptual problems to be faced before any kind of synthesis can be achieved. The first problem is whether the prophetic element in some accounts and its absence in other accounts should be treated as reflecting changes of substance or simply changes in reporting technique. As I have said, by Cicero's day the question 'What does the prodigy portend?' seems to have become a standard part of the problem the *haruspices* were expected to deal with; but if it is true that the question of ritual action was always more important than the question of prophecy, it would be very easy to imagine a recording convention which consistently under-reported or even omitted the prophetic element.

Secondly, even if it is true that the change is one of substance, not reporting, there is still a problem about how much emphasis should fall on the prophetic element as a determinant of the history of the institution. Cicero, admittedly, takes 'propositions about the future' as the criterion for his discussion of divination, but we have seen that it is philosophical influence that makes this the central issue for him; and his emphasis on the future in particular is refuted quite rapidly by the examples he gives, which include the discovery of a lost head of a statue (i.e. information about the present, not the future) and the identification of unnoticed past ritual error (i.e. information about the past, not the future).[25] Both these are perfectly normal activities of diviners; finding things was and is quite a normal job for the astrologer. If the emphasis is removed from this particular issue of predicting the future, then it is not so clear that there is a change of fundamental importance. The essential characteristic of Roman divination throughout the Republican period was a system of consultation with the gods, in which human action was constantly adjusted to this perception of the divine response. It may well be true that as time went by, there was an increasing tendency for this 'adjustment' to take the form of explicit warnings of danger. But, in this perspective, it is a minor issue when this change towards explicit rather than implicit expression took place.

The social functions of divination

Two possible models, derived from quite different situations, suggest themselves as providing a framework of interpretation within which to evaluate the system's value to the working of Roman society. Both

---

[25] Cicero, *Div.* 1,16 (head of Summanus' statue discovered in the Tiber by the *haruspices*); 1,33 (Gracchus' ritual error discovered by the *haruspices*).

provide starting points, though neither seems to me to take the question far enough. The first is the use of an oracle or divinatory system as a means of taking difficult or potentially controversial decisions by means of an arbitrative system perceived as (though it may not necessarily be) independent of the conflicting interests.[26] The second is the use of divination as a means of generating confidence, or restoring it after defeat, disaster or in any sort of crisis, recreating through the medium of ritual a sense of community and of external support and guidance to the community.[27] The first seems to apply only to a somewhat limited range of instances in Roman public life; it is possible that it might have been commoner and more important in private life, but we have no way of telling whether that was so or not. In public life, at least, the act of divination characteristically took place at predetermined points in political action, not at a moment specially isolated as a critical point of doubt or conflict. There was nothing properly corresponding to sending off to consult the oracle about what to do. The Romans did in fact sometimes send to Delphi for advice and there was, of course, a very famous oracle as close to them as Praeneste, which may have been consulted more often than we hear about.[28] But such consultations do not seem to have been a typical proceeding. There are occasions on which the gods were certainly consulted in the process of taking an important decision; this provides the nearest parallel, an interesting one, but with limited application. The best attested cases are the three war-declarations in Livy's fourth/fifth decades – that is in books 31, 36 and 42, corresponding to the declarations against Philip V, Antiochus the Great and Perseus.[29] The precise details of the procedure vary slightly and significantly, but in essence the same thing happened on these three and, presumably, many other occasions. The events of 191 BC will provide an example:

> At the beginning of the consulship of P. Cornelius Scipio and M'. Acilius Glabrio, the Senate, before dealing with the issue of the provinces, ordered the consuls to perform sacrifices, using the larger victims, at all the shrines where it was customary to carry out the *lectisternium*-ritual for most of the year. They were to pray that what the Senate had in mind with regard to the new war might turn out well and fruitfully for the

[26] The model is here derived from Evans-Pritchard's famous account (*Witchcraft, Oracles and Magic among the Azande* (Oxford, 1937)) of the working of the 'poison oracle'; see especially chs 7 & 8.

[27] For a full analysis on these lines, see Liebeschuetz, *Continuity*, 2-29.

[28] Recorded consultations of Delphi: the first certain case is the consultation of 216 BC, Livy 22,57; 23,11,1ff.; Plutarch, *Fab*. 18,3; cf. also Livy 29,11,5; there are several stories of consultations before the Second Punic War, but all to some extent suspect: see Latte, *RRG*, 223-4. For the oracle at Praeneste: J. Champeaux, *Fortuna, la culte de la Fortune à Rome et dans le monde romain* (Rome, 1982), 55-84; D. Briquel in Guittard, *Divination*, 114-20.

[29] 31,5-6; 36,1,1-6; 42,30,8-11.

Fig. 5. Two goddesses (perhaps the Fortunae) from Praeneste (Palestrina), the major oracular centre near Rome. This very unusual object is a small-scale representation of the images that would have been carried in procession and placed on a couch (shown underneath) to attend games and ritual banquets. The poles on which the statues of the goddesses would have been carried are visible near their feet.

Senate and the Roman people. All the sacrifices were favourable, the ceremony was fulfilled with the first set of victims: the interpretation by the *haruspices* was that the Roman peoples' boundaries would be extended and that a victory and a triumph were indicated. When all this had been reported, the Senate, their minds released from religious scruples, ordered that the question should be put to the popular assembly: whether it was their wish and command that there should be war against King Antiochus and those who had followed his lead; if this motion were carried, and if the consul so decided, they should bring the whole matter back to the Senate. (Livy 36,1)

This passage shows clearly that the gods were consulted before the decision was taken, indeed this was the first of the three steps – gods, Senate, *comitia* – before the negotiations by official legates took their course. The Senate might in the end vote against the proposed war, or it might be thrown out, as one actually was in 200 BC, by the popular assembly, the *comitia centuriata*.[30] Had the entrails (*exta*) at the sacrifices not given indication of success, the war-vote would presumably have been delayed, conceivably not taken at all. However, there is a remarkable ambiguity at this point in the wording of the prayer; the Senate had, of course, been involved in previous negotiations and debates; if there had not been a majority in favour of war, they would never have initiated the process of consultation at all. What was submitted to the gods was what the Senate already had in mind (*in animo*) about the new war. It seems to me very difficult to construe this as a situation in which conflict between groups needed to be resolved or avoided; rather it was a carefully prepared ritual programme, put into effect on the first day of the new consulship, and surely directed towards encouraging confidence in the floating vote at the *comitia*. Not the least interesting point in this passage is the fact that the *haruspices* certainly on this occasion produced a prophetic response, fairly specific in its character; but it is difficult to believe that this played any serious role in the making of the decision.

The second possible approach suggested above was the use of divination as a means of handling crises. Wolfgang Liebeschuetz, in the section of *Continuity and Change* which deals with these matters, lays a good deal of emphasis on this idea, that is on the maintenance of morale by sustaining the sense of common action with the gods and in particular (this is the part that works best) of the use of prodigies in crisis or after defeat to create a sense of a new reconciliation with gods or goddesses whose help has somehow been lost.[31] He has made a very considerable step forward by disposing of the long-lived misapprehension that the whole system was discredited by fraud and political manipulation;[32] not that there was no fraud in Roman religion, but that other societies illustrate clearly how awareness of fraud in individual instances can co-exist with continuing commitment to the system as a whole. Liebeschuetz's discussion of divination in relation to the maintenance of morale also marks real progress in interpretation. However, the usefulness of this particular hypothesis is limited: it is too unspecific to be very illuminating. After all, any

[30] Livy 31,6,3; the consul eventually persuaded the *comitia* to reverse the decision and follow the senate's wishes: 31,7-8.1.

[31] 7-29.

[32] See especially 20-24. M. Beard and M. Crawford, *Rome in the Late Republic* (London, 1985), 27-30.

common activity undertaken by a group will help to foster a sense of social solidarity and, if they persist in it in a crisis, that persistence itself will help them to retain a sense of unity and control. The trouble is that any form of regular behaviour will satisfy these conditions: it may be possible to generalize about human societies along these lines, but it becomes impossible to explain the specific religious phenomena of any particular time.

Both these functionalist approaches to understanding divination therefore have their contribution to make; but they depend on isolating particular religious phenomena at certain moments and seeking to assess their effects on the participants at the time. This is, of course, a perfectly valid set of questions to ask, and the answers are helpful in their own terms. But there may be other ways of looking at the same data.

Divination and Republic

One more fertile approach might be to look more broadly at the relationship between the activities of the different kinds of diviners and the socio-political system of middle Republican Rome. It is precisely because Roman priests were not separated from the rest of Roman life that this approach seems to offer the best opportunity of making progress. Their activities were an integral part of the political process in Republican Rome; they themselves were not just priests but also soldiers, politicians, administrators, lawyers;[33] in other words, the élite shared all these activities among its members, without using hereditary or other structural divisions, only on the basis of competition for honours. Nor does there seem to be any great separation between the actual proceedings of the diviners and the 'normal' rationality of their society. The obstacle to making much progress here is our lack of any first-hand documentation of what diviners actually did, how they arrived at their conclusions. In some respects, the *haruspices*, at least in so far as their practice is reflected in the Etruscan writings of which we have any record, evidently had elaborate systems of co-relating signs or natural events with particular predictions; and it is possible to show that they related their doctrine of lightnings with the latest developments of Greek astrology, so they were to some extent in touch with the latest progress in their field.[34] But the variations between the different systems in use in Rome were

[33] For lists of priests: G.J. Szemler, *The Priests of the Roman Republic* (Collection Latomus 127, Brussels, 1972).

[34] So S. Weinstock, 'Libri fulgurales', *PBSR* 19 n.s. vol 6 (1951), 122-53, especially 135-42; he made it certain that the Etruscan doctrine of lightnings had been modified in the course of the Hellenistic period under the influence of Greek astrology and the casting of horoscopes.

evidently wide and it is therefore not easy to generalize without far more detailed information than we have.

Despite these limitations on the information available, however, it is possible to say something about the way these priestly activities were presented. A feature common to augurs, *haruspices* and *XVviri*, that is both to Etruscans and to Romans (assuming that these are two distinct religious traditions), is that they were seen as working through written records. In the case of the *XVviri* this was just a question of finding the appropriate text in the Sibylline books – we do not know how exactly they proceeded in doing this. But the other groups had written works expounding their doctrines and preserving the experience of past periods; so there obviously was an underlying method of classification of the significant signs or responses. The Roman tradition was that religious books and written religious laws went back to the time of King Numa,[35] the originator of the whole religion; it is imposssible to say when this bookish tradition developed, though the fact that it is shared by Etruscans and Romans suggests that it belonged to the period of their mutual influence in the sixth and fifth centuries BC. One can only say for certain that by the end of the Republican period, the style of the priests' proceedings must share a good deal of common ground with the lawyers, historians and antiquarians, who were engaged in intellectual activities characteristic of the senatorial élite.

The implication of this discussion is that it would have been misleading to isolate priestly activity as 'superstitious' and hence different in kind from the other areas of Roman life which have been mentioned. It may suit us to read our Roman history in that way, because it is our preference to think of the Romans as rational administrators and imperialists – practical men to be contrasted with the idealistic Greeks. The reading is however a very biased one. It will be even clearer in the following discussion how priestly activity and the wider working of the state cannot be separated from one another; this takes us back to some of the issues raised earlier in this paper: the question is how far the divinatory system belongs in some characteristic way to the oligarchic system of the mid-Republic and how it relates to the power structures of the period.

What we have been discussing might be described as a particular style of divinatory activity. It is a style that (a) lacks emphasis on specifically prophetic utterance; (b) lacks identifiable prophets or holy men; (c) produces anonymous teams of diviners who display an oblique or reticent relationship to their divinatory techniques. The character of the ideology implicit in this will emerge sharply from a contrast with the role of the Greek *mantis*. To take a single example: there was in

---

[35] e.g. Livy 1,20,5, who describes Numa as giving detailed instructions on all aspects of religion when he set up the *pontifices*.

Sparta in Pausanias' day, a statue of the *mantis* Agias, born of a famous family of prophets;[36] the statue was in recognition of his achievements as diviner to Lysander, leading to the capture of the Athenian fleet at the battle of Aegospotami, at the end of the Peloponnesian War. Here we have the whole series of elements not to be found in the Roman tradition: the heroic achievement of the diviner; the recording of his name and his deeds; the public recognition of his glory. It cannot be assumed that no great prophets or holy men ever existed in Republican Rome, though there is no serious evidence that they did;[37] but, if they did, then it would be a striking tribute to the power of the accepted style, that their existence was 'ironed out' of the historical record.

There is at least a possibility of establishing this as more than just an unsupported speculation: the evidence comes from the haruspical inscriptions from Tarquinii republished (and identified as such) by Mario Torelli in his *Elogia Tarquiniensia*.[38] In these documents we find a series of fragmentary entries related to individual identified *haruspices*.[39] Torelli goes so far as to argue that these entries come from a list of members of the order of *haruspices* in Rome itself;[40] in my view, this theory goes well beyond the available evidence;[41] but it does seem to be certain that the priests listed were *haruspices* and were, at least in some cases, actively involved in the political life of Rome, not just in that of Tarquinii. What we have, therefore, is a local Etruscan record of individual priests; the entry in each case gives not just the name of office, but a brief account of the man's achievement as a diviner. In Roman records, the *haruspices* always appear as a group without any identification. Indeed, we scarcely know the names of any haruspices; even in the speech that Cicero devoted entirely to one of their pronouncements, he never mentions the name of a single *haruspex*.[42] Whether the Etruscans really kept records, or whether the entries from Tarquinii were based on memories, confusion or sheer fiction, does not matter for the present purpose. What does matter is that we have here an independent Etruscan perception, quite different from the Roman one. What in Roman records always appears as the

---

[36] Pausanias 3,11,5-8.

[37] For the brothers Marcii, who produced prophetic works in the Second Punic War period, see n. 24 above.

[38] *Elogia*, 105-35.

[39] That they are *haruspices* seems certainly implied by the fact that they are being celebrated in Tarquinii, while the technical language employed is Roman and hence the scene of their religious activities must have been Rome.

[40] 124-28.

[41] All we have is a succession of partial entries; they could as well be members of a particular priestly family, or distinguished Tarquinian *haruspices* some of whom had advised the Romans.

[42] See n. 4 above.

Fig. 6. Bronze model of a sheep's liver from Piacenza (in Etruria), *c.* 100 BC. The liver is divided into 42 sections, each marked by an inscription in Etruscan. It was perhaps meant to provide a guide for *haruspices* in the interpretation of the livers of sacrificial victims.

advice of an anonymous group of priests, in Etruscan eyes was the advice of individual, identifiable diviners, whose doings might be remembered and recorded. So the possibility arises that the 'anonymous team of diviners' should be seen as a construction, characteristic of the Republican system in Rome.

One of the effects of the system of divination in the Republican situation was to serve as a marker of the location of power. Not that divining was the sole prerogative of the state – it obviously was not. There was nothing in the system which could make it impossible for divination to be used in making an alternative claim to power. That would surely have been the situation during at least the early stages of the struggle between the patricians and plebeians for power in the Republic; it is inconceivable on my view that the tribunes could have held assemblies, passed decrees and elected magistrates without consulting the gods about what they were doing;[43] it would have been the view of the patricians that the tribunes had no right to do this. For early Rome it does not need proving that there was a close connection between the *auspicium*, the right to take the auspices, and the

[43] Some traces of their religious activities may survive into the later period: see J. Bayet, 'Les maledictions du tribun C. Ateius Capito' in *Hommages à G. Dumézil* (Collection Latomus 45, Brussels, 1960), 46-53 = *Croyances et rites dans la Rome antique* (Paris, 1971), 353-65.

magistrate's legitimate authority; it is quite specifically part of the legal structure of the republic.[44] Later on, the connection became less easy to specify, but evidently consulting the gods on the peoples' behalf remained a basic function of the magistrate or pro-magistrate, providing at least part of the ceremonial by which his power was represented or constructed. If that is right at all, it will not be surprising to find some kind of analogy between the style of Republican divination and the Republican system in general.

This distinctive Republican style can be characterized more sharply by contrast with the situation of divination and diviners both in the earlier monarchic period of Rome's history and in the period of the imperial monarchy that followed. In the myths of the regal period and even in later stories not concerned with Rome itself, there is no shortage of great diviners: Attus Navius, for instance – the augur who opposed the wishes of King Tarquin and then proved his powers by predicting that he would cut, and then cutting, his whetstone in half with his razor.[45] Significantly enough, he did have a statue and in the very centre of public life.[46] Or to take a later example, there is the story of the old man of Veii: Veii, according to Livy's story, could never be taken until the secret prophecy was known to the Romans; that was only achieved through the kidnapping by a Roman soldier of the old man who knew the secret.[47] So there was at all periods, not just an official divination enshrined in the structures of public life, but also an alternative mythical divination in terms of which other possibilities would be remembered or explored, an alternative which found room for great men, with miraculous powers and inherent skills. Later on, in the last years of the Republic and the early Empire, the great, named seer re-emerged; his arrival, as with the arrival of prophecies and prodigies connected with great men, is part of the reorientation towards the dynasts, which is surely a vital part of the collapse of the whole balance on which the Republic depended.[48] So once again we find named diviners now attached to famous individuals – to Gracchus or to Julius Caesar. This no doubt tells us at least something about the great man himself – for, whatever the reasons, he had chosen to be

[44] Mommsen, *Staatsrecht* 1³.76-116; P. Catalano, *Contributi allo studio del diritto augurale* 1 (Turin, 1960), provides exhaustive discussion of the terminological problems of *augurium* and *auspicium*.

[45] Livy 1,36,2-5 (and see Ogilvie, *Commentary*, 150-2): Dion. Hal., *Ant. Rom.* 3,71,1-5; see further, *PW* s.v. Navius(1) 16.1933-6 (Kroll); Linderski, *ANRW* 2.16.3.2207-8.

[46] Livy 1,36,5; Dion. Hal. 3,71,5; cf. Pliny, *HN* 34,21, who says the statue-base had been destroyed in the late Republican period.

[47] Livy 5,15 (with Ogilvie, *Commentary*, 661-3); see F.-H. Massa-Pairault, 'La rivalité Rome-Veies et la mantique. Quelques reflexions' in Guittard, *Divination*, 68-89.

[48] Gracchus' *haruspex* was Herennius Siculus (Val. Max. 9,12,6; cf. Vell. Pat. 2,7,2); Caesar's Spurinna (Cicero, *Fam.* 9,24; *Div.* 1,119; Suetonius, *Iul.* 81; Val. Max. 8,11,2); see Rawson, op.cit. in n. 4 above.

publicly associated with some particular divinatory system. Also, irrespective of his own thoughts, the diviner served as part of the legitimation of his position, as well as the sharer in his power, in his rise or fall. Consider the future *princeps* Tiberius, in exile on Rhodes, waiting for the ship bringing news of his recall:

> He was persuaded at this time of the powers of Thrasyllus the astrologer whom he had brought into his household as an expert in that art; for as soon as Thrasyllus caught sight of the ship, he said 'It is bringing joy'; and this happened at the very point when Tiberius strolling along with him and thinking how badly things were turning out and how contrary to Thrasyllus' predictions, had just decided to push him off into the sea, as a false prophet too rashly given access to his secrets. (Suetonius, *Tiberius* 14)

There is no need to take any particular view as to the historicity of this incident. It may very well not be true, and it does not matter for the present purpose whether it is true or not.[49] There does not, for instance, seem to be anything very astrological about Thrasyllus' announcement on setting eyes on the ship. But Thrasyllus' achievement is, all the same, of some importance. He was a distinguished practitioner of a reputable science, no village prophet.[50] He was personally linked with the aspiring *princeps* – strolling with him on the cliffs, privy to his secrets and hence potentially dangerous, on the very brink of being honoured by an imperial shove in the back. And, most important of all, as Tiberius triumphed and rose to power, so too did Thrasyllus. Whatever the sincerity of the evil old emperor's supposedly Republican vacillations, that day on the cliffs of Rhodes reeks of the monarchic divinatory style.

The general thesis argued in this chapter is that in this period a very close association existed between the character of the activity of diviners and the Republican system itself. Roman divination on this view should be seen not as a form characteristic of archaic Italy, surviving beyond its time; nor as some peculiar deformation caused by the narrow-minded and pragmatic character of the Romans themselves. Rather it is the expression in the religious sphere of some of the dominant characteristics of Roman Republicanism: there is an avoidance of the concentration of too much power on any individual; a tendency for decisions and actions to operate through groups or through changing individuals; a reluctance to recognize the special or charismatic qualities of special human beings. It must remain an open question at the end of this discussion how far this situation should be

---

[49] For other versions of the story, see Tacitus, *Ann*. 6,21; Dio Cass. 55,11,1-2.
[50] F.H. Cramer, *Astrology in Roman Law and Politics* (Philadephia, 1954), 92-108; *PW* s.v. Thrasyllus(7) neue Reihe VIA.581-4 (W. Gundel).

understood as the 'reality' of the time, how far as an interpretation imposed by the ruling élite and by the historians and commentators who shared their attitudes and preferences. In the particular case of the *haruspices*, we have even found reason to suggest that Etruscan observers might have seen the situation in a different light from the Romans themselves. On either interpretation, the religion of Rome has to be seen as the construction of a ruling élite, of the greatest value to them in sustaining political control, but always vulnerable, at least potentially, to the emergence of powerful religious initiatives outside the officially sustained system.

3

Priests and Power in Classical Athens

This chapter takes as its subject the priesthoods of Athens in the fifth and fourth centuries BC. This was the period of the most radical form of democratic government at Athens and the most radical known in the ancient world: power rested (both formally and in practice) with the assembly of adult male citizens, all of whom had the right to speak and vote; many officials of state, political and legal, were chosen by lot, so ensuring that executive authority was shared among the citizen body without favour to the rich or ambitious.

Priestly power is shown, once again, to have matched the distribution of political power. Whereas in Rome religious authority was diffused among the relatively small numbers of the élite, in Athens that authority was spread through the people (the *dêmos*) as a whole. The democratic system of government was mirrored in the patterns of religious office holding.

The close fit between 'political' and 'religious' authority in Athens necessarily raises the question of historical development. Athens had not always been a democracy; the radical democratic forms of the classical period developed from the aristocratic forms of government attested in the seventh and sixth centuries (the so-called 'Archaic period'). If Garland's thesis is correct, then we must assume that the character of religious authority in the earlier period was aristocratic and that it was 'democratized' at the same time as the Athenian political system, between the seventh and fifth centuries. We cannot now reconstruct the details of Archaic priesthood or of the assumed change, but (as Garland notes at the end of the chapter) there are sufficient hints in the ancient evidence to suggest a much more restricted élite control over religion in the seventh and sixth centuries BC. In Athens, as also at Rome and elsewhere, the overlap of politics and religion implies not a static view of religious authority, but dynamic changes in religious control linked to the well recognized 'political' changes in the state.

Priests and Power in Classical Athens
Robert Garland

This chapter is constructed around five questions which I believe to be central to a proper understanding of the structure of Athenian religion. Who had the right to issue authoritative pronouncements in the name of the state religion? Who exercised control over the religious life of the individual? By what mechanism and under which authority could innovations be introduced into the existing religious framework? What was the status of oracles and seers, and how could they intervene in the life of the community? Through what channels was mediation between gods and men conducted?

To borrow a phrase from John North (p. 52), there was no 'Church' to the Athenian 'State' – just the *dêmos*. There never was, nor could there have been, any clash between religious and non-religious power since power was not recognized as dividing along these lines. Furthermore, there was no Athenian category or Greek equivalent to our own word 'religion'. We are therefore faced at the start of our enquiry with a problem of language (writing in English, we must necessarily use English categories). Obviously, we cannot simply jettison the category 'religion' altogether, but we should see it as an analytical tool of modern scholarship, rather than as part of the Greeks' own thought-world. It may indeed correspond to their categories in part and at times, but essentially it is a modern introduction with false associations, Greek religion being, in Vernant's words 'more of a practice, a manner of behaviour and an internal attitude than a system of beliefs and dogmas'.[1] In fact, talking about Greek 'religion' is in some ways similar to talking about 'the Greek economy', likewise a conception no Greek ever possessed, but one which may help us better understand aspects of their life.

Religious function and religious authority in Classical Athens were diffused and non-centralized in a manner which in general outline resembles the Roman system, but which in its operative details is wholly distinctive. It will be my contention that the ability to act authoritatively in the name of and in matters of religion was not the preserve of any one class or caste, whether social or political, but was shared out among a multiplicity of specialist and non-specialist

---

[1] J.-P. Vernant, *Myth and Society in Ancient Greece* (London, 1980), 88.

Fig. 7. An Athenian vase of the early fifth century BC, showing a woman in front of an altar, on which a tall incense burner stands. The woman is playing, in our terms, a priestly role, although there is no way of knowing whether she is technically a priestess – or even whether she is a 'real-life' rather than a mythological figure. (Beazley, ARV² 199.)

institutions and individuals whose connection with one another, so far as we can judge, was essentially one of mutual dependency.

Priests

'Priest', etymologically a contraction of 'presbyter' from the Greek *presbuteros* or 'elder', is the conventional but somewhat misleading translation of the Greek *hiereus*. First and foremost this title denotes one who is in charge of the *hiera*, that is to say, the sacred objects stored within the sanctuary and the sacred rites connected with the cult, chief of which was the sacrifice. Both men and women served in this capacity, the general rule being that male deities were attended by male priests and female deities by female priests. The oldest and most venerable cults were 'gentile' – that is, their priesthood was reserved for members of a particular aristocratic kin-group or *genos*, as in the case of Athena Polias, whose priest had to be a member of the Eteoboutad *genos*. By *c.* 450, however, if not earlier, most if not all the priesthoods of new cults which gained official standing in the Athenian state became democratic, that is to say available to all Athenians depending only on the appropriateness of their sex, as in the case of Athena Nike, whose priestess was elected by lot 'from all Athenian women'. Priests generally only received a modest fee for their services, though they were also entitled to a special portion of the meat whenever they performed a sacrifice. While there is no evidence that they were required to undergo any formal training or ordination before assuming their duties, it seems inevitable that, at least informally, they received some instruction from their predecessors. So far as we can judge, the only positive qualification required of them was that they should be physically whole and in good health (*holoklêros*). No formal tie existed between priest and worshipper as it does in the Christian Church where the clergy are responsible for the spiritual well-being of their congregation, nor was the presence of a priest required at any of the *rites de passage* which mark the stages of a person's progress through life, most notable of which are those connected with birth, marriage and death.

As far as the present study goes, however, the most striking feature of Athenian priests and priestesses is their isolation. They were devoted to the cult of one god or goddess in one particular sanctuary and their authority was limited to issues related to that particular cult. Essentially their duties were liturgical and administrative. As the Stranger in Plato's *Statesman* (*Politicus*) states, priests 'understand how to offer our gifts to the gods in sacrifices in a manner pleasing to them, and they know, too, the right forms of prayer for petitioning the gods to bestow blessings on their worshippers'.[2] Priests were also responsible for the care and upkeep of the sanctuary over which they had control, and in particular for the cult statue, for conducting rites of purification (for instance after some pollution of the sanctuary), and for

2 290C.

safeguarding the treasures and gifts within their charge.[3] They also had the power to curse the enemies of the state, though never, it seems, except under express instruction from the *dêmos*. This is well-illustrated in the case of the alleged parody of the Mysteries in 415. Though it was the Eleusinian priesthood whose dignity was directly affronted on this occasion, they themselves did not rise up in holy fury and rain down curses upon the accused, but waited to be so ordered by the *dêmos*.[4]

Athenian priests never posed any threat to the legal or political authority of the state, chiefly, perhaps, because as a group they do not seem to have acknowledged any corporate identity. Or, to phrase it correctly, Athenian political life was so organized that there never developed anything remotely resembling a priestly perspective on any matter under consideration whatsoever. Only exceptionally do we hear of a member of the priesthood *qua* priest interfering in Athenian politics. A rare instance of this kind occurred in 480 when the priestess of Athena Polias announced that the sacred snake of Athena had already departed from the Acropolis, thereby lending support to Themistocles' proposal to evacuate the city in the face of the Persian advance.[5]

Our sources make it clear that a priesthood did not debar a man from holding political or military office. Callias, a priestly official of the Eleusinian Mysteries, fought at Marathon and later went to Persia on an embassy to King Artaxerxes; Demon, a priest of Asclepius, was active as a politician from 335-323; and Lycurgus, a priest of Poseidon Erechtheus, was director of Athens' finances in the 330s. In some cases, the priest might even make some public display of his priesthood in the military or political sphere, as Callias did at Marathon, fighting in his priestly garments.[6]

[3] For useful general accounts of the duties and responsibilities of priests, see Ph.-E. Legrand, 'Sacerdos' in Ch. Daremberg and E. Saglio (eds.), *Dictionnaire des antiquités grecques et romaines*, vol. 4 (Paris, 1877), 934-42; Martha, *Sacerdoces* and L. Ziehen, *PW* s.v. 'Hiereis'. References illustrating points referred to in the text include Herodotus 5, 72 and 6, 81; A. Walton, *The Cult of Asklepios* (Cornell Studies in Classical Philology 3, 1894, repr. New York, 1965), 96; *LSG* 35.16-20 (dated 350-320) and 36 (Piraeus, fourth cent.); *IG* II², 1163; Aeschines 3, 18; Aristophanes, *Birds* 864ff. For a theoretical description see Plato, *Laws* 6, 759. Not surprisingly, male prostitutes were debarred from holding priestly office, among other offices (Aeschines 1, 19).

[4] Plutarch, *Alc.* 22, with Clinton, 'Sacred officials', 16. Note the refusal of one priestess to obey the orders, saying that she was a priestess for praying, not for cursing. Other instances of Athenian priests being ordered to curse are in Lysias, 31, 44, 6 and Polybius 16, 31, 7. For priests ordered to pray, see *SIG³* 581, 2-8 = *Inscr. Cr.* 3, pp. 31-6, no. 3a, 1-7; *SIG³* 1003, 19-20 =*LSA* 37, 18-19.

[5] Herodotus 8, 41.

[6] For Callias (*dadouchos* – Eleusinian torch-bearer – from at least 490 to 446/5 or later) see Plutarch, *Aristides* 5, 6-7; Scholion on Aristophanes, *Clouds* 63; with further references in Clinton, 'Sacred officials', 47 and Davies, *APF*, 258-61; for Demon, *IG* II², 4969 (dated *c.* 350) with Davies, *APF*, 116-18; for Lycurgus, Davies, *APF*, 348-53. For priestly garments, see M.C. Miller in *Hesperia* (forthcoming).

Fig. 8. Part of the central slab of the east frieze of the Parthenon, Athens (between about 447 and 438 BC). This is the climax of the long procession running all around the Parthenon. On the right, a man, probably a magistrate, takes from (or hands to) a child the new *peplos* (robe) for the goddess Athena. On the left, a woman, perhaps a priestess, meets a girl carrying a stool at the head of the procession.

In any ancient city priesthood might confer public prestige on its holder, and in Athens we might *a priori* expect to find a distinction between gentile priesthoods and democratic ones.[7] Within the latter category, a further distinction in terms of prestige and its reverse might be suggested between those who served for life and those who were annually elected.[8] Certainly, in the case of some long-serving gentile priests and priestesses, we have evidence of particular prominence: if the suggestion is right that Lysimache, the gentile priestess of Athena Polias, who served the goddess for sixty-four years,

[7] For the origins and development of gentile and democratic priesthoods, I refer to my discussion in 'Religious authority'. Feaver, 'Priesthoods', 139, would lay it down 'with all probability' as a general principle that all gentile priesthoods were pre-Cleisthenic in origin and all post-Cleisthenic priesthoods democratic. This, I believe, is stretching the evidence too far.

[8] An example of the latter category are the two priests of Asclepius, one of whom was in charge of the city and the other of the Piraeic cult. In the third century the method of appointment was by sortition rotating in tribal cycles, i.e. allotments drawn each year from a single tribe, following the official order of tribes (cf. *IG* II² 1163.3f. dated 288/287). R. Schlaifer, 'Notes on Athenian public cults', *HSCPh* 51 (1940), 242-3, believes this method of election is quite likely to have been employed from the cult's inception in 420/419.

provided the recognizable model for Aristophanes' Lysistrata, it is
reasonable to suppose that this was due to the prominent position
which she occupied, at least informally, within the community as a
whole.[9] However, it would be a glib modern assumption to suppose
that, because democratic priests were selected by lot, they
automatically lacked the prestige of their gentile counterparts. It
might even be the reverse, in that the random choice made by the lot
could be interpreted (and certainly sometimes was) as leaving the
choice of priest or priestess to the deities themselves.

The Athenian priesthood was subject in some way to the authority of
the three major archons. These magistrates had from early times down
to the end of the sixth century BC been the senior officials of the
Athenian State: the *archôn eponymos* who was the chief executive
officer, after whom the official year was named, the *polemarchos* or
war-leader, and the *archôn basileus*, the successor of the old Kings of
Athens, who retained traditional legal and religious duties. Like
magistrates in most Greek states, these archons held their office only
for one year. In Athens, however, as ex-archons they joined an ancient
council, the council of the Areopagus, which was believed to have
wielded great power in the city in early times. Though we have too
little information to judge how it sustained and exercised this power, it
is conceivable that it was based partly on the control and manipulation
of religion.

By the democratic period with which this chapter is concerned, other
more modern magistracies had taken over many of the powers that the
archons and the Areopagus had once exercised. The Areopagus
remained the highest murder-court of the city as well as holding
jurisdiction over certain specified religious offences. Trials for impiety,
however, which were not infrequent, were heard by a normal
democratic court. The *archôn basileus*, like the Areopagus, retained
specific duties of a religious kind – oversight in the leasing of sacred
lands, jurisdiction between rival claimants to a priesthood, the
registration of impiety cases. These duties, combined with the
venerability of his magistracy, may perhaps have given him a certain
aura of sanctity, even in the later period; but it is abundantly clear
that if the archons and Areopagus had ever been the main religious
authority in Athens, they had lost that position by the fifth century

[9] Lysimache, daughter of Dracontides, of the deme of Bate, erected her statue on the
Acropolis and reared four children (Pausanias 1, 27, 4; Pliny, *HN* 34, 19, 76; Davies, *APF*,
170-1). The base of the statue survives (*IG* II² 3453). D.M. Lewis, 'Notes on Attic
inscriptions, xxiii. Who was Lysistrata?', *ABSA* 50 (1955), 1-12, believes that Lysimache
was in office when Aristophanes' *Lysistrata* was performed in 411 and that its heroine, who
'is meant to represent the oldest and best elements in Athenian life' (p. 3), may well have
been directly modelled on her.

BC.[10] The role of the Athenian priest as it has emerged from this account is, then, a very circumscribed one. The modern tendency is to evaluate the role of priests primarily in terms of the moral and spiritual guidance which they can offer. Of course, we cannot know about the private religious consciousness of individual Athenian citizens, nor about the influence on them which the activities of priests may have had. But it is clear from all our evidence that priestly office did not have the pastoral roles which are associated with the modern clergy. To conclude, it would not be right to think of the priest as a purely routine state official, discharging essentially mechanical functions, since that would be to underestimate the sensitivity attaching to their role as mediators between the city and its gods; but equally it would be wrong to assume a 'spiritual role' for which there was no outlet, given that piety in the Greek world was a condition not of moral or religious behaviour but of ritual obedience.

Exêgêtai

Alongside the priests, we find a group of expounders of the sacred law called *exêgêtai*: unlike the priests, they possessed the competence and technical skill to deal with difficulties arising from the practice of religious rituals.

Exêgêtai are defined by Jacoby as follows: 'interpreters who in dubious cases ... on the strength of their comprehensive knowledge of ancient ritual, utter an authoritative opinion as to how an act of cult is to be performed with ritual correctness.' Their sphere of expert opinion probably included such matters as the correct procedure for making sacrifices and, perhaps chiefly, the rules of purification to be adopted in cases of homicide. They expounded at the request of private individuals; whether they also expounded by order of the *dêmos* is disputed, the fourth-century evidence for their existence consisting wholly of private enquiries.[11] The fullest text for examining the board's *modus operandi* is provided by a speech attributed to Demosthenes in which the plaintiff claims that when an old nurse of his died at the

[10] For the religious functions of the basileus and Areopagus, see R.J. Bonner and G. Smith, *The Administration of Justice from Homer to Aristotle* 1 (Chicago, 1938), 258-61 and A.R.W. Harrison, *The Law of Athens: procedure* (Oxford, 1971), 8-9 and 37-9. The clearest statements on the religious role of the Areopagus in the classical period are Aristophanes, *Ath. Pol.* 60, 2 (trial of persons accused of destroying sacred olive trees) and [Demosthenes] 59, 80 (punishment of *archôn basileus* who had married an unworthy woman and had allowed her to perform sacrifices and administer oaths to priestesses). Its additional religious powers prior to this date remain a matter of conjecture.

[11] For discussion of *exêgêtai*, see H. Bloch, 'The exegetes of Athens and the Prytaneion Decree', *AJPh* 74 (1953), 407-18; Clinton, 'Sacred Officials', 89-93; Jacoby, *Atthis*, 8-51 (quote, 44-5); Oliver, *Athenian Expounders*, 24-52; M. Ostwald, 'The Prytaneion Decree Re-examined', *AJPh* 72 (1951), 35-46.

hands of the defendant, he consulted the *exêgêtai* 'in order to learn what ought to be done'. It seems from their response that they existed merely as an advisory body to clarify religious responsibility but without any powers of enforcement. In fact, in this case the client does not seem to have had any obligations to enlist their services or follow their advice. Even when the *exêgêtai* have delivered their exegesis and offered advice (it is significant that they distinguish between the two activities), their client is still free to act as he sees fit; he does this by looking up the relevant law-code and consulting his own friends.[12] *A fortiori*, it is improbable that the Athenian state was under any obligation to follow the advice of the *exêgêtai*.[13]

We would have a clearer picture of their activities, if we had a better picture of the development of the institution. However, our first clear evidence of the existence of *exêgêsis* comes only at the beginning of the fourth century BC. Though *exêgêtai*, in the sense of individuals willing and able to offer *exêgêsis*, may be as a formal institution a relatively late invention, it seems likely that the advice we find such persons offering in the fourth century would have been available from somebody in earlier periods. Notably some types of *exêgêtai*, such as the *exêgêtai* of the Eumolpidae, are closely connected with ancient aristocratic families. It may even be that *exêgêtai* were the aristocratic equivalents of the *chrêsmologoi* of democratic Athens – to whom we turn next.[14]

Chrêsmologoi and manteis

The other group of religious experts operating within the Athenian state were those who practised seercraft and divination, who were known variously and apparently indiscriminately as *chrêsmologoi* and *manteis*.[15] It is clear that these men could be perceived as a group with similar characteristics and functions. Indeed Aristophanes makes the *chrêsmologos* and *mantis* a frequent target of abuse for their importuning, greed and meddlesomeness. Yet analysis reveals that within this group there existed many very different types, inasmuch as *chrêsmologos* or *mantis* was, it seems, a title accorded to anyone who could command a following for his skill in divination, irrespective of the source of that skill.

[12] [Demosthenes] 47 (esp. chs 68-71).

[13] For other fourth-century references to *exêgêtai*, see Plato, *Laws* 12, 958d; Euthyphro 4C; Isocrates 8, 39; Theophrastus, *Char.* 16, 6.

[14] For the *exêgêtai* of the Eumolpidai, see Jacoby, *Atthis*, 26-7.

[15] The confusion is particularly striking in the case of Lampon who is variously referred to as *exêgêtês* (Eupolis, fr. 297); as *chrêsmologos* (Scholion on Aristophanes, *Peace* 1084 and *Birds* 988); as *mantis* (Plutarch, *Per.* 6; Athenaeus 8, 344e; Scholion on Aristophanes, *Clouds* 332; Suda s.v. *Thouriomanteis*); and even as *chrêsmologos* and *mantis* (Scholion on Aristophanes, *Birds* 521).

The possession of a list of oracular utterances was a common feature of seers. Lysimachus, the grandson of Aristides, earned his living from a tablet containing interpretations of dreams. Isocrates tells us of a certain 'wandering seer' called Thrasyllus who went into professional practice after being bequeathed books on the mantic art by one of his guest-friends, and who is said to have become the richest man on the island of Siphnos.[16] In this latter example we should note the foreign origin of the mantic texts, parallel to the foreign origin of seers themselves – some of whom (like Amphilytus, the *chrêsmologos* who had dealings with Pisistratus) came from Acarnania. In part then, we might suggest that the *chrêsmologos/mantis* appealed to religious authority from outside Athens.

While many seers perhaps relied exclusively on the technical skills embodied in written divinatory texts, the assumption that all *chrêsmologoi/manteis* were by definition persons whose 'claims to influence rest on learning, and mastery of the technical aspects of ritual rather than inspiration', is an oversimplification. Some at least seem to have relied on inspiration as well. Herodotus, for instance, comments on Amphilytos that he delivered his *chrêsmos*, or prophecy, 'being inspired' (*entheazôn*), and the mythical seer Tiresias in Sophocles' *Oedipus Tyrannus* was clearly possessed of a revelatory kind of wisdom, being described by Oedipus as 'you who comprehend all things, both those that can be taught and those which are unmentionable, whether of the sky or of the earth'.[17]

It is only in the military context that *manteis* may have been employed on a formal, regular basis, being required to supervise the sacrifices involving divination (*ta hiera*) which preceded any decision to join battle. As Pritchett rightly points out, however, in many such cases such a sacrifice would have been made at a time when it was militarily impossible to avoid battle.[18] It would, therefore, be unwise to assume that individually or as a group they exercised any influence in the counsels of war. As Jacoby commented, 'We should like to know whether at least the commander-in-chief was allowed to choose his own *mantis*, or whether the *mantis* was attached to the army by the Council or the Assembly.'[19] Clearly a *mantis* who was appointed by the state might have served as a check to the overall authority of the general, but it is not until the second half of the second century that there is evidence for such an official (*[man]tin tôn stratêgôn*), possibly

[16] Plutarch, *Aristides* 27, 3; Isocrates 19, 6.
[17] Herodotus 1, 63, 1; Sophocles, *OT* 300-1.
[18] W.K. Pritchett, *The Greek State at War* 1 (Berkeley etc., 1971), 10, with (for example) Thucydides 6, 69.
[19] F. Jacoby, *Die Fragmente der griechischen Historiker* IIIb, Supp. 2 (Leiden, 1954), 184.

reflecting at this date the influence of Roman military procedure and personnel.[20]

Chrêsmologoi/manteis sometimes gave their prophecies by order of the city *dêmos* (people) as well as at the request of individuals. In the former case it does not seem that they were in any sense constitutionally elected to serve the city; rather they are likely to have been – in Oliver's formulation – 'called upon for advice or for a special assignment, but when the assignment was over, their connection with the state was constitutionally no closer than that of other citizens of their class'.[21]

Their sphere of competence also included participation in the various ceremonies that might be perfomed in accordance with their advice. Thus the decree of Anticles passed in 446/5 after the Revolt of Euboea according to its most plausible reconstruction called upon 'three men, whomever the *boulê* (council) should choose from its own number with Hierocles (the *chrêsmologos*), to offer the sacrifices for Euboea, prescribed in the *chrêsmoi* as soon as possible'.[22]

Chrêsmologoi/manteis might also occasionally offer their advice to the city unbidden, and it is this element of their behaviour that in part, no doubt, gave rise to the charge of meddlesomeness frequently implicitly or explicitly levelled at them in Old Comedy. In Aristophanes' *Peace*, for example, the seer Hierocles turns up, unbidden, to question the legitimacy of the sacrifice which Trygaeus is performing on behalf of the new goddess Peace. Partly, however, that charge may be a reflection of a more general unease about their undefined position within the overall system of Athenian religious authority. By the latter half of the fifth century BC *mantis* could in a comic context be used as a by-word for certain forms of fraud, as in the case of the Hierocles referred to above, who is described as a charlatan or *alazôn*.[23]

In attempting to assess the degree of distrust and scepticism levelled by Athenians at seers, we should remember, however, that accusations of fraudulent practice are common in almost every form of oracular system; and that not even the enlightened few in Athens held a *consistent* view that divination was to be rejected. So not only the admittedly superstitious Nicias, but also the sophisticated Alcibiades made use of the service of seers.[24] In addition the career of Lampon gives us an example of a seer who was very well integrated into many of the aspects of public life in fifth-century Athens in that he played a

[20] See *IG* II², 1708, 5.

[21] Oliver, *Athenian Expounders*, 9.

[22] *IG* I² 39, 64-7 = Meiggs-Lewis, *GHI* 52, 64-7.

[23] Aristophanes, *Peace* 1045-126. There is every likelihood that this was the same man as is mentioned in the Decree of Anticles (n. 22).

[24] Plutarch, *Nicias* 13.

major part in the foundation of Thurii in 443, moved a rider to the decree regulating the offering of first-fruits at Eleusis, prophesied the political extinction of Thucydides, son of Melesias, and was one of the signatories to the Peace of Nicias in 421.[25]

Further evidence of the prestige, wealth and importance attaching to *manteis* in Classical Athens is provided by the fact that Theainetus, *mantis* of the general Tolmides (active in the middle of the fifth century), had a statue erected to him which stood on the Acropolis; and that one of the most impressive *peribolos*-tombs (family enclosures) of the fourth century belonged to a family from the deme of Myrrhinous in north-east Attica, which boasted among its numbers a *mantis* called Calliteles described as worthy, wise and just.[26]

To conclude, the role and influence of seers in Classical Athens was evidently considerable in both the public and private domains and the possibility that some of them owed their political prominence partly to their skill in divination cannot be discounted. The popular demonstration against them which attended the failure of the Sicilian Expedition in 413, to which they had evidently given their full backing, is merely a measure of the degree of unofficial confidence and trust which the *dêmos* reposed in their recommendation.[27]

The dêmos

In democratic Athens, the people – the *dêmos* – meeting in their regular assemblies, controlled all aspects of the city's life, including automatically the sphere of religion. It will be sufficient to take three areas in which religious authority can be conclusively demonstrated.

First, when a new cult was to be publicly recognized, it was necessary that the *dêmos* itself should approve the acceptance of the new deity, as for instance happened in the case of the Thracian goddess Bendis and the Epidaurian Asclepius, whose cults were introduced to Athens in the 420s.[28]

---

[25] Photius s.v. *Thouriomanteis*; *IG* I² 76.47-61; Plutarch, *Per.* 6, 2; Thucydides 5, 19, 2; Scholion on Aristophanes, *Peace* 1084.

[26] Pausanias 1, 27, 5. For a description of the *peribolos* and the persons buried within it, see R. Garland, 'A first catalogue of Attic peribolos tombs', *ABSA* 77 (1982), cat. no. Q3.

[27] Thucydides 8, 1, 1.

[28] For the *psêphisma* recording the establishment of the public cult of Bendis, see *IG* I³ 136 = *SEG* 10, 64 = J. Bingen, 'Le décret SEG X, 64 (Le Pirée 413/2?)', *RBPh* 37 (1959), 33f. For the establishment of the worship of Asclepius (under the auspices of the family of Telemachus of Acharnai), see *IG* II², 4355; 4960.8; 4961. It would be fascinating to know along what lines proposals for introducing new cults were argued in the *ekklêsia*, especially in the case of the exotic and outlandish Bendis. In practical terms, the case for her introduction was unanswerable: the Thracians were regarded by the Athenians as an important potential ally in the ensuing Peloponnesian War. This, to our minds, seems cynical bartering of an extreme kind. Should we then seek for a separate 'religious' argument behind the incorporation of Bendis within the Athenian pantheon? On the whole

Secondly, the *dêmos* exercised overriding authority in all matters which had to do with the financing of state cults. It fixed the emoluments to which the individual priests and priestesses were entitled, and, at least in the case of the priestess of Athena Nike, authorized the payment of a salary or honorarium.[29] More important, the *dêmos* had effective control over the use of wealth invested in public cults, which, though theoretically the property of the individual deity concerned, in practice became regarded as state property in times of national crisis. Thus Pericles included among the resources accruing to Athens on the eve of the outbreak of the Peloponnesian War not only the temple treasures but even the gold placed on the cult statue of Athena Parthenos.[30] It is to be noted that a marked increase in state interference in the finances of public cults is detectable in the second half of the fifth century. From then on responsibility for checking both the revenue and expenditure of public cults passed increasingly into the hands of officials answerable directly to the Athenian *dêmos*. In particular, the decision to retain the treasures of the Eleusinian goddesses on the Acropolis for safe-keeping from *c*. 460 onwards represents a dramatic and far-reaching move towards greater control of cult finance.[31] Finally, the *dêmos* subjected both gentile and democratic priests to a financial audit at the expiry of their term of office. In the event of any malpractice on the part of the holder of a gentile priesthood, the *dêmos* regarded not only the individual but also the whole *genos* accountable.[32]

Thirdly, it was the state which prosecuted most crimes of a religious nature. There were four categories of offences: misconduct in connection with certain religious festivals, theft of temple property, *asebeia* and atheism. It is instructive, in view of what has been said about Athenian priests above, that they too were liable to charges of *asebeia* (broadly speaking, any offence against established religious custom or usage). The fourth-century *hierophant* Archias, for instance, was tried and punished for illegally performing a sacrifice at the festival of Haloa.[33]

To sum up, it would be valid to think of the Athenian *dêmos*, sitting

---

I think not: to secure the goodwill of the Thracian people was inseparable from securing the goodwill of their front-rank goddess. Such thinking need not and does not imply the manipulation of religion for political advantage. On the contrary, it is expressive of the inseparability of the religious and political domains within the city-state.

[29] See *IG* I², 24 = Meiggs-Lewis, *GHI* 44; *IG* I², 25 = Meiggs-Lewis, *GHI* 71. See also the epitaph to Myrrhine, priestess of Athene Nike (*SEG* 12, 80).

[30] Thucydides 2, 13, 3-5.

[31] *SEG* 10, 6, Face C, 115-21.

[32] Aeschines 3, 18.

[33] [Demosthenes] 59, 116.

in *ekklêsia* (assembly), as a focus of communication between men and gods. The religious significance of the meeting was marked by the sacrifice of piacular pigs, by the uttering of a curse and a prayer by the herald at the dictation of the secretary, and by the precedence given to sacral matters.[34]

The *boulê*, no less than the *ekklêsia*, possessed responsibilities and authority in religious matters as in everything else. It dealt with the boards of *hieropoioi* who cooperated with priests in the management of public festivals, and at least in some cases appointed these officers from among its own ranks. In addition, the *boulê* received reports from a variety of religious officials including priests, *hieropoioi* and *epimelêtai* (religious overseers).[35] With the express authorization of the *ekklêsia*, it could be empowered to investigate crimes of a religious nature, as occurred in the case of the alleged parody of the Mysteries, though significantly, this extension of power did not include the actual sentencing of those who were found guilty, which was handled by the *dikastêria* (lawcourts).[36] Further evidence of the subordinate religious role of the *boulê* in relation to the *ekklêsia* is provided by the grant of *enktêsis* (land tenure) to the *emporoi* (merchants) of Cition in Cyprus for the purpose of establishing a *hieron* (sanctuary) for the worship of their goddess Aphrodite, a measure that seems to have been passed by the *ekklêsia* in defiance of a negative recommendation by the *boulê*.[37]

Oracles

Within Athens itself, then, the *dêmos* was the supreme arbiter of religious observance. But the authority to make changes in that observance was very often, if not invariably, derived from instructions received from an oracle. Thus, for example, a new sacrifice or new cult would have its regulations, its timings and its procedures legitimated from outside the city. This is no doubt why Plato in his description of the ideal state puts all legislation in matters of religion under the general supervision of Delphic Apollo whom he describes as 'the interpreter of the religion of our fathers' (*patrios exêgêtês*).[38] In Aristophanes' *Peace* the *chrêsmologos/mantis* Hierocles demands of Trygaeus who is performing a sacrifice: 'By what oracle did you burn those thigh-pieces to the gods?'[39] *Manteiai* or oracular pronouncements

[34] See, for example, Aeschines 1.23.

[35] For *hieropoioi* and *epistatai* generally, see my account in 'Religious authority' (with bibliography). For their connection with the *boulê*, see Rhodes, *Athenian Boule*, 127-32.

[36] See the detailed discussion in Rhodes, *Athenian Boule*, 159 and 186-8.

[37] *IG* II², 337 = Tod, *GHI* 2, 189. For further discussion, see J. Pečírka, *The Formula for the Grant of Enktesis in Attic Inscriptions* (Acta Univ. Carolinae Philosophica et Historica Monographica, 15, 1966), 59-61.

[38] *Republic* 4, 427bc. Cf. *Laws* 6, 759c.

[39] *Peace* 1088.

Fig. 9. The central figure of this later fifth-century vase is an image of the god Dionysus. In front of him stands a table of offerings and on either side are two women, probably maenads, the mythical followers of the god. They carry various pieces of cult equipment, including (on the right) a large sacrificial basket in which offerings would be brought to the altar. (Beazley, ARV² 1073.)

were preserved among the state archives and could be produced at a trial as evidence that the *patrios nomos* (traditional lore) had been breached.[40] Not even the Eleusinian Mysteries were exempt from oracular control, as is revealed in the case of the sacrifice to the goddesses made from the collection of first-fruits which had to be carried out 'in accordance with *ta patria* (traditional practice) and the oracle at Delphi'.[41] Apollo's overall responsibility where pollution is concerned is conclusively demonstrated by the fact that the *pythochrêstos exêgêtês* who gave advice about purification was directly appointed by Delphi, probably from a short list of candidates submitted by the *dêmos*.[42] Delphi, however, was not an unrivalled source of religious authority for the Greek world. In the 420s, when it became inaccessible because of hostilities during the Peloponnesian War, the oracle of Zeus at Dodona was almost certainly consulted regarding the inauguration of a public cult to the goddess Bendis. So, too, there was oracular consultation of Zeus' oracle at Ammon at the oasis of Siwa in the Libyan Desert.[43]

Delphic authority, or authority proceeding from any other oracular shrine, though extensive, was not unlimited. The ultimate safeguard against excessive interference in the affairs of other states lay in the system of 'petition response' which prevented an oracle from being proffered unless first requested. At least this seems to have been the case until the very end of the Classical period. The verb *automatizô*, which, as Parke notes, means 'to speak a prophecy without (or before) being questioned' and hence 'to prophesy spontaneously', first occurs in regard to a prophetic ill-omen uttered shortly prior to Philip II's death in 336.[44] No other instance of spontaneous prophecy securely predates the Hellenistic period. The oracle, was, moreover, careful to avoid posing as a threat to the legal authority of the state. This attitude is summed up in what Socrates says in Xenophon's *Memorabilia*: 'You know that the god of Delphi, whenever anyone asks him, "How can I show my gratitude to the gods?", replies, "In accordance with state law." '[45]

It has to be admitted that the importance of the oracle's influence is not always apparent in the evidence which happens to survive in our sources. A speech, for example, is extant, attacking the way the

[40] Demosthenes 21, 51-4 and 43, 66.

[41] *IG* I², 76, 4-5 = Meiggs-Lewis, *GHI* 73, 4-5.

[42] For the *pythochrêstos exêgêtês*, see Jacoby, *Atthis*, 28-33 and Oliver, *Athenian Expounders*, 35-46.

[43] See H.W. Parke, *Greek Oracles* (London, 1967), 90-6; 109-11 for discussions of Dodona and Ammon. The first Athenian consultation of Ammon was made at the time of the Sicilian Expedition (Plutarch, *Nic.* 13 and 14, 7 with n. 46 below).

[44] H.W. Parke, 'A note on *automatizô* in connection with prophecy', *JHS* 82 (1962), 145; Diodorus Siculus 16, 92.

[45] Xenophon, *Mem.* 4, 3, 16.

Athenians carried out a major revision of their calendar of religious
festivals in the years following the end of the great Peloponnesian War;
it alleges that illegalities were committed by Nicomachus, the official
in charge of the revision. The allegation is explicitly made that
Nicomachus lacked authority from the *dêmos*, not from the oracle, for
his omissions from and additions to the calendar. At first sight that
would seem to suggest that the *dêmos* had not bothered on this
occasion to obtain approval for the revision. More likely, however,
Delphi here as elsewhere merely gave its general consent to the
religious changes envisaged, while leaving the complex, technical
details to the state concerned, which had the competence and expertise
necessary for such a complicated exercise. If this is correct then
reference to oracular authority would not have helped in the attack of
Nicomachus. Further on the same subject, it is salutary to reflect that
in the case of the introduction of the cult of Bendis, the details of which
are preserved in a lengthy but mutilated inscription, it is only because
of the survival of half a dozen words that we happen to know that the
cult was authorized by the oracle of Zeus at Dodona. It would not
therefore be surprising if in other cases this (for us) crucial information
has simply not survived.

To conclude, oracular authority was limited by the following factors:
first, there was a number of different oracles representing different
sources of oracular authority; secondly, an oracle was only supplied
upon request; and thirdly, the practical details about how to
implement its recommendation were left entirely under state control.[46]
Moreover, at least in the case of Athens, the seeking of approval from
the god for the sanctioning of any change or innovation in cultic
procedure never led to any challenge to the power of the *dêmos*.

Religious authority in Classical Athens was the monopoly neither of
the citizen body as a whole nor of any particular group of individuals
within it. It was a discrete prerogative shared out among a number of
groups comprising amateurs as well as experts, priests as well as
'laity'. No one group could act wholly on its own initiative without
reference to or consultation with at least one other group. The
priesthood performed, the *exêgêtai* expounded and the *chrêsmologoi/
manteis* interpreted by command of the *dêmos*, the *dêmos* sought the
sanction and approval of the god for any religious innovation, and the
god was debarred from undertaking any initiative except at the

---

[46] The very obscurity of oracular utterances, and the fact that they did not only refer to a
present, but also to a future situation must have militated further against divine
interference through this medium. Cf. Plutarch's reference to the oracle of Zeus Ammon
issued at the time of the Sicilian Expedition to the effect that the Athenians 'would take all
the Syracusans', interpreted by some seers as signifying merely that Athenian generals
had formed an accurate assessment of Syracusan manpower (*Nic.* 14.7).

express invitation of the *dêmos*.

It is pertinent to enquire whether the procedural circularity – or circuitousness – outlined here was largely inherited from an ancient, traditional system of ordering religious affairs which became established in the Archaic city state, or whether it owed its origins chiefly to the democratic revolution which took place in Athens from c. 462 onwards. Only a tentative answer can be formulated to a question of this nature, inasmuch as we possess no first-hand contemporary evidence on the subject from the period covering the eighth to sixth centuries BC. Lack of contemporary source material notwithstanding, it is a reasonable assumption that the central political institutions of early Athens as outlined above (p. 80), namely the archonship and the Areopagos, can be regarded as élite groups occupying the central ground at the intersection of political-religious authority. Possessing such a vantage point they also controlled the major cults established with the *genos*, the phratry and the city.

In further support of the hypothesis that in Archaic Athens religious authority was not diffused among the many but consolidated within the few, it is evident from Herodotus that aristocratic *genê* were careful to control access both to oracles and seers, whom they manipulated freely in order to acquire and sustain political power. It was, for instance, with the assistance of an oracle delivered by the seer Amphilytus that Pisistratus finally established tyranny in Athens in c. 540-539, and it was by outright bribery of the Delphic oracle that the Alcmaeonids, an Athenian *genos* exiled by the Pisistratids, succeeded in ridding Athens of that tyranny thirty years later.[47]

There is therefore a strong case for arguing that progress towards radical democracy in Athens was accompanied by a parallel readjustment in religious authority marked by (a) a reduction in the power and influence of élite groups and (b) a new ambiguity, even distrust, on the part of the city in regard to oracular authority emanating from outside its walls.

Hence, in conclusion, the diffusion of religious authority in Classical Athens mirrors the diffusion of political authority in the same period through large numbers of boards of magistrates with many members performing minor, routine tasks. In the matters that count, however, in both the political and legal, no less than the religious sphere, the *dêmos* arrogated to itself as much power as possible. Thus the study of the evolution of Athenian religion provides a novel, yet complementary perspective to the study of that same process by which the citizen body came to establish a unique degree of control over its own affairs through the expression of its collective will in the assembly and lawcourts.

[47] Herodotus 1, 62, 4; 5, 63, 1.

PART II

Outside the City-State

4

The High Priests of Memphis
under Ptolemaic Rule

This chapter remains focussed on the Graeco-Roman world of the Mediterranean – but not this time on the life and institutions of the traditional city-state. Dorothy Thompson's theme is the religious and political organization of Egypt during the last three centuries before the Christian era, first under the rule of the Ptolemaic dynasty, then – after a period of increasing Roman influence – under open Roman control.

The familiar image of Egypt is, of course, the Egypt of the Pharoahs, immediately calling to mind the pyramids and the sphinx, hieroglyphic script, the treasure of Tutankhamun and the traditional Egyptian deities – Ptah, Osiris, Horus and the jackal-headed Anubis. But all this belongs to the distant past, to Egypt of the third and second millennia BC. This chapter is concerned with a much later period when Egypt had long been subject to foreign conquerors – first as part of the Persian Empire; then under the sway of Alexander the Great, who won the throne from Persia in 332; and finally under the Greek dynasty of the Ptolemies, who gained control of the country in the wars that divided Alexander's vast conquests following his death in 323 BC.

The Ptolemaic dynasty was Macedonian Greek in origin and introduced into Egypt not only Greek officials and settlers, but also Greek culture and traditions; so, for example, the greatest library of Greek books in the world was established at Alexandria (the city established by Alexander the Great on the Nile Delta) by the first Ptolemies. But this introduction of Hellenizing culture by no means extinguished Egyptian ancestral traditions. We find right through the Ptolemaic period the continuance of Egyptian language alongside 'official' Greek; we find traditional Egyptian political themes still important under the Ptolemies – particularly the rivalry (which stretched back to the old Pharaonic period) of Upper (that is, Southern) Egypt, with its capital at Thebes, and Lower Egypt, with its chief city of Memphis; we find the continued worship of the traditional gods – prominent among them Ptah (the patron deity of Memphis and, according to Memphite theology, the creator of the world) and Amun (principal deity of Thebes, equated with the Greek Zeus or Roman Jupiter). In fact, in many ways the most interesting aspect of Ptolemaic Egypt is the interaction between traditional Egyptian and Ptolemaic Greek culture.

This chapter investigates the relations between the traditional Egyptian high priests of Memphis and the new Ptolemaic dynasty – revealing a complex interplay between royal 'interference' in the temple administration and royal 'dependence' on the legitimation of their position provided by the traditional priests. This interplay ceased, Thompson argues, only with the Roman conquest of Egypt, at the death of the famous Cleopatra VII. As an absentee dynasty (quite unlike the Ptolemies), the emperor Octavian/Augustus and his successors could dispense with the favour of the high priests of Memphis – of whom, strikingly, throughout the Roman period, we hear no more.

The High Priests of Memphis under Ptolemaic Rule

Dorothy J. Thompson

On 27 November 197 BC the fifth king of the dynasty of Ptolemies, the thirteen-year-old Ptolemy Epiphanes, was enthroned as king in the old Egyptian capital city of Memphis. Recently hailed as sovereign in the Greek capital of Alexandria, he now claimed recognition according to Egyptian rites. After Alexander the Conqueror, Epiphanes was probably the first of the Greek rulers of Egypt so to be crowned, and the high priest of Ptah who officiated was likewise the fifth of his line, Harmachis the son of Anemhor II and of Heranch, and the younger brother of Teos who had preceded him in office (see Table 2).

At this time all the priests of Egypt, delegates from every temple, gathered in Memphis to celebrate a recent victory over rebels, whose punishment in the city was combined with the coronation. The coronation ritual, once preserved (we may assume) in the library of the high priests, has not survived the years; only a few elements are known. The king, in residence in the royal palace north of the main Ptah temple in the valley city of Memphis, had first to yoke the Apis bull and lead it through the city. Then, in the temple of Ptah, Ptolemy met with the priests and took his seat on the royal throne, while the high priest Harmachis placed on his head the Pschent crown, the double crown of Upper and Lower Egypt. The king wore a special tunic; the high priest had the wig of Ptah on his head and wore the ceremonial dress of linen robe and panther-skin with golden crook and mace. In the words of a contemporary decree, the rites performed on this occasion were those 'needful to the succession to the throne'. This ceremony and this moment when 'secular' and 'religious' authority came together to affirm their interdependence may serve to introduce the subject of this chapter.

First I am interested in the high priests themselves, in their family and their standing within the priestly hierarchy of Egypt. For Egypt was a country where cult and temples were organized to a high degree and the priesthood might enjoy an influential role within society. In the fifth century BC the Greek historian Herodotus spoke of the priests of Egypt as the first of the seven major occupations which made up the population of Egypt.[1] Drawn up in priestly panels within a strict

[1] II, 164; the others were soldiers, cowherds, swineherds, merchants, interpreters and pilots.

Table 2. High Priests of Memphis in the Ptolemaic period

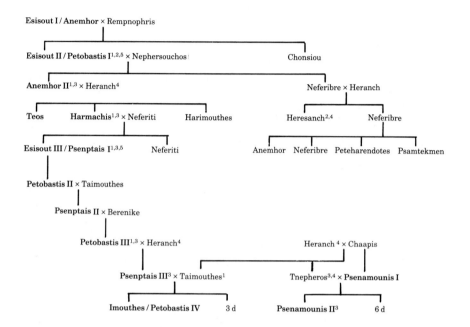

Esisout I / Anemhor × Rempnophris

Esisout II / Petobastis I[1,2,5] × Nephersouchos   Chonsiou

Anemhor II[1,3] × Heranch[4]   Neferibre × Heranch

Teos   Harmachis[1,3] × Neferiti   Harimouthes   Heresanch[2,4]   Neferibre

Esisout III / Psenptais I[1,3,5]   Neferiti   Anemhor Neferibre Peteharendotes Psamtekmen

Petobastis II × Taimouthes

Psenptais II × Berenike

Petobastis III[1,3] × Heranch[4]   Heranch[4] × Chaapis

Psenptais III[3] × Taimouthes[1]   Tnepheros[3,4] × Psenamounis I

Imouthes / Petobastis IV   3 d   Psenamounis II[3]   6 d

High priests appear in **bold** type
[1] priest of Arsinoe
[2] priest(ess) of Philotera
[3] priest(ess) in the dynastic cult
[4] priestess musician
[5] priest of Horos lord of Sakhebou
[6] high priest of Letopolis

hierarchy, they divided between themselves the responsibility for the practice of cult. The profession of priest was regularly passed on from father to son. Most priests were full-time cult officials involved in ritual activities within the temples to which they enjoyed an exclusive right of entry. In lesser cults, however, part-time service was not infrequent, and attached to the temples as agricultural workers, craftsmen, temple cleaners and in many other roles came a large number of non-priestly workers. The temples themselves were big landowners, in the New Kingdom owning up to 15 per cent of the country's land,[2] and even in the Hellenistic period they retained much of their earlier importance. Temple workshops produced linen, faience,

---

[2] H.J. Breasted, *Ancient Records of Egypt*, vol. 4 (Chicago, 1906), 98, from the twelfth century BC.

Fig. 10. The black basalt 'Rosetta Stone' of March 196 BC, on which was inscribed in hieroglyphic, demotic and Greek, the decisions of the convocation of priests of all Egypt who met in Memphis for the coronation of Ptolemy V Epiphanes in November 197 BC.

gold and metal-work which supplemented the income from agriculture, offerings and the dedications of pilgrims. Connected with a whole range of gods, temples were found in all parts of the country. Now, however, under the Ptolemies, the capital was on the Mediterranean coast in Alexandria, and the priesthood of Ptah at Memphis was adapting to this new situation.

With the conquest of Alexander and the establishment of a new, immigrant dynasty the traditional role of this priesthood was redefined. My second concern in this chapter is to investigate and characterize the nature of this redefinition, the process by which relations between the power of the temples and the priests and that of the king and the royal administration which governed the country of Egypt changed in aspect and over time. For when the priests gathered for the coronation of Epiphanes they all stayed on in Memphis for a further four months. In March 196 BC the decree was finally issued which is preserved on the 'Rosetta stone'.[3] Representing the result of hard bargaining over the months, this decree, in the name of the king, may be seen to represent a concordat of priestly and secular power. Similar decrees were to follow, particularly from Memphis, but how far were these traditional in content and what in them was new? Besides such official gatherings, a growth in personal relations between the two families of the Ptolemies and of the Memphite high priest may be observed. What, if any, were the implications of this for the country as a whole?

The high priests of Memphis

The high priest of Memphis was 'first prophet' in the cult of Ptah and stood at the head of the hierarchy of Ptah priests. It was his particular title 'chief of artificers' which distinguished this senior priest from other high priests. The family is known from a variety of different sources but primarily from their Egyptian grave stelae written in both scripts, in hieroglyphic and in demotic, and from other related objects connected with the priests which must have come from Saqqara, the Memphite necropolis. Reaching the antiques market early in the nineteenth century, these records are now scattered among the major collections of Europe.[4] For Harmachis who crowned Epiphanes a coffin also survives, for others a Book of the Dead (an Egyptian guide to the after-life) or an offering table inscribed with the priestly titles of its dedicant. These records cover the whole of the Ptolemaic period apart

---

[3] *OGI* 90; Sethe, *Hieroglyphische Urkunden*, 183, no. 36.
[4] See Quaegebeur, 'Genealogy' and *PP* III². Reymond, *Priestly Family*, conveniently collects these – but her interpretations have been questioned; see D. Devauchelle, review of Reymond, *CE* 58 (1983), 135-45.

from a break of almost 90 years in the second century BC. The genealogical information of the grave stelae and other monuments allows the reconstruction (see Table 2) of a complete stemma of high priests throughout the period.

The first recorded high priest of Ptah from Memphis is Esisout, otherwise known as Anemhor, whose wife was Rempnophris. Nothing is known of either the family or the office in the immediately preceding period,[5] but Esisout/Anemhor heads a stemma of ten generations with thirteen holders of the office (see Table 2). The most striking feature of this stemma is the closed family group within which the post is held. Once the office devolved on a brother (to Harmachis from Teos in the fourth generation); and once, in the ninth generation, with the accession of Psenamounis I, it devolved on the half-brother (and brother-in-law) of a high priest's wife.[6] This high priest had only two years in office and on his death the office reverted to the young son of Psenptais III, Imouthes/Petobastis IV, who was in turn succeeded by his cousin, Psenamounis II, the son of Psenamounis I and Tnepheros. The case of Anemhor II in the third generation shows that early retirement from office was possible for high priests; Teos who succeeded Anemhor in fact predeceased his father, to whose position he had earlier succeeded. More often, however, holders died in office and their sons regularly inherited the priesthood. As was the case with the royal house these sons were often very young. Psenptais III was fourteen when in 76 BC he became high priest of Ptah, and his son Imouthes/Petobastis was only seven and ten days when named high priest on 23 July 39 BC. It would indeed seem likely that hereditary appointment to the office was more important than the capacities of the individual who filled the post.

High priests were related by blood and members of the family were likely to hold a similar range of priesthoods, gathering together a collection of priestly offices. Indeed an enumeration of the many varied appointments of the high priest of Ptah constitutes a listing of the major cults of Memphis and the surrounding countryside. The concerns of this particular family spread very wide indeed. Harmachis, for instance, is described on his coffin as:

> Prince, chief of artificers, god's father, beloved of the god, sem-priest, servant of Ptah, follower of him-who-is great of power (and) pleasant of scent, priest of the gods in the mansion of the white walls, prophet of the gods Euergetai, of the gods Philopatores, and of the gods Epiphaneis, member of all five priestly orders of Ptah, chief of the month of temple

---

[5] I follow the stemma of Quaegebeur; see Devauchelle (n. 4) for yet another interpretation, with the same number of high priests but one generation less.

[6] In marrying his half-sister Psenamounis I stands alone in a practice more common among the Ptolemies.

service and the 15 days of the temple service of all five priestly orders in the temples of Memphis, likewise in the temple of Arsinoe Philadelphus which is within the white walls, overseer of the mansion of Ptah, senior priest, skilled in his temple duty.

He was also, we learn from his tombstone:

prophet of the window-of-appearance, prophet of Horos of the window-of-appearance, minister of the records office, superintendent of confidential affairs in the domain of Ptah in Rosetau.[7]

The high priest regularly held office in the dynastic cult of the kings; on occasion he also served as scribe in the popular cult of the goddess Arsinoe, now worshipped together with Ptah as a temple-sharing deity, *sunnaos theos*. Among the many other titles held were sometimes that of 'priest of Horos, Lord of Sakhebou' and 'high priest of Letopolis', a neighbouring centre of cult. Such an accumulation of offices would seem to be a reflection of high standing and would also, no doubt, bring financial rewards. Cult was supported by the state, as well as by the offerings of the faithful. High priests with a multiplicity of offices might thus be in receipt of significant stipends.

Their wives too were priestesses, often priestess-musicians who played in processions; and when in 44-43 BC Tnepheros, wife of Psenamounis I, already a sistrum-player of Ptah, was designated 'wife of Ptah'[8] this new appointment seems consciously modelled on the earlier Theban appointment of 'wife of Amun'. And in this innovation are echoes of an age-old rivalry of Thebes and Memphis, with Memphis now on top. Whereas for the later years of Ptolemaic rule the home of Amun became a centre of trouble and secession, the consistent loyalty of Memphis and its priesthoods was recognized by the queen Cleopatra VII in the creation of this honorific post for the wife of the high priest of Ptah. The importance of the high priests' wives suggested in this appointment is marked also by the survival of funerary stelae which record their lives and families. Almost as much is known of the women of this family as of their high-priest husbands.

This small number of families linked by intermarriage would seem, in their monopoly of key office, to form an élite among the numerous priestly families in Memphis. Each new Memphite stele published adds to the growing prosopographical picture, though we are never likely to know what proportion of the city's population were priests. Not surprisingly in a privileged group like this the ranks were closed; the priesthood remained hereditary and exclusive, barely penetrated by the Greek settlers of Egypt.

[7] *PP* III[2], 5358; Reymond, *Priestly Family*, 95-102; Quaegebeur, 'Genealogy', 67, no. 16.
[8] *BM* 184 (British Museum stele); Reymond, *Priestly Family*, 223-30, no. 29.

A further striking feature of the family of high priests of Ptah is their use of double names, Esisout/Anemhor, Esisout/Petobastis, Esisout/Psenptais and Imouthes/Petobastis, four out of thirteen holders of the office. Double names, with one native name and one Greek name (Menches/Asklepiades for example), are not infrequent in Ptolemaic Egypt; they are normally taken to represent a stage in the process of hellenization for Egyptian members of society.[9] Most commonly found within the administration, occasionally this practice is to be seen amongst the priesthood too. Dorion, officer and priest, honoured in 112-111 BC by the Idumaeans of Memphis, was at least in part Egyptian, the son of Dorion and of a priestess Heranch also known as Herakleia.[10] So too Horos also known as Dorion, the son of Berenike, whose Book of the Dead now lies in Assisi, may have come from a priestly family: for the name Dorion is one of the few Greek names taken up by those of the priestly community prepared to compromise, and even hellenize, with the adoption of double names.[11]

Among the high priests, however, the double names are both Egyptian, never Greek; the same feature is found in the later generations of the family of high priests of Letopolis, perhaps following the Memphite suit. This unusual practice may have been a conscious echo of royal usage, where multiple Egyptian names were normal. In this case, their nomenclature set the high priests of Memphis apart from the rest of the population and gives us some indication of the importance of these particular priestly families.

This primacy of the high priest of Memphis under the Ptolemies would seem to derive as much from the geographical and historical importance of the city as from the postion of Ptah within the Egyptian pantheon. Throughout Egyptian history Memphis and Thebes, with their respective deities (Ptah and Amun), alternated as capitals of the country; the occasional exception (Amarna for instance or Sais later) serves only to highlight the rule. The old divisions of Upper and Lower Egypt were as important under the Ptolemies as ever before, and the close relationship between Memphis and Alexandria may be contrasted with the break-away tendencies of Thebes and the south already mentioned. A series of rebels and native kings in the south probably benefited the city of Memphis whose priests were consistently loyal. The appointment of a 'wife of Ptah' at this time – as an honour for Memphis – has already been noted.

Among the Memphite temples, the temple of Ptah was supreme. Its

[9] D.J. Crawford, *Kerkeosiris: an Egyptian village in the Ptolemaic period* (Cambridge, 1971), 134-5.

[10] *OGI* 737 (112-111 BC); P. Vernus, *Athribis* (Bibliothèque d'étude, 74, Le Caire, 1978), 214-18, with H. de Meulenaere, 'Prosopographica Ptolemaica', *CE* 37 (1962), 73-5.

[11] G. Rosati, 'Antichità egizie ad Assisi', *OA* 25 (1986), 59-67 with J. Quaegebeur 'Osservazioni sul titolare di un Libro dei Morti conservato ad Assisi', *OA* 25 (1986), 69-80.

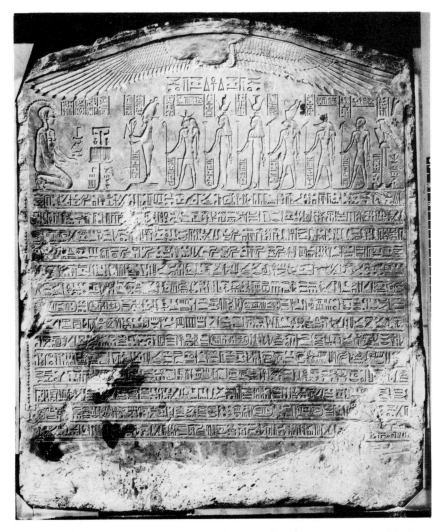

Fig. 11. The hieroglyphic funeral stele of the Memphite high priest Psenptais III, son of Petobastis and Heranch (90-41 BC). The priest is shown on the left kneeling before an offering table. Facing him stand the deities Osiris, Apis, Isis, Nephthys, Horus, Anubis, Imhotep son of Ptah and the Goddess of the Necropolis, who are all addressed in the introductory invocation. (BM 886.)

wealth was based on land, though the extent of its holdings cannot now be known. Much earlier, in the twelfth century BC under Ramses III when the temples owned so much of the country's land (p. 98 above), Thebes had 81 per cent of this land and Memphis only 1 per cent. Yet even this 1 per cent represented 10,154 arouras, approximately 2,540 hectares or 6,275 acres of land, scattered throughout the districts of

Fig. 12. Detail of Fig. 11, showing the high priest in his ceremonial dress: a long linen robe with panther's skin across the shoulders and wig of Ptah on his head. Facing him is the god Osiris.

Lower Egypt. There was livestock and geese in addition, for temples were more than simply places of cult and worship. Within their large enclosures there lived families engaged in multifarious activities – barbers (priests went clean-shaven), shepherds, gold- and silver-smiths, bakers, sellers of water and fuel and many, many others. There were storehouses and a treasury, and other dependent animal cults (the baboon of Thoth, for instance, lived in the temple of Ptah, as did the Apis bull and the Isis cow, its mother). The temple of Ptah at Memphis covered around 20 hectares (*c.* 50 acres) while, depending on it administratively, up on the desert edge were other large temple enclosures, the Serapieion, the Anoubieion, Boubastieion and Asklepieion (the temple that is of Imhotep whom the Greeks called also Imouthes) and the sacred animal necropolis with its ibis, hawk, baboon and cow catacombs. The Ptah temple with its council of elders and high priests dominated a city which Egyptians recognized as a major centre of cult. For foreigners the city of Memphis with its well-established immigrant communities – Phoenicians, Persians and Jews, Carians and Ionians, as well as the later Greeks who followed Alexander – was a magnet for pilgrims and visitors who came to see its sights. Like Herodotus, they wondered at the temple of Hephaistos, that is the temple of Ptah.

Within this temple context the role of any high priest, with access to the central shrine, consisted of ceremonies concentrated on the statues of the god. Anemhor II was known as director of the wardrobe[12] and Teos, we are told, clothed the gods with the products of his handiwork (from the temple looms perhaps).[13] In dressing the statues priests were involved in the daily ritual of the cult which was inaccessible to the people on whose behalf the cult was practised. Yet besides these daily rituals, on special occasions the high priest represented his god in relation to that other god, the king. At the centre of this relationship stands the ritual of the coronation, and through this ritual role the high priest of Ptah dominated the other priests of Egypt. Under the Ptolemies Ptah (combined always with Apis) in this way reigned supreme.

The first certain Ptolemaic coronation is that of Epiphanes already described, though according to the *Alexander Romance* Alexander himself had been crowned at Memphis. Besides the high priests' tombstones and the Rosetta decree it is somewhat surprisingly in a Roman source of the first century BC, Nigidius Figulus, that the few known details of the contemporary ceremony are preserved. The Romans of that date were as fascinated by the mysteries of Egypt as were the Greeks before them, as they tried to understand the wealthy kingdom of the Ptolemies. The temple of Memphis, writes Nigidius Figulus, is the spot where Typhon (i.e. Seth) was buried. (The place of royal enthronement in this account is thus linked to the mystery of Osiris, the mystery central to the religion of Egypt.) First, Nigidius' account continues, in this temple the king is initiated in sacred matters. Next, dressed in a special ceremonial costume, he must yoke the Apis bull. By leading the bull through a district of the city, he can be seen to have had experience of human toil; he is required to refrain from any form of cruel dealing with all beneath his sway. Led by a priest of Isis to the inner sanctuary (called the *adytos*), kings are bound by oath to refrain from interference with the calendar, intercalating neither month nor day, nor changing any feast day, but completing the 365 days as instituted of old. Then a further oath is added, that they will always care for the protection and provision of both land and water. Finally the diadem is put in place, and the king controls the land of Egypt.[14]

Much in Nigidius' account is obscure; a diadem has replaced the double crown of the Rosetta decree, a priest of Isis the high priest of Ptah. Nevertheless it is clear that this covenant of the king with his

[12] *PP* 5352.
[13] *PP* 5573.
[14] *De sphaera graecanica et barbarica* (ed. Swoboda) fr. 98.

people, a covenant mediated through his priests, in which the calendar and control both of the flood and of agricultural land are guaranteed by the king's physical prowess and by his oath, dates from an Egypt long before the Greeks arrived. In continuing the age-old ceremony Ptolemy recognized the important role such a ceremony could fulfil in a land where ceremony was always strong. In the eyes of Egyptians this was no less true of the period of the Ptolemies, and the importance of such ceremonies should not be underestimated. In the rites of coronation king and country were closely bound. And the high priest of Ptah in Memphis played a focal role in mediating between his king, his people and the gods in an effort to ensure the well-being of the land of Egypt – the annual flood and the crops it brought.

Ptolemies and temples

The interplay of divine and secular power seen in the coronation ceremony was not always so close. In relation to the traditional gods of Egypt, represented through their priests, not all Ptolemies showed equal zeal or concern. Nor were all temples as concerned as those of Memphis to accept and adopt the immigrant rulers of Egypt. The interaction of powers changes over time, differing area by area.

The scene may be set with a papyrus found amongst the debris excavated on the western edge of the North Saqqara headland, part of the Memphite necropolis and the location of several temples. A nail-hole shows that the papyrus, written in large clear letters, was once posted up, and the orders it records are those of Alexander's military commander, Peukestas the son of Makartos:

Orders of Peukestas. Out of bounds. Property of the priest.[15]

Fig. 13. Papyrus written in large letters, presumably for display. Peukestas, the Macedonian military commander, gives orders to his troops to keep off the priestly property.

[15] E.G. Turner, 'A Commander-in-Chief's order from Saqqara', *JEA* 60 (1974), 239-42.

The Ptolemaic take-over of Egypt involved the substitution of a Macedonian general for an Egyptian pharaoh, and of Greek as the language of administration for demotic or Aramaic. The king was the main recipient of wealth and honour in the country and the economic autonomy of the temples was reduced. The temples were left in control of their land but they now paid an annual tax, in the form of one artaba to the aroura (about one tenth of the annual yield). Within the temples the priests remained in control of cult and religion. Priestly offices were sold and ceded as before, and the traditional organization of the native priesthood went unchanged until Ptolemy III Euergetes added to the existing four classes an extra class of priests in honour of his daughter Berenike.[16] However, the innovation with perhaps the most serious implications for temple independence was the appointment of state (or royal) representatives within the temple administration. How this worked in practice may in part be seen from the Memphite evidence.

From the third century BC, the third Ptolemaic high priest of Memphis, Anemhor II, is recorded with the office of *royal* scribe for all financial matters in both temple and temple estate of Osiris-Apis and, similarly in the valley, in the temple of Memphis (that of Ptah) and of Arsinoe Philadelphus.[17] The recruitment of a high priest to such a wide-ranging position of authority is a clear sign of royal concern both to exercise some measure of control within the temples and to work with and through this prominent priestly family. The cooperation found in Memphis is unusual in its extent.

By the second century BC a royal subvention, *syntaxis*, financed the cost of much of temple cult. The crown's concern for the proper use of this support is shown in the appointment of specific officials to represent its interests. As is clear from their names and titles these officials were Egyptians, not Greeks, and, like Anemhor II earlier, they were also priests. These Egyptian 'royal scribes' and 'fiscal scribes of Pharaoh'[18] were probably responsible to a Greek official in Alexandria, known, even in Greek, by his Egyptian title *pheritob*.[19] It seems that, in the use of Egyptians and of Egyptian titles, the central administration was showing some concern for Egyptian sensibilities.

Details of the areas of competence of these overseers are found in both Greek and Egyptian archives from the second century BC. Known in Greek as *epistateis*, these 'agents of Pharaoh' were involved in both fiscal concerns (in particular the *syntaxis*) and more general cult

---

[16] *OGI* 56; Sethe, *Hieroglyphische Urkunden*, 142-6; Ch. Onasch, 'Zur Königsideologie der Ptolemäer in den Dekreten von Kanopus und Memphis (Rosettana)', *APF* 24-5 (1976), 137-55.

[17] Quaegebeur, 'Genealogy', 65-6, no. 6.

[18] *PP* 5677e; 5829e (both appointments); 5694a; 5519; 5658e; 5677e; 5510; 5354.

[19] *UPZ* 51. 18 (161 BC); cf. *P. Lond.* vii 2188. 61 (148 BC) and *Hor* 22. 3-4 (165 BC).

responsibilities within the temples of Memphis. One such official, Amasis son of Petenephtimis, in June 172 BC presided over a council meeting of the elders of the Ptah priests who were investigating alleged abuses within the ibis cult of the sacred animal necropolis, and again in June 165 BC another, Psintaes son of Piomis, played a similar advisory role.[20] A Greek archive from the Serapeum well illustrates the responsibility of Psintaes, here called *epistatês*, for the proper distribution of *syntaxis* to cult personnel within the temple.[21] He was for instance responsible for the payment of a daily ration of bread loaves to the Egyptian twins who played a ceremonial role in the mourning for the Apis bull who died in April 164 BC. When there were problems over the payment of the loaves the first appeal was to Psintaes – who did nothing. The episode however is even more significant in illustrating the reality of Greek power and the overriding control of the central administration in temple affairs. For in the episode of the twins and their food allowance it was orders from the *dioikêtês*, the chief financial administrator of the Ptolemies, that had reduced their rations by one half. And, while recognizing the responsibility of Psintaes for the actual payment of their loaves, it was the deputy finance-minister, the *hypodioikêtês*, to whom they finally turned in the hope of positive action in their interest. In practice therefore the actual appointment of royal representatives (like Amasis or Psintaes) within the temple probably interfered little with a traditional area of Egyptian influence; it was rather the subordination of the temples to the financial departments of the royal administration that represented the more significant diminution of an earlier position of power and independence.

Interference however might be matched by Ptolemaic patronage. Ptolemy son of Lagos had not been long on the throne when the Apis bull of the time died of old age. The cost of burial was high, and in addition to the lavish allowance already made, a further 50 talents of silver was borrowed from the king. While in good tradition, the king's readiness to come forward with subventions for this sacred cult proved a sure sign of things to come, and, in their patronage of both cult and temples, the dynasty may well have helped to reconcile the native population to the fact of foreign rule.[22] In this way cults might receive supplementary finance and support, while the temple-building record of the kings suggests a significant level of commitment to the religious life of Egypt. The relationship seen here of divine and secular powers is a complex and reciprocal one that changes over the passage of time. At

---

[20] *Hor* 19 recto. 16-17 (*PP* 7376a); *Hor* 20 recto. 6-7 (*PP* 7472a).

[21] *UPZ* 20. 55 (163-162 BC); 42. 23-4 (162 BC); 43. 16 (162-161 BC); 46. 8, 19; 47. 12, 24; 48. 10-11 (162-161 BC); 50. 27-8 (162-161 BC); 52. 22; 53. 23 (161 BC).

[22] Diodorus Siculus 1, 84; cf. Crawford, 'Ptolemy, Ptah and Apis', 15-18.

stake were power and influence, but the players were not equal in this game, for kings were also divine.

The official dynastic cult of the Ptolemies, developed under Ptolemy II Philadelphus, was primarily connected with the Greek cities of Alexandria and Ptolemais where Greek (or Macedonian) priests and priestesses played a civic role. Developing separately from the Greek dynastic cult, royal cult for the Ptolemies in Egyptian temples started under Ptolemy II Philadelphus when Arsinoe Philadelphus was introduced into the temple of Egypt as a *sunnaos theos*, to share cult with the chief god of the individual temples. This was a bold and innovative move. Egyptian-style cult of the new goddess, funded by a tax on orchards and vineyards known as the *apomoira*, was physically located in already existing temples; her close association with the well-established gods might serve to press her claim to acceptance among the population at large. Such a degree of direct interference in the religious life of Egypt had probably not been seen since Akhenaten, the heretical pharaoh of the fourteenth century BC. The initiative in establishing this queen cult depended on the political acumen of Ptolemy Philadelphus and of his close associates. A generation later the deification of Arsinoe was followed by that of Berenike, the daughter of Euergetes I, whose death occurred during a national gathering of priests at Canopus in 238 BC. Assimilated with Tefnut, daughter of the god Helios/Ra, Berenike was deified in full Egyptian style; the priests gave her father instruction in the new cult, the details of which are recorded in the Canopus decree.[23] The emphasis found here on apparel and on cult procedures (the head-dresses to be worn, the bread to be served or the boat processions) well illustrates Egyptian priestly functions.

Also ratified in this same decree was the introduction to the Egyptian temples of a regular Ptolemaic ruler cult of an entirely traditional type. The reciprocal emphasis is strong in all Ptolemaic synodal decrees, and at Canopus it was in return for royal benefactions that it was agreed that all priests now became priests of the *Theoi Euergetai*, of Ptolemy III Euergetes I and his consort Berenike. While according to the Canopus decree all priests were now in addition priests of the ruler gods, the *Theoi Euergetai*, in practice the title was only given to particular individuals. In Memphis, as we have seen, the high priest regularly held the post (see Table 2); the periods of silence about this cult coincide significantly with the loss of the high priests' stelae.

In the first century BC, when evidence returns for royal cult in Memphis, a 'first prophet of the lord of two lands' (that is a priest of the king) is now recorded for the first time. The designation is that of

Fig. 14. Arsinoe II Philadelphus portrayed as an Egyptian goddess, together with her husband/brother Ptolemy II Philadelphus. Besides a kilt and collar, the king wears the double white and red crown of Upper and Lower Egypt; the queen wears a long clinging robe and a vulture headdress, beneath a composite crown (incorporating the red crown of Lower Egypt, the high plumes of Isis, the cow's horns of Hathor and the ram's horns of Amon). Both hold sceptres and their names are inscribed above. (BM 1056.)

Psenptais III, the high priest son of Petobastis III and of Heranch. This title might simply be an archaism, a return to the language of earlier days now used to describe the office of high priest, but more likely here it represents a new and special appointment, made perhaps at the instigation of Ptolemy XII Neos Dionysos (Auletes) who in March 76 BC named Psenptais III as his priest.[24] There are two particular indications that this new title reflects a new degree of royal deification: first, the cult of Auletes has been detached from that of his wife; second, Auletes was the first of the Ptolemies to appear in Greek inscriptions with the world 'Theos' ('god') among his personal titles for normal use. Whereas the office of prophet in the royal cult of earlier couples might be extended throughout the priesthood, the prophet of the living pharaoh appears in contrast as a rather special, personal appointment.

A particular interest of the Ptolemaic dynastic cult derives from its different forms and operations in different sections of the population. It pervaded many areas of life, serving perhaps to bind together the disparate elements of the kingdom. Within the bureaucracy, predominantly Greek at least in its upper levels, the regular sacrifices made at the start of an official's day on behalf of the king and his offspring (always 'on behalf of' and never directly 'to'), perhaps served to reinforce any written guarantee which, in the form of a royal oath, might accompany official appointments.[25]

Dynastic cult penetrated daily life outside the sphere of the central administration. The guarantee, for instance, of the ruler gods was sometimes invoked in the penalty clauses of contracts. For penalties might include the requirement to make payment not only direct to the injured party, but also for the benefit of the royal cult, in the Greek terminology the payment of 'sacred drachmas'.[26] So, in a release document from 78 BC in which four undertakers cede burial rights over an extended family in favour of five others, detailed provisions are made for corpses brought to the wrong group of undertakers. Initially four days are allowed for the redirection of such corpses. In the event of failure to redirect within the following five days those drawing up the contract are required to pay the rightful owners 5 deben of silver (i.e. 100 drachmas) in coined money, and in addition 5 deben of silver for sacrifices and libations on behalf of the everlasting rulers.[27] The royal dimension of such day-to-day contractual arrangements among the Egyptian population – undertaker, tradesman and temple worker alike – may testify to the pervasiveness of ruler cult in the lives of both

---

[24] *BM* 886. 6 (British Museum stele); Crawford, 'Ptolemy, Ptah and Apis', 30-1.

[25] *BGU* VIII 1767. 1-2; 1768. 9 (first century BC); *P.Tebt.* 27. 52-4 (113 BC).

[26] e.g. *UPZ* 31. 13-14 (162 BC).

[27] *P.Leid* 374. i 10-12 (78 BC) = P.W. Pestman, 'Les documents juridiques des "chanceliers du dieu" de Memphis à l'époque ptolémaïque', *OMRL* 44 (1963), 18.

rulers and ruled. The additional levy of 'sacred drachmas' besides the regular fine in a penalty clause presumably added weight to its operation. While benefiting from such clauses, the crown could then be approached in an appeal for justice. Revenue levied from these fines was fed back into the system in a process of reaffirmation of the ruler's divinity; and in the eyes of his subjects Ptolemy was known as both god and king.

The recognition of this royal role is nowhere more clearly seen than with the recipients of *syntaxis*. Through this block grant to the temples, as through the *apomoira*-tax levied for the cult of Arsinoe, the Ptolemies ensured the continuation of their own royal cult; within the temples recipients reacted favourably, recognizing the ultimate source of their support. So those twins of the Serapeum-archive who played their part in the mourning of the Apis bull also served for the Mnevis-bull, making additional sacrifice to the god Imouthes/ Asklepios. As they themselves report, this complex service was performed 'on behalf of the king'.[28] Others felt the same, and so the royal cult became well embedded in the outlook of at least the priestly sector of the native population.

By involving a broad spectrum of the social scale in the ruler cult, the Ptolemies seem to have captured the imagination of their subjects. Now sharing a temple with the main god of the place, the king was the recipient of both cult and respect from priest and population alike. Through ruler cult, especially in its Egyptian form, the ruling family had encroached on the traditional power of the temples. The success of this development may be further reflected in the surviving quantity of small, cheap terracotta busts of various Ptolemies; their poor quality suggests mass production for popular consumption.[29]

As gods then, and as kings, the Ptolemies were recognized in the temples of Egypt. How divine support and ceremonial authority might be translated into political power is a complex question. In the case of the Ptolemies it is further complicated by the fact that the political capital of the country – where Ptolemy mainly functioned – was now separate from the religious centre – where Ptolemy was crowned and where the high priest of Ptah was also his priest. The third-century BC foundation of a Serapeum in Alexandria did little to modify the earlier pre-eminence of the Memphite temples. To overcome this problem of the gap between the new and the old, the Ptolemies made royal visitations to Memphis with increasing frequency, or took up residence

---

[28] *UPZ* 17. 5-6 (163 BC); 20.41 (163 BC); cf. 14. 28-30; *Hor* 7. 11-12.

[29] e.g. R.A.L. Scheurleer, 'Ptolemies', in *Das Ptolemäische Ägypten* (Mainz, 1978), 1-7; cf. D.B. Thompson, *Ptolemaic Oinochoai and Portraits in faience. Aspects of the Ruler Cult* (Oxford, 1973), 78-101. In contrast the small ruler heads of plaster (e.g. O. Rubensohn, *Hellenistisches Silbergerät in antiken Gibsabgüssen* (Berlin, 1911), no. 12) represent the prototypes of bronze and silver portraits made for wealthier clients.

in the city. And when they visited, they acted as pharaoh, making the proper sacrifices to the gods and making themselves available to their subjects.

From the second century BC the Ptolemies were regularly found in Memphis to mark the start of the new Egyptian year. Another recurrent context for royal visits to the city was provided by times of uncertainty and transition in royal power, times when divine legitimation was particularly needed by the king. Such a need presumably lay behind the Memphite coronation of Epiphanes described at the start of this chapter. Later Ptolemies followed the practice of Memphite coronations and under Ptolemy IX Soter II came the first recorded Sed-festival of the dynasty – that is, a thirty-year jubilee in the Egyptian style. Originally crowned at Memphis shortly after his succession in 116 BC, in 107 BC Soter II fled the country, ousted from the throne by his younger brother. After years in Cyprus in 88 BC he returned to power in Egypt. He found the country in distress and split in loyalties, for as so often in the past Thebes and the south were in revolt. Reacting swiftly to a need for confidence in the countryside, Soter made for Memphis where he called on the religious strength and support of Lower Egypt which this city might provide. Hierax his general was despatched south to the home of Amun, and in early 86 BC Soter II was crowned a second time in Memphis. In this ceremony, conducted by the high priest Petobastis III, Soter II was the first of the Ptolemies to celebrate the traditional thirty-year jubilee, as a reaffirmation of his royal power.[30] Soon after, Thebes was finally defeated and destroyed. Memphis and Lower Egypt had once more triumphed over the south. In this and other ways the complicity of king and Memphite high priest may be seen as an important feature of the last century of Ptolemaic rule.

In this relationship between the Memphite priesthood and the king the advantages accruing to the king are clear. Such advantages however are likely be mutual, with individual priests also benefiting from royal support. The tensions and rivalries within the temple organizations and among members of the major priestly families are rarely explicit in the sources that survive, but good relations enjoyed between high priest and king seem to have played their part as weapons in such rivalries. So, for example, Psenptais III on his hieroglyphic tombstone[31] parades his friendship with Ptolemy XII

---

[30] Recorded on an Apis stele, H. Brugsch, 'Der Apis-Kreis aus den Zeiten der Ptolemäer nach der hieroglyphischen und demotischen Weihinschriften des Serapeums von Memphis', *ZÄS* 24 (1886), 32-3, no. 50, cf. *Thesaurus inscriptionum aegyptiacarum. Vol. 5, Historisch-biographische Inschriften altägyptischer Denkmäler* (Leipzig, 1891), 871; J. Bergman, *Isis: Ich bin Isis. Studien zum memphitischen Hintergrund der griechischen Isisaretalogien* (Acta Univ. Upsal., Hist. Rel. 3, Uppsala, 1968), 114 n.3.

[31] *BM* 886 (British Museum stele); Reymond, *Priestly Family*, 136-50.

Auletes. After the Memphite coronation of the king this high priest visited Alexandria, the occasion already mentioned when he was named 'prophet of the lord of two lands'. The king then came to Memphis on a feast day:[32]

> He passed up and down in his ship that he might behold both sides of the place. So soon as he landed at the quarter of the city called Onkhtawy, he went into the temple escorted by his magnates and his wives and his royal children, with all the things prepared for the feast; sitting in the ship he sailed up, in order to celebrate the feast in honour of all the gods who dwell in Memphis, according to the greatness of the goodwill in the heart of the lord of the land, and the white crown [of Upper Egypt] was upon his brow.
>
> I was a great man, rich in all riches, whereby I possessed a goodly harem ...

boasts the high priest. Readers of this tombstone would include the family and priestly colleagues of Psenptais III. So under the last of the Ptolemies such interaction between king and high priest would seem important to them both. Cooperation rather than conflict was the key-note here.

Meanwhile Rome grew strong in Egypt, and finally on 3 August 30 BC, Octavian seized Alexandria. Imouthes/Petobastis IV, the sixteen-year-old high priest of Memphis, had died two days before. The contrast between Ptolemaic and Roman rule is evident in Octavian's attitude to Memphis, its priests and its gods. As Octavian he refused to enter the presence of Apis, remarking that he was accustomed to worship gods not cattle. The high priest lay unburied and it was only two and a half years later under Augustus that a successor was appointed.

The successor, Psenamounis II, came from the same family of high priests and he held the further appointment of 'prophet of Caesar'; his mother Tnepheros, wife of Ptah since 44-3 BC, was now made 'prophetess of Caesar'.[33] Such appointments were probably put into effect only after the events in Rome of 13 January 27 BC. And in this dynastic cult at Memphis Augustus followed straight on Ptolemaic precedent. There is no sign of the goddess Roma and many of the other mechanisms of deifying Roman power so familiar from the Greek world. In 23 BC (another crucial year in Rome) in Memphis, on 9 April, the last Ptolemaic high priest (Imouthes/Petobastis IV) was finally buried, after almost seven years of waiting in the House of Embalming. The occasion was the funeral of his aunt Tnepheros; his cousin, the

---

[32] S.R.K. Glanville in E.R. Bevan, *A History of Egypt under the Ptolemaic Dynasty* (London, 1927), 348.

[33] Quaegebeur, 'Genealogy', 70-1, nos. 29 and 36.

current high priest Psenamounis II, performed the ceremony.[34] In a key province no expense was spared and after initial suspicions Augustus now, briefly, was playing the role of pharaoh. But this double burial with all its pomp and circumstance proved a last gesture of the old style. As an absentee dynasty, the Roman approach to rule was very different. After Psenamounis II no more is heard of the family of high priests of Memphis.[35] The temples soon were taken over, their power and wealth reduced. In the imposition of this new authority the old ways were regularly abandoned and local sensibilities ignored. The fate of the temples and of the Memphite priesthood is but one sign of the wholesale change the Romans introduced.

---

[34] *BM* 188 (British Museum stele); Reymond, *Priestly Family*, 214-21, no. 26.
[35] P.J. Parsons, 'Ulpius Seranianus', *CE* 49 (1974), 142-5; A. Bülow-Jacobsen, 'The archiprophetes', *Papyrologica Bruxellensia* 19 (1979), 124-31.

5

Nabonidus and the Babylonian Priesthood

In the sixth century BC (while Rome was still ruled by Kings and the Athenians by the tyrant family of the Pisistratids) Babylon was enjoying a brief period of renewed independence after many years under the domination of the Assyrian Empire. The Babylonians had played an important part in the final overthrow of the Assyrians and their new Empire sought to revive the glories of the age of Hammurabi a thousand years before, when they had themselves been the dominant power of the area. But it was in these same years of the first half of the sixth century BC that a new power was growing in the Middle East, that of the Persians led by Cyrus the Great. In 539 BC Cyrus defeated Nabonidus, the last king of Babylon, and incorporated his kingdom into the Empire that was to dominate the East for two hundred years. These dramatic events find their reflections not only in surviving Babylonian and Persian sources, but also in the Bible, since the fall of Babylon rescued the exiled Israelites, who had been brought to Babylon after the destruction of Jerusalem by Nebuchadnezzar, one of Nabonidus' predecessors.

This chapter is concerned above all with contemporary reactions to and interpretations of the fall of Nabonidus. In modern discusssion, these events have often been seen as a classic example of a priestly group acting as a powerful political element in the state, pursuing its own policy and objectives. King Nabonidus, the argument goes, had developed heterodox religious ideas; the 'priests' therefore, acting in defence of orthodox views, supported the invader and brought about the swift collapse of Babylonian resistance. There is far more at stake in this debate than the interpretation of these particular incidents: the occasion provides a test-case for the whole theory that priesthood in these early Middle Eastern Empires was radically different from that more familiar in the Graeco-Roman world, that the priests controlled great resources and, not unlike modern churches, represented an autonomous area of power within, or even potentially opposed to, the state.

In relation to the history of these early empires, this theory of priestly power provides a tool for interpretation of events which has been much employed, but which can hardly ever be tested against detailed evidence; it is Kuhrt's contention that in the case of the fall of Nabonidus our information is good enough and varied enough to provide such an assessment. Of course, an analysis of the fall of one king cannot by itself prove that the standard view of priestly power is wrong: but, by starting from the detailed analysis of a single set of events, Kuhrt is trying to develop new ways of thinking about the whole subject. The result is a challenge to received ideas about the nature of priesthood, its relations with the king and with society in general.

Nabonidus and the Babylonian Priesthood
Amélie Kuhrt

The impression that Babylonian cities were dominated by large-scale temples and their attendant staffs, i.e. 'priests', described by ancient writers as 'Chaldaeans',[1] was widespread in classical antiquity and has continued to enjoy a certain vogue. The notion has, in fact, appeared to receive further confirmation from exciting archaeological discoveries in Iraq (approximately equivalent to the ancient area generally called Mesopotamia, which included Assyria in North Iraq and Babylonia in the South); these discoveries, made from the early nineteenth century onwards, and also the progress of decipherment of texts written in Akkadian, the Semitic language of the area, and that of the even earlier Sumerian documents from South Iraq, have all served to strengthen the prevailing view.

Already in the fifth century BC in Herodotus (1,181-3), the 'Chaldaeans' are presented as learned priests who were in a position to inform him of the precise history of Babylonia and of its religious practices. When Alexander entered Babylon in 331 BC, according to Arrian (3,16), he followed the advice of the 'Chaldaeans' on how to comport himself in all matters of ritual. The clearest description of these 'priests', however, is contained in Diodorus Siculus (1,28,1) who compared their position to that of Egyptian priests, holding a privileged social and economic position and set apart from other members of society by virtue of their extraordinary learning. Another illustration of the kind of power achieved by Babylonian priests is given by Diodorus (probably deriving the story from Ctesias, who wrote in the early fourth century BC): in his account of the successful attack made on the Assyrian Empire by an alliance of Medes and Babylonians, he presented the Babylonian king (Belesys) as a Chaldaean, whose only contribution to the war was to foretell correctly the success of the Median ruler, for which he was rewarded with Babylonia to govern.[2]

Archaeological exploration has uncovered in the course of the past hundred and fifty years a number of temples in the Mesopotamian area together with their ziggurats – 'temple-towers'. Not only are these

---

[1] The term became synonymous with 'astrologers': cf. Voigtlander, *Survey*, 50-1; Kuhrt, 'Synthesis', 545-6.
[2] Diodorus Siculus 2,24,2-3; cf. Kuhrt, 'Synthesis', 544-5.

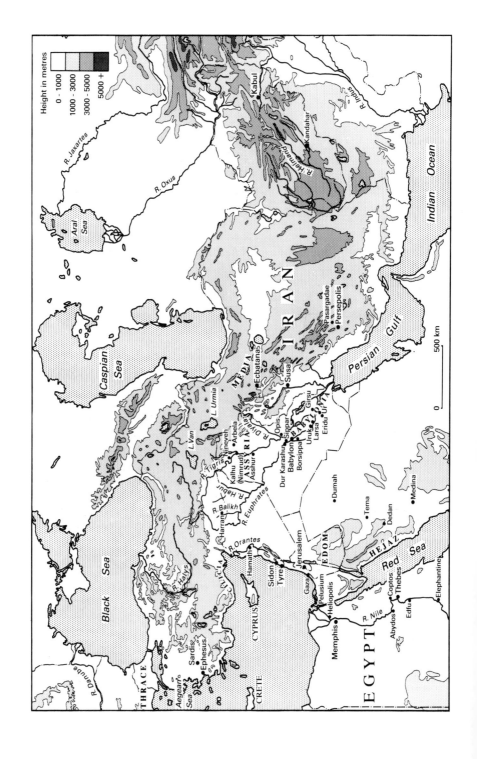

Height in metres

0 - 1000
1000 - 3000
3000 - 5000
5000 +

R. Jaxartes

R. Oxus

Aral
Sea

Caspian
Sea

Kabul

Kandahar

R. Helmand

R. Indus

Indian
Ocean

I R A N

Pasargadae
Persepolis

Ecbatana

Susa

MEDIA

Persian

Gulf

500 km

0

L. Urmia

L. Van

Opis

Sippar

Girsu

Nineveh

Arbela

R. Diyala

R. Tigris

Babylon

Borsippa

Uruk

Larsa

Eridu

Ur

Kalhu
(Nimrud)

Asshur

ASSYRIA

BABYLONIA

Dur Karashu

R. Habur

R. Balikh

R. Euphrates

Dumah

Tema

Medina

Dedan

Black

Sea

R. Halys

Sardis

Ephesus

Aegean
Sea

THRACE

Danube

CRETE

CYPRUS

Harran

R. Orantes

Hamath

Sidon

Tyre

Gaza

Jerusalem

EDOM

HEJAZ

Red

Sea

Pelusium

Heliopolis

Memphis

R. Nile

Abydos

Coptos

Thebes

Edfu

Elephantine

E G Y P T

Fig. 15. Limestone vessel probably from Uruk, dating to c. 3000 BC. It shows a 'hero' figure with his arms placed protectively around cattle, the whole group intricately sculpted in very high relief to form the base of this 'cult vase'. Iconographically and technically it can be associated with other items found within the temple area at Uruk and dating to this period.

Fig. 16. Schist-type stone object (the so-called 'Blau Monument'), possibly from Uruk, dating to the late fourth millennium BC. The central, tall figure with cross-hatched skirt is usually interpreted as a 'priest-king'. Similarly dressed figures appear in prominent positions on other elaborately worked objects of around this date from the temple precincts at Uruk. Note the early pictographic signs on the extreme right and just behind the main figure. The reverse has more writing and shows the same figure with an elaborate hairdo making a presentation; the purpose of the object is unknown.

sacred structures huge and elaborate, they also appear at a number of
sites to be the earliest buildings: a complex series of temples dating to
the end of the fourth millennium and beginning of the third
millennium BC was excavated at Uruk and associated with them were
remarkably finely worked and precious cult-objects.[3] Even more
striking was the discovery at the old Sumerian city of Eridu of a series
of temples overlying each other and demonstrating the continuity of
sacred buildings on the same spot from the Ubaid period (*c.* 5000 BC) to
c. 2000 BC.[4] The importance of the Eridu temple is not limited to
demonstrating a direct development from the prehistoric into the
historical period; it was also, it appears, the only structure of solid
building materials in the earliest phases of the site, thus
distinguishing it from the light structures used for domestic
habitation.[5] Taking all this evidence together, one might well assume
that all technological, material and labour resources were invested in
the temple and its equipment. The number, size, complexity, elaborate
decoration and antiquity of temples all combine to emphasise the
primacy and central importance of these institutions in the
Mesopotamian communities.

Support for this reading of the archaeological record seemed to come
also from the documentary evidence: the earliest indications of writing
came from temple contexts,[6] and it appeared that in some cities the
rulers originated from the ranks of the temple-hierarchy.[7] Most
startling were the results of the pioneering studies by Deimel[8] of
archives dating to *c.* 2500-2400 BC from the Sumerian city of Girsu.
These seemed to reveal that virtually the entire city-state and almost
all arable land was owned by the 'city-god', i.e. by the temples and their
staff – the priests.

Added to all this material evidence was the influential theory,
propounded by Wittfogel,[9] of state-formation in areas such as South
Iraq, where agricultural exploitation of the environment is dependent
on irrigation. The need for these large-scale installations, it was
argued, necessarily resulted in a centralized, complex organization
that could initiate and direct the difficult and expensive work of
canal-digging, dredging, flood-protection and regulating access to
water-supplies. Given the centrality of temples at the very earliest
periods in South Iraq, given their vast staffs and their overriding
control of resources both agricultural and commercial, it seemed

[3] See, e.g., Strommenger, *Art*, Pls. V, 13-33; pp. 378-86.

[4] See, e.g., D. Oates and J. Oates, *The Rise of Civilization* (Oxford, 1976), 122.

[5] Strommenger, *Art*, 377-8; H.E.W. Crawford, *The Architecture of Iraq in the Third Millennium B.C.* (Mesopotamia 5, Copenhagen, 1977), 74-5.

[6] Uruk: see Falkenstein, *Texte*.

[7] Uruk: cf. Jacobsen, *Early Political Development*, n.32; Adams, 'Factors'.

[8] *Tempelwirtschaft*, 71-113.

[9] *Despotism*.

obvious that it would have been the temples and their associated bureaucracy that fulfilled this role.

With the expansion of population resulting from irrigation works, the development of stratified society and the increasing incidence of inter-city conflicts, kingship emerged.[10] Once firmly institutionalized, the rulers of the various city-states vied with the temples for power and influence. The rich documentation from Girsu even suggests that for a while the rulers triumphed in this struggle and transgressed against the temples by 'illegally' exploiting sacred land for their own purposes.[11] It was inevitable that ultimately the 'secular' power of the state as represented by the kings would predominate, so that the temples came under their patronage and were dependent on them. But given the expertise of the 'priests' in learning, rituals, divination, writing and law, as well as their continuing, if slightly diminished, importance as controllers of the large land-owning institutions, they still represented an intellectual and economic force to be constantly reckoned with. As one scholar[12] has put it:

> ... in general, the power of the priesthood waxed or waned with the waning or waxing of the civil power of the state. Under the powerful Assyrian kings (c. 900-600 BC) the influence of the priesthood was strictly limited to its proper sphere, but in Babylon, owing to the pre-eminent place which that city held as the religious capital of Mesopotamia, even after its political importance had declined, the priesthood always exercised great power, especially during the closing days of the Neo-Babylonian Empire (c. 610-539 BC) ...

Though never made absolutely explicit, the long history of Mesopotamia, and especially of Babylonia, has thus been characterized as reflecting a dichotomy, at times even a struggle, between 'Church' and 'State' on the model of European history; classical writers, archaeological finds and local documentary evidence all appear to complement each other and confirm this picture as essentially correct.

Yet, over the last thirty years or so, this presentation has been seriously challenged and much of the evidence on which it rests shown to be either deficient or capable of alternative interpretations. Both Deimel's interpretation[13] and the theories of Wittfogel[14] have been

---

[10] Jacobsen, *Early Political Development*, 137-9.

[11] S.N. Kramer, *History begins at Sumer: thirty-nine firsts in man's recorded history* (Philadelphia, 1981), 45-50.

[12] Hooke, *Religion*, 54.

[13] Diakonoff, *Society and State*; Gelb, 'Economies'; B. Foster, 'A new look at the Sumerian temple state', *JESHO* 24 (1981), 225-41.

[14] K.W. Butzer, *Early Hydraulic Civilization in Egypt: a study in cultural ecology* (Chicago, 1976); Adams, *Evolution*; H. Helbaek, 'Samarran irrigation agriculture at Choga Mami in Iraq', *Iraq* 34 (1972), 35-48.

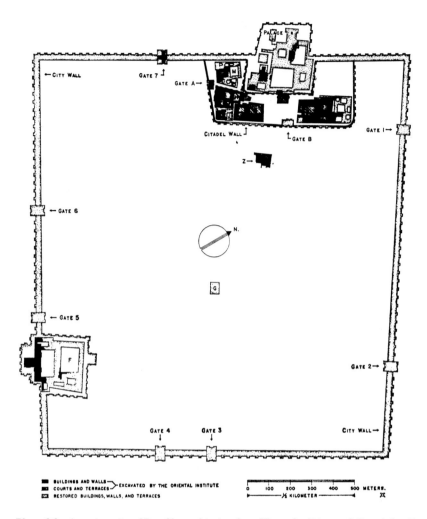

Plan of the Assyrian city of Dur Sharrukin (modern Khorsabad) in north Iraq (after Loud and Altman 1938). The palace and main temples including the ziggurat (temple tower) are situated on the north-western edge of the city enclosed within a separate wall on a kind of acropolis and dominating the rest of the city.

seriously challenged; this makes a re-assessment of state-development in South Iraq essential. Further, it needs to be emphasised how partial excavations have been: the number of sites explored is relatively small; very few have provided an unbroken sequence from the earliest chalcolithic phases of settlement into the historical periods; and, most important, the areas investigated within sites have often been extremely limited. The latter factor in particular has caused a serious distortion of our understanding of Babylonian history. The sites on which attention has most frequently been focused have been the

Plan of Babylon (after Unger 1931). The main temple (Esagila) and ziggurat (Etemenanki) are located squarely in the centre of the town with the colourful processional way, along which the public New Year processions moved, linking them to the Ishtar gate and the route to the festival house (beyond the city). The palace straddles the northern city-wall at a considerable distance from the main temple.

temples and their precincts; through their size and their continuous re-building in the same place, these have formed eye-catching *tells* as opposed to humbler dwellings. Meanwhile, royal palaces and government buildings in Babylonia appear quite often to have been situated on or near the city-walls, often at a considerable distance from the main temple and associated ziggurat which was located in the centre of the city. This has meant that the greater part of the material – artifactual, architectural and documentary – has been recovered exclusively from temples. It is instructive to compare the situation briefly with that in Assyria to the north, which was culturally and politically closely intertwined with Babylonia, though exhibiting a number of distinctive traits. Here the royal palace, the main temple with its ziggurat and the government buildings were built closely together on a kind of acropolis at the edge of the city and often, indeed, walled off from it. As a result, the documentary evidence and material remains from Assyrian sites are far more mixed, so that the impression received is that the king was able to 'control' the power of the priests and temples, as Hooke[15] argued. So the traditional picture of Babylonia dominated by its temples may not reflect any historical reality, but just the pattern of archaeological discovery.

Yet despite the shrivelling of the Sumerian temple-state theory, the limitations of the archaeological record and the repeated admonitions of text-books that modern distinctions 'between "religious", "social" and "economic" reflect modern attempts to analyse the structure and behaviour of societies and...would have had no meaning in ancient Mesopotamia',[16] the very size and location of temples, the number of religious rituals the king had to perform, the royal emphasis on piety, often expressed concretely through gifts to and embellishments of temples, has meant that the notion of priests able to wield effective power and to form a political counterweight to the king is inherent in the analysis of a number of Mesopotamian historical events.[17]

The evidence on which such approaches are based is usually inferred rather than direct. There is, however, one event in a later period of Babylonian history, namely the conquest of Babylonia by Cyrus the Great of Persia in 539 BC, for which there exist diverse, fairly full and virtually contemporary sources, emanating both from the conqueror and from the defeated king, Nabonidus. These sources appear to support the concept of priests as holders of political influence and as effective opponents to the existing regime. The documents and the related arguments about their interpretation fall into two distinct categories.

The first and most frequent approach focuses on the official inscriptions produced by Nabonidus and on those of Cyrus, composed after his conquest, vilifying the defeated ruler in traditional Babylonian fashion.[18] These latter mention, though in a distorted form, a number of events of Nabonidus' reign attested to by his own inscriptions, thus suggesting that the conqueror was not just uttering empty phrases but exploiting genuine criticisms levelled against Nabonidus by the inhabitants of Babylonia. As these texts of Cyrus are composed in the standard Akkadian of the time, which he probably did not speak, they must have been composed by Babylonians. As the

[15] See above p. 123
[16] Oates, *Babylon*, 25.
[17] A good example of this is the so-called 'secularization' thought to have taken place in the reign of Hammurabi of Babylon (1792-1750 BC); see R. Harris, *Sippar: a demographic study of an Old Babylonian city (1894-1595 BC)* (Istanbul, 1975).
[18] Kuhrt, 'Conquest'.

repositories of literacy and learning were the temples with their priests, it must be they who were the real authors. Finally, as some of the acts of Nabonidus attacked in them involved apparent deviations from Babylonian religious norms, it was obviously priests who had been most offended by this and who took the opportunity publicly to express their opposition to these deviations and their consequent support for Cyrus' contrasting behaviour.[19] The issue at stake, according to this interpretation, was a theological one: Nabonidus attempted to introduce changes into some aspects of Babylonian religious practice and thus incurred the hostility of the priests whose interests lay in maintaining the religious *status quo*. Central to this analysis is, of course, the notion that there was a concept of separate spheres of activity – one proper to the king and a separate one subject exclusively to religious authority. A further elaboration of the 'theological conflict' argument is the suggestion, based on Isaiah (41-8), that before the conquest the Persians had carried on an active propaganda campaign within Babylonia.[20] Through the use of *magi* (Persian learned men) able to converse with the Babylonian scholars (priests), the Persians were able to whip up and sharpen the discontent of the Babylonians with their king to the point that, when the attack on Babylon actually began, the Persian armies met with practically no opposition and were, indeed, welcomed as liberators.[21] Apart from requiring wholesale acceptance of the 'theological conflict' argument as a base, it is also essential to the viability of this theory that priests should be conceived as having been politically effective enough to disseminate the propaganda and substantially to influence the course of events.

The other approach is often combined with the first in an attempt to create a fuller picture of the events or to analyse the underlying 'true' reasons for Babylonian disaffection.[22] This argument centres on the wealth of administrative documents from temple archives; it puts forward instances of royal interference in the running of the temples and of increased royal control over their resources as a major contributory factor in the lack of support given to Nabonidus and in the ease of Cyrus' victory. Despite the different focus and material used, the analysis again depends on assuming that priests were powerful enough to mobilize a general opposition to the reigning king when their economic interests and independence were threatened.

It is this nexus of documentation and interpretation that will be

[19] Smith, *Historical Texts*, 32; Garelli, 'Nabonide', 274.
[20] Smith, *Isaiah*; Boyce, *History*, 43-7.
[21] Smith, *Historical Texts*, 61; Voigtlander, *Survey*, 199. The argument has been expanded through analogy with the (assumed) functioning of Second Isaiah in relation to the exiled Jews in Babylonia.
[22] Labat, 'Assyrien', 107-8; Voigtlander, *Survey*, 183ff.; Garelli, *Empires*, 156.

examined in what follows. For the sake of clarity and space, it will be
necessary to limit detailed examination of the large number of
inscriptions and texts to a small selection only. The first section will
consider the political situation immediately preceding Nabonidus'
reign in order to place him in a historical continuum; this will be
followed by a brief discussion of his reign according to the one
unbiased[23] source available, the so-called 'Nabonidus Chronicle'.[24]
This will serve the further important purpose of considering whether
there is any real evidence for the widely-held view that Cyrus'
conquest was regarded as a liberation and that it proceeded almost
unopposed – this is crucial to *all* arguments. In the second section, I
shall look at some of the most important of the documents to see
whether the 'theological conflict' analysis can be maintained; this in
turn entails considering whether any evidence exists to show that real
disaffection was felt by priests, which could be exploited by the
Persians. This will be followed, in the third section, by a necessarily
brief examination of the 'economic' argument to see whether temples
and their staffs suffered any real diminution of their resources and of
control over them.

The question around which the entire problem revolves is, of course:
who were the priests in Babylonia? Did they wield the power with
which they have been credited and is there any validity in the concept
of a separation of 'political/civic' and 'religious' authority? If this
separation provides a feasible hypothesis, is the documentation
available of a type that provides real insights into 'the nature of the
internal dissension which led to the final fall of Babylon'?[25]

The fall of Babylon

Nabonidus was the last king of what is called the Neo-Babylonian
Empire; he reigned from 556 to 539 BC, in which year Cyrus of Persia
conquered Babylon. The Neo-Babylonian Empire came into being as a
result of the fall of the Assyrian Empire: the Babylonians co-operated
with the Medes to mount attacks on the capital cities of Assyria (Assur,
Nimrud (Kalah), Nineveh: see map) and defeated the last Assyrian
king at his Western stronghold, Harran in North Syria in 610/609 BC.
By the time the Babylonian king Nabopolassar died in 605 BC, he,
together with his son and designated successor Nebuchadnezzar (II),

---

[23] Or apparently unbiased: *contra* B. Landsberger and T. Bauer, 'Zu neuveröffentlichten
Geschichtsquellen der Zeit von Asarhaddon bis Nabonid', *ZA* 37 (1927), 61ff.; Garelli,
'Nabonide', 274; W. von Soden, 'Kyros und Nabonid, Propaganda und Gegenpropaganda'
in *Kunst, Kultur und Geschichte der Achämenidenzeit*, ed. H. Koch and D.N. Mackenzie
(AMI Ergänzungsband 10, Berlin, 1983).
[24] Grayson, *Chronicles*, no. 7.
[25] Smith, *Historical Texts*, 83.

Fig. 17. Fragment of the Babylonian chronicle series, usually called the 'Nabonidus Chronicle'. Despite its fragmentary state it is the most important source for the reign of Nabonidus and his defeat by Cyrus, king of Persia, in 539 BC.

had established his control over the major part of what had constituted the Assyrian Empire, the main difference being that the imperial capital was now at Babylon in Southern Iraq. Sixteen years of his reign had been spent in fighting the Assyrian army, much of the time within the area of Babylonia itself; the results had been serious ravages of the countryside, destruction of harvests and even, at times, starvation for some city-dwellers.[26] His son Nebuchadnezzar II, who had conducted campaigns on behalf of his father during the later part of his reign, was accepted on Nabopolassar's death as a worthy successor, and he

---

[26] A.L. Oppenheim, ' "Siege Documents" from Nippur', *Iraq* 17 (1955).

inaugurated a brilliant and prosperous period in Babylonian history. As far as one knows, the wars that were fought henceforth took place far from the central Babylonian area;[27] booty and war captives provided both resources and manpower to carry out magnificent building schemes, especially in Babylon itself;[28] and the re-establishment of peace resulted in the stimulation of extensive overland trade[29] and a gradual normalization of agricultural activities. Unfortunately, Nebuchadnezzar's son, Amel-Marduk, does not appear to have had the opportunity to establish a reputation for himself in the manner of his father and was deposed by his uncle by marriage, Neriglissar, after less than two years of rule. Neriglissar was both an ardent campaigner and a restorer of sanctuaries in the tradition of Nebuchadnezzar,[30] but died after four years of rule. He was succeeded by a young son (posssibly still a child), Labashi-Marduk, who was murdered after only a few months on the throne – some cities, in fact, never seem to have accepted him as king at all[31] – by a group of powerful Babylonians (unfortunately it is impossible to define them more closely), who chose as king Nabonidus, a man bearing no family relationship to his predecessors[32] and of mature years; he had an adult son called Bel-šar-uṣur, better known as the Belshazzar of the Book of Daniel.

Although the names of both Nabonidus' father and mother are known, it is impossible to define his background more precisely. It seems *likely* that both parents played a role at court, but otherwise nothing is known, though much imputed;[33] nor is there any evidence of Nabonidus' career before his elevation to the kingship.[34] Fortunately, the main events of his reign are largely known from the 'Nabonidus Chronicle'[35] which, though now severely broken in places, originally covered (with lacunae) all seventeen years of his reign, then described Cyrus' capture of Babylon and continued into Cyrus' first year of rule. From this text it is plain that Nabonidus campaigned vigorously in the West (Cilicia, Hamath, Edom) early in his reign, thus continuing and maintaining the policies and frontiers of Nebuchadnezzar and

---

[27] Grayson, *Chronicles*, no. 5.

[28] R. Koldewey, *Das wiedererstehende Babylon* (4th ed. Leipzig, 1925).

[29] Oppenheim, 'Essay on overland trade in the first millennium BC', *JCS* 21 (1967), 236-54.

[30] Langdon, *Königsinschriften*, 45-6; 208-19; Berger, *Königsinschriften*, 108-10; Wiseman, *Chronicles*, 37-42; 74-7; Grayson, *Chronicles*, no. 6.

[31] cf. Parker and Dubberstein, *Chronology*, 13.

[32] One should note the emphasis put in the epitaph for Nabonidus' mother at Harran (Gadd, 'Inscriptions', 56-62) on her activity in carrying out the cult for deceased Neo-Babylonian kings – an activity usually performed by the male heir (M. Bayliss, 'The cult of Dead Kin in Assyria and Babylonia', *Iraq* 35 (1973), 115-25). It could perhaps be interpreted as one of the elements used by Nabonidus to justify his irregular accession.

[33] Dougherty, *Nabonidus*, 16-28.

[34] *pace* Dougherty, *Nabonidus*, 29-70; Voigtlander, *Survey*, 161-5.

[35] Pritchard, *Texts*, 305-7; Smith, *Historical Texts*, 110-18; Grayson, *Chronicles*, no. 7.

Neriglissar. Probably in his fourth regnal year, he mounted a massive and lengthy expedition into Arabia. Certainly by 540/539 BC,[36] Nabonidus was back in Babylonia and making final preparations to defend it against Cyrus' attack. By October 539, Cyrus was installed in Babylonia and the whole area that had comprised the Empire fell into Persian hands.

Apart from Nabonidus' military endeavours, his own extensive and numerous building inscriptions provide a wealth of information on his pious acts of building, repairing, beautifying and endowing Babylonian sanctuaries in the manner of his royal predecessors, Nebuchadnezzar II and Neriglissar, whose work he in many instances completed. Much of this building activity was, in fact, connected with re-establishing sanctuaries destroyed during the 'war of liberation', waged between Assyria and the Medo-Babylonian confederacy,[37] including the major rebuilding of the moon-god's temple (É.hul.hul) in Harran.[38]

The impression of Nabonidus gained from texts either contemporary with his reign or having a good claim to be considered objective and reliable,[39] is that of an able and vigorous ruler, brought to the throne as the result of a coup carried out by Babylonians opposed to having a child as king. He was presumably chosen because of his proven abilities; in what is unknown, but his active campaigning policy would suggest that he was an experienced soldier and military commander. He certainly did not disappoint his supporters in this respect, as he followed up his active securing of the boundaries of the empire by expanding Babylonian control into the Northern Hejaz area, where he conquered and occupied the strategic oasis city of Tema[40] and brought under his sway other oases (e.g. Medina), which were major centres of the important Arabian caravan trade.[41] This activity appears to be an extension of earlier Assyrian and Neo-Babylonian relations with the region generally, which reflect both commercial (*ABL* 1404) and military interests.[42] The campaign was very long-drawn-out –

---

[36] If not earlier – 542/541 – cf. Tadmor, *Inscriptions*.

[37] Langdon, *Königsinschriften, Nbn.* no. 8.

[38] ibid. col.x.

[39] i.e. the 'Nabonidus Chronicle', cf. Grayson, *Chronicles*, ch.2.

[40] A massive site: cf. G. Bawden, C. Edens, R. Miller, 'Typological and analytical studies: a. Preliminary archaeological investigations at Tayma', *Atlal* 4 (1980), 69-106; G. Bawden, 'Recent radiocarbon dates from Tayma', *Atlal* 5 (1981), 149-53; A. Livingstone, B. Spaie, M. Ibrahim, M. Kamal, S. Taimani, 'Researches: A. Taima: recent soundings and new inscribed material', *Atlal* 7 (1983), 102-16.

[41] Gadd, 'Inscriptions', 59; Briant, *État et pasteurs*, 160.

[42] cf. generally I. Eph'al, *The Ancient Arabs: Nomads on the borders of the fertile crescent, 9th-5th centuries BC* (Jerusalem, Leiden, 1982), 74ff.; for the importance of the Arab campaigns in the late Assyrian Empire, cf. M. Weippert, 'Die Kämpfe des assyrischen Königs Assurbanipal gegen die Araber. Redaktionskritische Untersuchung der Berichte in Prisma A', *WO* 7/I (1973), 39-85. Berossus (third century BC) seems to have referred to military activities by Nebuchadnezzar II against the Arabs (*FGH* 680, Fgt.8; cf. *FGH* 685, Fgt.6). There is certainly some evidence for settlements of Arabs in Babylonia during the

Nabonidus stayed in the Hejaz for ten years – but markedly successful; in his absence, the Empire was ably and smoothly administered by his son, Bel-šar-uṣur,[43] including the completion of the major rebuilding and renovating projects in Babylonian temples and cities, some begun before Nabonidus left, others begun in his absence but with his blessing. One major rebuilding project which was almost completed during Nabonidus' absence was that of the temple of É.hul.hul in Harran, a site of strategic importance for the control of northern Mesopotamia, destroyed by the Babylonians themselves in the final battles against Assyria.[44] Within Babylonia itself preparations for safe-guarding the Empire were also not neglected: a new fortress was built[45] upstream from Sippar on the Euphrates – a vulnerable point in Babylonia's defences at all times, as it is here that the Diyala (last stage of the major Khorasan route)[46] flows into the Tigris, while the Tigris and the Euphrates approach each other most closely; it was thus the main route for entry into the most populous and agriculturally developed heartland of the country,[47] both from the north (Assyria) and the east (Iran).[48] All in all, the picture one has of Nabonidus' reign from the contemporary records, eked out by the chronicle where preserved, is of a period when the policies initiated by Nabopolassar and especially Nebuchadnezzar II were brought to fruition and completed. The Empire was larger than it had ever been, the rebuilding of sites destroyed in the earlier war against Assyria was completed, and tactical measures for ensuring the realm's safety were taken.

Yet in 539 Cyrus, apparently in the space of a few days, gained control of this immense area[49] and little opposition seems to have been offered to his invasion. Should one then reinterpret Nabonidus' reign

---

reign, but whether as traders or as deportees is unclear (Eph'al, op.cit., 189-90). Further, Temaites are found settled there at the same time: Dougherty, *Nabonidus*, Pl.I, 117 (Nebuchadnezzar RY 7); BIN I, 151 (Neb. RY 15); cf. Eph'al, op.cit., 188.

[43] Dougherty, *Nabonidus*, 105-37.

[44] Langdon, *Königsinschriften, Nbn.* 8, col.x; cf. Grayson, *Chronicles*, no.3, ll.63-4.

[45] Grayson, *Chronicles*, no.7, col.ii, l.13; cf. *RLA* 2, 246; Voigtlander, *Survey*, 194.

[46] cf. P. Briant, *L'Asie centrale et les royaumes proche-orientaux du premier millénaire (VIIIe-IVe siècles avant notre ère)* (Paris, 1984), 39.

[47] S.S. Ahmed, *Southern Mesopotamia in the Time of Assurbanipal* (The Hague, 1968), 17-26.

[48] It was almost invariably in this region that major set battles between Babylonians and invaders were fought, e.g.: Dur Shulgi (Kurigalzu II (1345-1324) against the Elamites); Mt. Ialman (Adadnirari II (1307-1275) and Babylonians); cities in the area were seized from Babylonians by Shamshi-Adad V (823-811); Der (720: Sargon II against Elamites and Babylonians); Halule (691 or 690: Sennacherib against the Elamites). Some of the war between Assyria and Babylonia leading to the ultimate fall of the Assyrian empire (626-610) was centred in this region too: cf. Grayson, *Chronicles*, no.2, ll.19 & 29. Not least is, of course, the battle of Opis (539) in which Cyrus defeated Nabonidus.

[49] Grayson, *Chronicles*, no.7, col.iii, ll.12ff.

in the light of this easy defeat, arguing that his self-presentation in the royal inscriptions masked serious disturbances and crucial weaknesses in his control of the Empire and especially of Babylonia? The question hinges to a large degree on one's reading of the relevant chronicle passage: Smith, in his initial publication,[50] rendered the passage as:

> Cyrus, when he did battle at Opis on the Tigris against the troops of Akkad, *burnt the people of Akkad with fire, he killed the people* [my italics] ... Sippar was captured without a battle.

which suggests a battle followed by a massacre. In a note,[51] he added that it might be rendered instead as 'the people of Akkad revolted', which would agree with Xenophon's account in the *Cyropaedia* 7,5,20-6; this was, unfortunately, the interpretation taken up by, for instance, Oppenheim,[52] who went one better by translating the line:

> the inhabitants of Akkad revolted, but he (Nabonidus) massacred the confused inhabitants.

Thus, by means of an interpretation intended to bring the renderings into line with what one was *expecting* to find, the passage was changed to provide a dramatic picture of the Babylonians mutinying as soon as battle was joined and of a despotic king, in dire straits, turning on his own subjects. Fortunately, a careful re-editing of the text by Grayson[53] has both improved understanding of the text and restored some of Smith's original rendering:

> ... when Cyrus did battle ... against the army of Akkad, the people of Akkad retreated. He carried off the plunder (and) slaughtered the people.

What one is left with, then, is a rather more 'normal' course of events: the invader attacks, battle is joined and the Babylonians defeated; the victor then loots the city and massacres the population. This brutal image is *not*, of course, in keeping with that of Cyrus the 'merciful liberator', and hardly supports the picture of a people so oppressed that they prefer foreign domination to the hated yoke of their own ruler. That the extreme measures used by Cyrus at Opis paid off is shown by the fact that Sippar, the city next in line of attack, surrendered to him; Nabonidus fled to Babylon, just downstream, where he was captured

---

[50] *Historical Texts*, 117; col.iii, 12-14.
[51] ibid. 121, l.14.
[52] in Pritchard, *Texts*, 306.
[53] *Chronicles*, no.7, col.iii, ll.12-14.

by Cyrus' general,[54] who disposed his troops within the city to maintain peace and to ensure that it would formally welcome the conqueror as its new king. This was part of an established procedure practised by earlier Assyrian conquerors[55] and cannot therefore be taken to reflect the 'real' feelings of the inhabitants of Babylonia as a whole, or of Babylon in particular.

One objection that could be raised against this view is that, while Cyrus may have had to fight an initial bloody battle, the entire conquest of Babylonia took only about a month. Surely, this must indicate that Nabonidus was woefully unaware of the threat represented by the Persians, that he failed to make any proper preparations earlier and was instead frittering away valuable resources and time in Arabia. But the refurbishing of Harran, the foundation of the fortress at Dur Karašu and the presence in Babylonia during Nabonidus' Arabian campaign of the capable Bel-šar-uṣur argue against such neglect. It has also been plausibly suggested[56] that from 550 onwards, when Cyrus defeated Astyages of Media and became heir to the vast regions he controlled (from the River Halys to at least central Iran), there had been some occasional conflict between Babylonia and the Persians in frontier areas.[57] If this is correct, then Cyrus' conquest would be the outcome of prolonged, though intermittent, warfare rather than of the lightning campaign it appears at present to be, on the basis of the very fragmentary and, in this respect, inadequate chronicle text.

One important element in building up a picture of Cyrus as able to exploit and manipulate opposition to Nabonidus should thus be questioned, and perhaps entirely discarded: as far as reliable, relatively unbiased evidence based on material virtually contemporary with events is concerned,[58] Cyrus did not walk unopposed into Babylonia, nor did he liberate it. Rather, when he eventually entered Babylonia, possibly after years of border skirmishes, he had to fight a battle, ending in severe reprisals against the population; in response to this brutal example, Sippar and Babylon surrendered and, after investing the capital with Iranian troops, a carefully orchestrated,

---

[54] There is no evidence, apart from the doubtful later testimony of the *Cyropaedia* 4,6,1, that Gubaru (Gobryas) was a Babylonian traitor: the fact that he was governor of Gutium, a vague location north-east of Babylonia, would suggest that it was his physical proximity that led to his playing an important role in the conquest, for which he was rewarded by being installed as Babylonian governor (though he died three weeks later). Cf. Kuhrt, 'Babylonia'.

[55] Kuhrt, 'Conquest'.

[56] Voigtlander, *Survey*, 194 & 8.

[57] cf. also G.G. Cameron, 'Cyrus the "Father" and Babylonia', *Acta Iranica* I/1 (1974), 45-8.

[58] Grayson, *Chronicles*, 8-9.

ceremonial welcome by the capital city to Cyrus was engineered by his general.

Nabonidus' 'religious reforms'

Although a careful scrutiny of the actual process of Cyrus' conquest of Babylonia somewhat undermines the notion that it was a virtually bloodless transition from one king to another, the complexities of what people may or may not have felt about their former ruler could well be masked by the 'official' character of the presentations of Nabonidus' reign given in his inscriptions and by the terseness of the chronicle entries. This is the view held by many scholars who have argued that a text that takes particular issue with Nabonidus' religious policy was not composed merely as the result of Cyrus' successful conquest, but allows insight into the grievances of the priesthood (of Babylon, in particular) against him. The reason for this is that 'the document does not accuse Nabonidus of imaginary crimes. Where one can confront it with the inscriptions of the king himself, one observes that there has been no systematic deformation ... Nabonidus' piety was heterodox.'[59]

The accusations levelled against Nabonidus in this tract, generally known, after Smith's publication of it, as 'A Persian Verse Account of Nabonidus', have been most successfully compared with an inscription of Nabonidus recording his rebuilding and dedication of the temple of the moon-god in Harran. It has been thought that both some references in the chronicle and certain specific statements in the Harran text combine to show that traditional Babylonian religion was 'flouted by Nabonidus',[60] and that this roused the opposition of the priesthood who 'were able to express themselves after Cyrus' victory'[61] in this 'Verse Account'. To test this widely held supposition, I propose to look briefly at the texts in turn and assess each on its own merits first. It will then be possible to draw the results together and see whether the established view is vindicated or requires some modification.

(A) The text erected by Nabonidus at Harran is extant in two versions.[62] It was clearly composed to commemorate his rebuilding there of the moon-god's temple (É.hul.hul), possibly also to provide an explanation for his delay in doing so;[63] the text is remarkable for the great prominence it gives to the moon-god (Sin) in comparison to the other gods of the Babylonian pantheon. The outward form of the text is

---

[59] Garelli, 'Nabonide', 274.

[60] J.M. Cook, 'The rise of the Achaemenids and establishment of their empire', *CHI* 2 (1985), 200-91, esp. 212.

[61] Garelli, 'Nabonide', 274.

[62] Gadd, 'Inscriptions'; Pritchard, *Texts*, 562-3; Röllig, 'Erwägungen'.

[63] Tadmor, 'Inscriptions', 357-8.

that of a normal royal building inscription, but some unusual features have been inserted.[64] The contents state that Sin called Nabonidus to the kingship and having done so revealed in a dream that Nabonidus must rebuild his temple in Harran and that Sin would give control of all lands to him. The next section states that the *mār banê* of six prominent cities in Babylonia and the *šangê* (a term usually translated 'priests') of the dwelling-places of Akkad (i.e. Babylonia) sinned against the godhead of Sin by a number of blasphemous acts: they neglected rituals, they spoke lies and they ate each other like dogs. As a result they were struck by fever and drought, so that many people died. Nabonidus left Babylonia and went to Arabia at the command of Sin and stayed there for ten years. All Nabonidus' ventures in Arabia during this time worked out remarkably well, through Sin's agency, and eventually the auspicious day dawned when he returned to Babylon in peace and joy. He then proceeded to build Sin's temple in Harran.

Now the most obvious interpretation of this text would seem to be that the coup that had raised Nabonidus to the throne of Babylon met, not unexpectedly, with a certain amount of opposition in Babylonia, although this does not seem to have been a united effort, but rather led to disagreements among various groups of inhabitants. It is possible that a virulent disease and bad harvest, which befell Babylonia around this same time, was exploited by Nabonidus to demonstrate to the trouble-makers that the gods wished him to rule and that their opposition would only bring suffering on the malefactors themselves. Having brought the situation under control, he left his son to govern Babylonia and undertook an extraordinarily successful campaign in Arabia, conquering oases along important trade-routes and subjugating various troublesome bedouin tribes. The fact that his kingship met with divine approval was borne out by Nabonidus' achievements, which are described as:

(1) a miraculous rainfall resulting in bumper harvests (two in one year)
(2) all rulers of foreign countries made friendly overtures to Nabonidus
(3) hostile raiders and plunderers (i.e. bedouin groups) were prevented from continuing their acts of robbery
(4) the frontiers, even the most distant and difficult ones, were safe and well-guarded.

---

[64] Röllig, 'Erwägungen', 232.

Fig. 18. Neo-Babylonian agate cylinder seal and impression. The impression shows the Babylonian moon-god Sin on the left depicted as a male figure standing on the crescent moon. The creature on the right is the dragon (*mušhuššu*) associated with Marduk, the patron-god of Babylon, supporting the spade which is another of Marduk's symbols.

This peaceful and prosperous situation was attributed to the activities of different Babylonian gods (Adad, Ishtar, Nergal, Shamash), who carried them out in Nabonidus' interest at the command of Sin, the moon-god, who had given Nabonidus the kingship in the first place. Therefore, when the auspicious day arrived for Nabonidus to return to Babylonia, he gratefully complied with Sin's command to rebuild his temple in Harran – or rather to inaugurate it, since the actual building had presumably been going on while Nabonidus was in Arabia. On this occasion, the text describing what led to the building was set up and Sin, who was patron deity of Harran, was not surprisingly given a very prominent place in the account.[65]

The striking element in the text is the reference to opposition encountered by Nabonidus; the question is who were the groups expressing opposition and what were they opposing? Does the text support the contention that they were priests and objecting to Nabonidus' building of the temple to Sin at Harran?[66] Although the term *šangê* is often translated as 'priests', this meaning is in fact not certain. A word as such for 'priests' does not exist in Akkadian, as has been noted by several scholars,[67] and in some contexts *šangê* certainly appears to describe temple-administrators rather than cultic personnel.[68] The word was rendered neutrally by Oppenheim as

[65] cf. Cyrus' attribution of his successful conquest of Babylonia to Marduk in Babylon (Cyrus Cylinder) and to Sin in Ur (U.8837 = *UET* 1, 307); in neither case can these texts reveal Cyrus' personal religious convictions. See further Kuhrt, 'Cyrus Cylinder'.

[66] Röllig, 'Erwägungen', 241-2.

[67] Kümmel, *Familie*, 147 n.1; Brinkman, review of G.J.P. McEwan, *Priest and Temple in Hellenistic Babylonia* (Wiesbaden, 1981) and *Texts from Hellenistic Babylonia in the Ashmolean Museum* (Oxford, 1982) in *JCS* 35 (1983), 232.

[68] *AHw* s.v. *šangû*.

'administrators',[69] a translation receiving some support from the so-called 'court calendar' of Nebuchadnezzar II,[70] which gives a list of the main officials and governors of the Neo-Babylonian Empire: among these figure a group of *šangê*. The other dissident group are called the *mār banê*; though its precise meaning remains uncertain, the term certainly characterized juridically free land-owning individuals and it was from their ranks that the assemblies that heard legal proceedings within certain cities were drawn.[71] Though the meaning in either instance is not completely certain, an identification of these groups as priests is *not* a necessary one. As to the object of their opposition, a close reading of the text does not bear out the interpretation that these groups objected to Nabonidus' worship of Sin or his plan to rebuild É.hul.hul in Harran. Rather, it was directed against Nabonidus' assumption of kingship, which is described in the text (given the context of its composition – i.e. the inauguration of the newly completed Sin temple) as the 'plan of Sin'. What Nabonidus is saying in effect is that their opposition to himself as king constituted an offence against the moon-god because it was the god who had elevated him to the throne. Any specific objection to Nabonidus on a purely theological level would thus appear to be entirely absent.

Thus far the evidence of the Harran stele. But the issue is more complex because some of Nabonidus' other building works comme-morated in inscriptions also seem to give the moon-god an over-riding importance[72] compared with other Babylonian gods, so that he appears at times to be displacing Marduk, the patron-god of the city of Babylon and traditional head of the Babylonian pantheon. Also important is the fact that the epitaph for Nabonidus' mother was set up in Harran too, and in this her constant devotion to the god Sin is dwelt upon at length.[73] As Nabonidus' mother may have played a particularly important part (see n.32 above) in Nabonidus' claims to legitimacy as king, this may all reflect a specific devotion on the part of the Nabonidus family to the city of Harran and to its major cult.

There are, however, some objections to this: first, the rebuilding of Harran was strategically and economically a major undertaking of prime importance and entirely Nabonidus' achievement as opposed to other building works at, for example, Ur, Sippar, Babylon, Uruk and Kish – to mention some of the main ones[74] – where Nabonidus was following in the footsteps of, and completing work already begun by,

[69] in Pritchard, *Texts*, 562.
[70] E. Unger, *Babylonien die heilige Stadt nach der Beschreibung der Babylonier* (Berlin, 1931 (repr. 1970)), no.26, col.v.
[71] Oelsner, 'Erwägungen', 134-5; Dandamaev, 'Citizens'; Kümmel, *Familie*, 162-3.
[72] Tadmor, 'Inscriptions', 359-63.
[73] Pritchard, *Texts*, 560-2; Gadd, 'Inscriptions', 56-62.
[74] cf. for the details Berger, *Königsinschriften*, 108-10.

his predecessors. Secondly, in only a very few of Nabonidus' inscriptions is Sin given a position of paramount importance; these are the Harran texts, where (as I am arguing) this should be related to the location, and also in a text from Ur,[75] another centre of the Sin cult, where the same argument applies. Two other texts relate to the major work done by Nabonidus on the sun-god's temple (Ebabbara) at Sippar,[76] but only one of these assigns Sin very exalted epithets; finally, Sin is prominent in a text similar in several respects to the Harran texts, but of unknown provenance[77] – for all one knows it may have come from a centre of the worship of Sin. Thirdly, in accordance with a notion that Nabonidus himself came from Harran and was therefore a 'foreigner' in Babylonian terms[78] – both of which are very questionable assumptions – it has been suggested that he at first kept his religious inclinations hidden, but that, as his reign progressed, his personal devotion to Sin was more and more blatantly displayed. On the basis of this structuring of Nabonidus' development, his inscriptions have been dated by Tadmor[79] to reflect an increasingly obvious favouring of Sin and a diminution of the traditional Babylonian pantheon. This is, however, to prejudge the issue, as pointed out by Lambert,[80] and at least one of the crucial texts[81] has been dated earlier by Berger[82] than Tadmor's proposed date.

To conclude: it is conceivable, though of course not certain, that the exalted position given to Sin by Nabonidus in two of the texts relating to the rebuilding of the sun-god's temple at Sippar[83] may be a reflection of the enormous importance of the Harran building project, rather than an indicator of Nabonidus' personal religious proclivities. One must bear in mind that out of twenty-six longer building inscriptions in only one[84] is Sin given a hugely superior position to the other Babylonian gods, despite the fact that the text relates to a site unconnected with the moon-god. Further, there is no clear indication from the evidence so far discussed that his projected rebuilding of Harran caused any opposition among the population, nor can one really maintain that the elevation of Sin to a premier position in the pantheon was part of a deliberate plan of religious reform.[85]

---

[75] Langdon, *Königsinschriften, Nbn.* 5.
[76] Langdon, *Königsinschriften, Nbn.* 1; id.,'Inscriptions'.
[77] L.W. King, *Babylonian Boundary Stones* (London, 1912), no.37.
[78] e.g. Smith, *Historical Texts*, 46-9.
[79] 'Inscriptions'.
[80] W.G. Lambert, 'Nabonidus in Arabia', *PSAS* 6 (1972), 53-64.
[81] Langdon, *Königsinschriften, Nbn.* 1.
[82] *Königsinschriften*, 111-12.
[83] His other major building project, cf. A.L. Oppenheim, 'The Babylonian evidence of Achaemenian rule in Mesopotamia', *CHI* 2 (1985), 529-87.
[84] Langdon, 'Inscriptions'.
[85] As was assumed by Oppenheim, *Mesopotamia*, 108-9.

(B) Some references in the Nabonidus Chronicle[86] have been interpreted in conjunction with the notion that Nabonidus was a fanatical devotee of Sin, to show that he deliberately interfered with traditional Babylonian rituals, with the result that the hatred of the population and in particular of the priests was aroused against him. The references are to the fact that Nabonidus omitted to perform the annual New Year festival in Babylon for several years, although a curtailed ceremony is, in one instance, reported.[87]

A number, though not all, of the Babylonian chronicles display a particular interest in this festival and whether it was performed or not; its importance cannot be gainsaid. It reaffirmed the *status quo*, the position of Marduk as king of the gods, the privileges of Babylonian citizens, the king as a guarantor of order and prosperity, as well as being an occasion for the king to display his military forces and booty taken abroad. It was a long and, more importantly, a public festival involving gods from other cities too[88] and for a full performance, required the participation of the reigning king. In no way, however, did the recognition of a king as the legitimate ruler depend on his officiating in the ceremony.[89] An earlier Assyrian king, for example, who was an acknowledged ruler of Babylon as well and who seems to have been rather favourably thought of among at least some of the Babylonians,[90] never once performed the New Year festival in Babylon. An obvious reason for omitting the festival was the absence of the king on campaign, and this must certainly be the reason for the ten-year interruption of the festival in Nabonidus' reign as he was away establishing his control of Tema and the desert caravan routes. He certainly performed the festival before leaving[91] and after his return,[92] as one would expect. It would therefore be quite false to accept, for example, Smith's statement[93] that: '(because of his devotion to Sin) Nabonidus ordered the cessation of the New Year festival; ... an evidence of his own personal dislike of the ceremony once he had officiated in the rites. But this cessation of the sacred yearly festival must have caused much discontent among both priests and people ...'. Nothing that is known, either about the function of the festival or from the chronicle's references as preserved, allows of such an interpretation.

[86] Grayson, *Chronicles*, no.7.
[87] col.ii, ll.7-8.
[88] Texts: Thureau-Dangin, *Rituels*, 127-54; Pritchard, *Texts*, 331-4. Discussion: Labat, 'Caractère religieux', 166-73; A. Falkenstein, 'akiti-Fest und akiti-Festhaus', in *Festschrift Johannes Friedrich zum 65 Geburtstag*, ed. R. von Kienle *et al.* (Heidelberg, 1959); Grayson, 'Akitu Festival'; J.A. Black, 'New Year ceremonies', 39-59; Kuhrt, 'Conquest'.
[89] Grayson, 'Akitu Festival'; *contra*, Smith, 'Sennacherib'.
[90] Grayson, *Chronicles*, 30-2.
[91] Langdon, *Königsinschriften, Nbn.* 8 col.ix.
[92] Grayson, *Chronicles*, no.7, col.iii, ll.5-8.
[93] *Historical Texts*, 48-9.

(C) It is now necessary to examine the text that has been in large measure responsible for imposing this view of Nabonidus' reign and the notion that he was violently detested, especially by the priesthood and, in particular, that of Marduk, i.e. the 'Persian Verse Account'.[94] The text is an unusual one in that it is a propaganda text with a definite poetic structure, suggesting possible public recitation.[95] Most of the text concerns the wicked deeds of Nabonidus during his reign; the last column is devoted to praise of Cyrus, who put right what Nabonidus had done wrong, thus causing joy and well-being for all Babylonians. Among the criminal acts committed by Nabonidus is the fact that he made a sacrilegious statue of the moon-god and then built a place to house it, called É.hul.hul. Moreover, he declared that no New Year festivals should take place until his building plan was completed. But that was not all: the king's mounting insanity eventually resulted in his asserting that the temple of Marduk in Babylon (Esagila) did not belong to Marduk at all but to Sin.

This would seem at first sight to lend support to the view that Nabonidus was attempting to introduce religious changes and that this attempt was disliked in Babylonia. But his activities in relation to the cult of the moon-god are only some of the crimes of which he is accused; the list of these is in fact much longer and more varied.[96] The text states that Nabonidus was abandoned by his *šēdu*, his protective deity, thus causing his own downfall through a series of blasphemous acts and bringing the country to ruination. These acts are then given:

He made the unnatural cult-statue, to which he gave one of the names of the moon-god.

He decided to build É.hul.hul and to stop all New Year festivals until it was finished. In doing that, he made É.hul.hul as beautiful as Esagila.

He then decided to go off to Tema in Arabia, where he ruined the inhabitants so that he could build Tema into a residence like Babylon; he built walls for it and made the inhabitants labour for him.

(A column is here maddeningly broken; when the text can be read again:)

Nabonidus was completely off his head: he claimed victories he had not achieved and the conquest of peoples who, as everyone knew, were subject to Cyrus.

---

[94] See above, p. 135; text: Smith, *Historical Texts*, 83-91; Pritchard, *Texts*, 312-15.

[95] E. Reiner, 'Die akkadische Literatur' in *Altorientalische Literaturen*, ed. W. Röllig (Neues Handbuch der Literaturwissenschaft 1, Wiesbaden, 1978), 151-210; Voigtlander, *Survey*, 179, no.28.

[96] Only cols.ii and iv are preserved with something approaching completeness; of cols. i and vi, the second halves of most lines (c.34?) are preserved. By contrast, only a few words at the beginnings of eleven lines are preserved from cols.iii and iv.

Nabonidus also began to claim enormous wisdom for himself, but was quite incapable of getting a single ritual right and in fact put a stop to regular ritual activity.

He reinterpreted a symbol on Marduk's temple in Babylon to indicate that Esagila really belonged to Sin. (Two high-ranking officials are actually named at this point as having accepted this as truth – it is not clear whether the text is implying that they were forced to do so, or whether one should regard them as toadies.)

There can be no doubting the propagandistic nature of the text nor the fact that it was composed and circulated after Cyrus' victory in 539 BC, as Smith[97] was careful to emphasise.[98] But does it have the historical value that Smith[99] also imputed to it, because (as he said) 'it shows the nature of the internal dissension which led to the final fall of Babylon'?

The list certainly appears to add up to a damning indictment; but several points must be emphasised. First, the text concerns the insanity of the king – a creature forsaken by his god and thus no longer really part of human ordered society. Thus anything he did was bound to be bad and this included a number of military and political exploits, as well as his attentions to the moon-god. The latter, by the same argument, cannot possibly have been a normal act of devotion, but was bound to have been a travesty of divine worship. Secondly, the two comparisons made in the texts may be significant: namely, that É.hul.hul was made as splendid as Esagila and that Tema was built as a second Babylon. This is an accusation also levelled at a much earlier famous king (Sargon of Agade) and intended, almost certainly in that instance, to explain why his dynasty, despite his achievements, did not endure.[100] In other words, the accusation in that context has quite palpably no historical value,[101] but was an explanation offered for the dynasty's ultimate lack of success. Thirdly, the naming of the two officials who accepted Nabonidus' ritual changes has implications for the question of whether there was any active dissenting by priests from Nabonidus' supposed religious 'reforms': the titles that they are given are ones usually associated with temple administration,[102] so that this *could* be a reference to the behaviour of the temples and their staffs in relation to the king. If so, the passage would either indicate that opposition to the king's policies emanating from religious institutions was not unanimous or, on the supposition that they were

[97] *Isaiah*, 21.
[98] *pace* Voigtlander, *Survey*, 179, n.28.
[99] *Historical Texts*, 82-3.
[100] Grayson, *Chronicles*, no.19, l.51.
[101] Güterbock, 'Tradition', 57.
[102] San Nicoló, *Beiträge*.

forced to accept the royal cult-provisions, that royal control over the priesthood was very effective. The fourth point relates to Nabonidus' interpretation of the sign 'u₄.sar' on Marduk's temple Esagila, which is in fact correct: both of the usual readings of this sign would result in an epithet commonly applied to Sin either as 'the heavenly lamp' or describing him as the 'moonsickle'. In what way this could be read as an accusation against the king is quite obscure. Finally, the fact that Nabonidus interrupted rituals until É.hul.hul had been built was possibly correct behaviour in cultic terms:[103] the order from a god received in a dream by a human king required checking and confirmation; thus, ideally, the king wore sack-cloth and left his hair unkempt until the dream-portent was confirmed through favourable omens; if this conduct was not observed, he risked dire consequences. If this interpretation is correct, it has important implications for understanding the passage concerning the interruption of the New Year Festival: it would not be the ceasing of its celebration as such that was sinful; rather it was one of the many acts of Nabonidus' reign that were simply bound to be blasphemous because of his, literally, god-forsaken character.

What I would suggest is that the main point of the text was to provide an explanation of why Nabonidus was defeated by Cyrus. This did not happen because any one of his individual acts was in itself sacrilegious or caused offence to a definable group of the Babylonian population such as the priesthood; rather the *fact* of defeat indicated the support of the Babylonian gods for Cyrus and their condemnation of Nabonidus; they 'abandoned' Nabonidus, so that whatever he had done was, by hindsight, doomed. Although the literary character of the text appears to be unique, it has been compared at times to another text promulgated by Cyrus, the famous Cyrus Cylinder,[104] which is in the form of a building inscription. Here, too, a long introduction (unfortunately badly damaged) vilifies Nabonidus, describes the abandonment of Babylon by Marduk, who seeks out Cyrus and conducts him to Babylonia to restore order. Though this latter text has often been interpreted as demonstrating a radical departure from earlier Assyrian and Neo-Babylonian imperial policy,[105] this quite

---

[103] I owe this suggestion to a talk given by Professor T. Jacobsen (Seminar on Near Eastern and Egyptian Topics, 21.11.1983, Warburg Institute, University of London) relating to an unpublished text as well as to the course of events in the 'Curse of Agade' (cf. J.S. Cooper, *The Curse of Agade* (Baltimore, 1983).

[104] F.H. Weissbach, *Die Keilinschriften der Achämeniden* (Leipzig, 1911), 2-11; Pritchard, *Texts*, 315-16.

[105] e.g. M. Leroy, 'Eternel Iran', *Acta Iranica* I/1, 24-8; most recently, J.M. Balcer, *Sparda by the Bitter Sea: imperial interaction in Western Anatolia* (Brown Judaic Studies 52, Chico, Calif., 1984), 119.

definitely is not the case:[106] it can be demonstrated that it contains
exactly the same standard statements as those made by earlier
Assyrian conquerors and Babylonian usurpers. In fact, the Cyrus
Cylinder in less detail, the Verse Account in a fuller, detailed exposé,
both present *post eventum* justifications for the defeat of a perfectly
legitimate, regular Babylonian ruler. Neither they nor any other
evidence indicate any real reversals of Nabonidus' policies under the
Achaemenids; but no more can they be used to support the notion that
there was any real or effective opposition to Nabonidus expressed
during his reign that helped to bring about his defeat.

(D) At this point, it might be in order to consider briefly the
prophecies of Deutero-Isaiah concerning the fall of Babylon at the
hands of Cyrus, 'the annointed one of Yahweh', which has been
connected at times[107] with the Verse Account and the Cyrus Cylinder.
Such a comparison certainly holds as far as some of the expressions are
concerned. Thus, for example, Isaiah 42:6:

> I am the Lord, I have called you in righteousness, I have taken you by the
> hand and kept you; I have given you as a covenant to the people.

may be compared directly to the Cyrus Cylinder, ll.11-12:

> He searched through all the lands, sought a righteous ruler who would
> please him. With his hand he took Cyrus, the king of Anšan, and called
> him; for the kingship of the totality he named his name.

Isaiah 42:6-7:

> (I have given you) as a light to the nations, to open the eyes that are
> blind, to bring out the prisoners from the dungeon, from the prison those
> who sit in darkness.

may be compared to Verse Account, col.iv:

> To the inhabitants of Babylon a (joyful) heart is given now,
> They are like prisoners when the prisons are opened
> Liberty is restored to those who were surrounded by oppression
> All rejoice to look upon him as king.
> (translation by Oppenheim, in Pritchard, *Texts*, 314)

which provides a direct contrast to the situation at the broken

---

[106] J. Harmatta, 'The literary pattern of the Babylonian Edict of Cyrus', *AAAS* 19 (1971),
217-31; P.-R. Berger, 'Der Kyros-Zylinder mit dem Zusatzfragment BIN II nr.32 und die
akkadischen Personennamen in Danielbuch', *ZA* 64 (1975), 192-234; Kuhrt, 'Cyrus
Cylinder'.
[107] Smith, *Isaiah*; Boyce, *History*, 43-7.

beginning of the Verse Account, where the unhappiness of the country under Nabonidus is described and the population compared to prisoners.

Because of the edict of Cyrus preserved in Ezra 1, ordering the rebuilding of the Jerusalem temple and the return of exiles, the Isaiah prophecies have been taken to reflect an active propaganda campaign among the Jewish deportees in Babylonia, perhaps disseminated in the form of Flugblätter.[108] This, it has been suggested, was part of a more widespread campaign initiated by a Persian magus able to influence the attitudes of Babylonian priests and to exploit their discontent with Nabonidus, as well as to play on the longings of deported groups to return home.[109] Deutero-Isaiah would thus constitute the one preserved piece of evidence of this much bigger and more complex process, with the Verse Account providing evidence of the way in which resentment was moulded among the Babylonian priesthood slightly later on. The generally presumed date of the speeches of the prophet is some time between the conquest of Lydia by Cyrus (mid-540s BC) and the fall of Babylon in 539 BC.[110] There are, however, some objections to these interpretations of Deutero-Isaiah. It must be remembered that both the character and dating of the prophecies are exceedingly uncertain, as demonstrated recently by Vincent,[111] who has argued for a cultic context for the prophecies, rather than connecting them with historical events. Also, having emphasised that the Verse Account and the Cyrus Cylinder were *post eventum* reconstructions of Nabonidus' reign and the Persian conquest, and in view of the similarities of phraseology with the Isaiah passages, I would suggest that the prophecies too might well be exhortations to loyalty to the new Persian conqueror rather than subversive propaganda predating his victory. Moreover, in relation to the particular concerns of this chapter, even were one able to demonstrate that they were genuine prophecies heralding Cyrus' victory, neither the context nor the figure of Deutero-Isaiah are clearly enough known for arguments to be built upon them concerning effective opposition offered by priestly circles as such. To conclude this discussion of what I dubbed in the introduction the 'theological conflict' argument, let me summarize the results.

---

[108] Smith, *Isaiah*, 20.

[109] Boyce, *History*, 46-7.

[110] Smith, *History*, 20; P.R. Ackroyd, *Israel Under Babylon and Persia* (Oxford, 1970), 105-6.

[111] J.M. Vincent, *Studien zur literarischen Eigenart und geistigen Heimat von Jesaja, Kap. 40-55* (Frankfurt-am-Main, 1977). Cf. also the emphasis on Deutero-Isaiah's lack of historical precision in P. Ackroyd 'The Biblical portrayal of Achaemenid rulers', 7th Achaemenid History Workshop, to be published as *Achaemenid History V: the roots of the European tradition*, ed. H. Sancisi-Weerdenburg and J.-W. Drijvers (Leiden, forthcoming).

Although Nabonidus does appear to have exalted the moon-god Sin on occasion, this is the exception rather than the rule and may perhaps be related to the obvious importance of his enormous reconstruction project at Harran, rather than indicating his personal religious proclivities. The interruption of the New Year Festival by him was caused by his absence on campaign in Arabia; it was not a deliberate part of his religious policy as, on his return, he performed the festival again. The Verse Account is a text composed well after Cyrus' victory and explained the reasons for Nabonidus' fall in terms of his abandonment by the gods in favour of the new ruler. This was a standard way of solving the problem, with which the Babylonians were not infrequently presented, as to why an apparently successful and legitimate king should be defeated; the defeat was seen, in retrospect, as a judgment on him by the gods. It therefore follows that the text cannot reflect any contemporary opposition to Nabonidus; by the very fact of his defeat, Nabonidus' acts were also condemned. Although Deutero-Isaiah shows some marked similarities to the Verse Account and to the Cyrus Cylinder, the uncertainty over its dating makes it difficult to argue for effective undercover propaganda activity in Babylonia by Persians predating the conquest. In fact the similarities of formulation might rather argue for a post-conquest date. Moreover, the precise social setting of the prophecies is also unclear, so that they cannot be used to support arguments that Babylonian and other priestly circles were infiltrated, or their presumed resentments manipulated, by Persian *magi*.

Nabonidus and the Babylonian temples

On the basis of the royal inscriptions, literary texts and historiographic material, it would seem difficult to maintain that there was any opposition to Nabonidus 'by priests and people', apart from some initial unrest, related to the coup that brought him to the throne. But this on the whole negative result may, of course, simply be due to the specific limitations of the source material. If one were to amplify this material by drawing on the wealth of documentation available for the functioning of temples and the activities of their staffs, might one not find evidence for changes at a more mundane level suggesting that the priests did have good reason to detest Nabonidus? And surely priests, as guardians of learning and ritual, must have been able to wield a subtle yet powerful influence on the king, which he would have disregarded at his peril, since that would have alienated the priests and the community? Did Nabonidus 'exasperate' the priests by 'increased royal control', which together with his interest in Harran and its god 'pushed (them) to revolt'?[112] The question may best be considered in two parts: first, what changes can be seen to have taken place within the temples in Nabonidus' reign and were they of a type to excite the anger of their staffs? Secondly, how did kings and priests interact? The corollary to both these questions and the most difficult problem is, of course, who the priests themselves actually were. I propose to look at each of these aspects in turn.

(A) Using the extensive evidence available for the important Eanna sanctuary in Uruk, it is argued with some justification that the temples were by far the largest and most important landowners in Babylonia.[113] By Nabonidus' third regnal year new officials, royally appointed, appear in the very highest echelons of the temple administration; this suggests a close, permanent, royal supervisory presence to ensure that the income of temple estates was fully recorded.[114] Simultaneously, leases of extensive tracts of temple land were granted by the king (or central authority) to individuals outside the regular temple staff who, while still obliged to make the regular deliveries to the temple, were able, through personal investment (land-reclamation, date-orchard planting etc.), to make immense profits out of temple-lands for themselves and for the king, to whom they paid taxes or rather tithes.[115] These two developments – tight royal control on temple finance and the use of temple-land to produce increased revenue for the central government and profit for people outside the traditional temple structure – resulted, it is suggested, in the angering of the priesthood.

But these measures could also be interpreted differently. The general policy of Assyrian rulers over Babylon was to strengthen the position of old cities with important temples.[116] This was partly achieved by bestowing more land on the temples, partly by respecting certain civic privileges claimed by the cities. The purpose was to ensure their allegiance and to counteract the political power of the Chaldaean and Aramaean tribal groups in Babylonia. As a result of this policy, the temples owned enormous tracts of land which they were not exploiting fully. In addition to this, the ravages wrought by the war of liberation against Assyria had resulted in the neglect of some land and the devastation of date-groves; it probably required a massive investment of labour and other resources to put everything into full production again.[117] One should therefore interpret Nabonidus'

---

[112] Garelli, *Empires*, 156.
[113] e.g. Labat, 'Assyrien', 106.
[114] San Nicoló, *Beiträge*, 18-21.
[115] Labat, 'Assyrien', 107; Dougherty, *Nabonidus*, 117-24.
[116] Brinkman, 'Babylonia', 237.
[117] Cocquerillat, *Palmeraies*.

intervention in temple-administration in the light of this situation and hence as intended primarily to ensure that the accounts were properly kept and the work on the temple-estates efficiently carried out.[118]

The leases of temple-land that were granted must also be viewed against this back-drop: the temple could only benefit by this institution, since it made the gathering of outstanding obligatory deliveries on temple-lands into the responsibility of the new overall lease-holder;[119] the temple administration was thus able to rely on a much smaller number of people who guaranteed to deliver certain temple-supplies regularly, instead of having to expend enormous effort on chasing up innumerable small-scale tenant-farmers, who might frequently not be in a position to meet their obligations. Further, it is quite clear from a number of lease-contracts representing this type of agreement (generally known as *Generalpacht* or *ferme générale*) that members of the temple-staff were themselves involved in these transactions[120] and the institution remained in force throughout the early Persian period.[121] Moreover, the practice of levying a temple-tithe from the population[122] would mean that some of the profit made by investors would in any case come back to the temple in the form of such a tax.

It has also been suggested that the institution of a 'king's basket' in the temple, whereby part of the temple income was set aside supposedly for the king[123] and which was supervised by a royal official, effectively constituted a reduction in the temple's income. On the other hand, it is possible that the 'basket' was in fact used to provide a certain amount of income for some of the higher temple officials themselves.[124] In the absence of any clear evidence as to how precisely the 'basket' functioned, it cannot be used to support arguments that royal interference in temple administration constituted such a weakening of their economic power that they became major foci of opposition to Nabonidus' rule. One might also note that the massive documentation – mainly from Eanna in Uruk – available from Nabonidus' reign shows the economy to have been exceptionally prosperous in this period. Moreover, not one of these institutions created or developed further by Nabonidus in relation to the functioning of temples was reversed by the Persian conquerors; if anything, the measures begun by Nabonidus were strengthened and extended,[125] yet there is no sign of a concerted temple or priestly

---

[118] Saggs, 'Officials'; Kümmel, *Familie*, 137ff.; San Nicoló, *Beiträge*, 18-21.
[119] Kümmel, *Familie*, 160.
[120] Cocquerillat, *Palmeraies, passim*; Kümmel, *Familie*, 103-7.
[121] Cocquerillat, *Palmeraies, passim*.
[122] Dandamaev, 'Tempelzehnte'; 'State and temple', 593.
[123] San Nicoló, *Beiträge*, 31 n.91.
[124] Garelli, *Empires*, 159; San Nicoló, *Beiträge*, 69 n.4; Voigtlander, *Survey*, 169-70.
[125] San Nicoló, *Beiträge*; Kümmel, *Familie*; Cocquerillat, *Palmeraies*.

opposition to the Persians later.[126]

(B) One important limiting factor, in assessing both the real effects of increased involvement by the central authority in temple affairs and also the relationship between royal power and the temples, is the very one-sided nature of the evidence available. It comes mainly from Uruk; there is practically no information on the Marduk priesthood in Babylon and no royal archives are extant, so that one cannot gain much clarity on the interaction of king and cultic experts in Babylonia at this time, as one can, for instance, for the Assyrian Empire approximately a hundred years earlier. If one makes the probable assumption that the relationship between the king and the religious experts, learned men or scholars was similar in Babylonia to that which had existed in Assyria,[127] important conclusions emerge. On the basis of the Assyrian material, it was quite difficult to falsify reports or to keep unfavourable omens and portents hidden from the king, because he had reports sent from a large number of different areas and could compare them for consistency. Another important feature of the relationship was the tendency of the scholars to keep the king happy, as this helped them to find royal favour. Also, reports made to the king were usually made at the command of the ruler himself; they concerned almost exclusively a variety of ominous events and the prescribing of the appropriate rituals to counteract adverse signs, including such action as intercalating months when necessary. Finally, it was ultimately the king himself who was responsible for making cultic arrangements and appointments to temple offices. The conclusion from the Assyrian material is that the activities of religious experts were directed by and towards the monarch and that the experts themselves were dependent on him.

There is, in fact, some slight evidence that the relationship between palace and temple in the Neo-Babylonian Empire was not greatly dissimilar. Thus the king is seen to issue instructions concerning months to be intercalated and when rituals, thus delayed, should be performed.[128] Early in his reign (555 BC) Nabonidus issued orders to the Eanna temple in Uruk that the regular daily offerings made to four female deities should be made 'as it was of old in the time of Nebuchadnezzar, king of Babylon';[129] in his eighth regnal year,

---

[126] It may be interesting just in passing to note that the full names taken by the Babylonian rebels against the Persians in 521 were, in both instances, 'Nebuchadnezzar, the son of Nabonidus'.

[127] Parpola, *Letters*, xvi-xxi.

[128] *YBT* III 152; cf. Saggs, 'Officials', 38; for more examples, see Parpola, *Letters*, 504(6.2); 505(6.3).

[129] Princeton Theological Seminary no.2097 (the text was presented at the 31. Rencontre Assyriologique Internationale in Leningrad by Dr. G. Frane, who kindly sent me a copy of his paper and has allowed me to refer to it).

548/547 BC, Nabonidus was sent a petition by the chief temple administrator of Eanna, asking that the allocations of the temple perquisites, established by Nebuchadnezzar II to conform with the practice in the Marduk and Nabu temples in Babylon, be continued.[130] Another example of the interaction of the two institutions is a letter ordering the chief administrator of Eanna to set up stelae, possibly recording the king's building works, in an 'appropriate place' in the temple.[131] These indications, limited though they are and coming from a very different archival context from the Assyrian palace archives, show clearly both how detailed were the matters of temple activity with which the king appears regularly to have dealt in person and – conversely – how dependent the temples were on him in all such matters. It is difficult to see how, in these circumstances, it would have been possible for staffs of the temples to develop an independent, effective opposition to the sovereign.

Temple matters both of an economic and of a cultic nature were the king's concern; just as they were dependent on him for funding and initiating temple building and repairs, and their resources swollen by gifts from his war-booty and land,[132] so their day-to-day activities were closely controlled and regulated by him; and this was certainly no innovation made by Nabonidus, as is shown by the references to earlier arrangements made by Nebuchadnezzar II.

(C) Having reappraised the relationship between Nabonidus and the temples and suggested a different way of interpreting his 'interference' in their affairs, I now confront the crux of the problem, which is who the priests actually were. The first point to stress is that, as already mentioned, the category 'priests' as such in relation to Babylonia must be dropped – there is no term that defines priests in any general sense whatsoever. The upper echelons of the temple consisted primarily, it appears, of administrative officials, who functioned together with officers appointed by the king, from Nabonidus onwards, and who co-operated in some way with this 'civil' authority; it is a vexed question how the two were separated and what might have been their respective spheres of competence.[133] Cultic personnel and ritual experts together formed just one category, a poorly defined one, within the temple; the category included lamentation-singers, liturgy-singers, the *šangê* of specific deities, exorcists and possibly, though the evidence is entirely inferential, astronomers, diviners and omen-experts. It is possible that this group of cultic personnel was in part known as the 'temple-enterers' (*ērib bīti*),[134] but this is disputed as the term may be

[130] *YOS* VI, 10; cf. San Nicoló, *Beiträge*, 66-9.

[131] *YOS* III, 4; cf. Tadmor, 'Inscriptions', 361.

[132] Dandamaev, 'State and temple', 593-4.

[133] For a discussion of this problem in the Seleucid period, cf. Doty, *Archives*, 21-5.

[134] J. Renger, 'Notes on the goldsmiths, jewellers and carpenters of Neobabylonian Eanna', *JAOS* 91 (1971), 407-8; G.J.P. McEwan, *Priest and Temple in Hellenistic Babylonia* (Freiburger Altorientalischer Studien 4, Wiesbaden, 1981, 7-8).

a general one, defining all those allowed to enter the temple in order to carry out a wide variety of duties.[135] The sources of income for these groups are not always clear: the exorcists seem to have had allotments of land (*isqu*), but whether this was true for the others is not known. Among the small executive group responsible for regulating temple affairs, the *šešgallu* is the only functionary at this time who probably, though not certainly, had some religious duties as well.[136]

Apart from these groupings of what one would regard as religious actors – and hence 'priests' in our sense – there are a very large number of people who at first sight seem to be quite separate from them. These, according to their professional designations, seem simply to be suppliers of necessities to the temple rituals, but not themselves participants in the ceremonies. One group included cooks, bakers, brewers, oil-pressers, fishermen, herdsmen (of two types), gate-keepers and those responsible for supplying first-quality dates for divine offerings. All of these held land allotted to them (*isqu*), which formed the income associated with their office. In this respect, then, they are indistinguishable from some of the 'cultic personnel', such as the exorcists. And there are some indications that they were in fact much more deeply involved in the religious ceremonies than one would imagine simply from looking at their professional names. Thus in a ritual from Hellenistic Uruk, concerning the daily offerings made to the gods, the butcher is enjoined to recite when he slaughters the ox and sheep for the ceremony, the prayer: 'The son of Šamaš (sun-god), the lord of beasts, has made a pasture in the plain',[137] while the baker is to utter a specific prayer over the freshly prepared ceremonial loaves: 'Nisaba (goddess of grain), exuberant abundance, pure food'.[138] Clearly people with these mundane-seeming designations were knowledgeable, not just in a specific activity such as butchering or baking bread, but also in the ritual for which they were supplying the temple: they had to be aware of what to supply (the regulations are very precise), at what hour and in what section of the temple it was required and precisely what prayers to recite over which items of prepared foodstuff. Given this evidence it would be feasible to assume that the other personnel in this category were similarly closely involved in the temple-ceremonies. It is thus difficult to see how or why one should separate these people from those who seem to us to be the obvious 'cultic actors': our own traditional distinction seems not to be applicable to Babylonia.

Similar problems arise when one considers what seems to be a third category of people involved within the temple: the 'craftsmen'

[135] D.B. Weisberg, *Guild Structure and Political Allegiance in Early Achaemenid Mesopotamia* (YNER 1, New Haven, 1967); Brinkman, op. cit. in n. 67 above, 232.

[136] Kümmel, *Familie*, 134.

[137] Thureau-Dangin, *Rituels*, 78; 83-4, ll.9-10.

[138] ibid, 77 and 83, ll.46-7.

Fig. 19. Part of the text prescribing the course of the New Year Festival in Babylon. The text has had to be reconstructed from several fragments and is even now not complete, although enough survives to indicate the important role played in it by the king and the parts played by a whole range of cultic functionaries, including craftsmen and butchers. The date of the preserved versions of the text is hellenistic.

(*ummânu*). These include carpenters, jewellers, metal-workers, seal-cutters, masons, goldsmiths, weavers, launderers, bleachers, cane-weavers and leather-workers. Their income seems generally to have consisted of an entitlement to regular rations (*kurummatu*). They too played an important part in religious ceremonies, a good example being the New Year Festival at Babylon. Here the metal-worker, goldsmith, carpenter and weaver all received specified cuts of meat from Marduk's offering-table for four days of the festival; this issue of meat, different for each craftsman, was assigned to them for preparing two elaborate statuettes, which played an important part in the festival.[139] The craftsmen again, but this time without distinction as to profession, prepared the golden canopy under which the statue of Marduk was, at a later point of the festival, enthroned; and also, either during or after the act of enthronement, they recited an incantation together with the *šešgallu*.[140] Still later, after the god Nabu had been ceremonially conducted by the king himself to Babylon from the nearby city of Borsippa, it was again the craftsmen who administered the meal that was offered first to the god on his arrival, then to the king.[141]

These different groups of temple-staff can, then, be easily classified according to the specific needs they satisfied for the deities – such as understanding and interpreting their orders, feeding them, providing them with clothing and with furniture; but there is no obvious way in which any one group was considered closer to the divine and hence more sacred or more 'priestly'. Each appears to have played a role as important in relation to cult and as intimate as the others. The only clear distinctions in temple-hierarchy that can be arrived at are:

(1) the small group of temple administrators who between them were responsible for directing all temple affairs, which included transmitting orders received from the king;
(2) the officiants of *all* types discussed above;
(3) below these, temple oblates (*širku*)[142] and employees such as shepherds, cowherds and tillers of the soil.[143]

An important fact that needs to be borne in mind is that most of the text material available at present comes itself from temple-sites, while there is virtually no such material for the civic context, whose various needs and requirements the temples met.[144] Those who supplied the higher levels of the temple-staff, i.e. above the level of the oblates and employees, seem to have been drawn from a specific juridically defined group, the *mār banê* sometimes described as 'citizens' (see above p. 138). These, as suggested already, usually consisted of fairly prosperous, land-owning families, many of them connected tradition-ally with certain specific temple offices. As a result of this entitlement, they were able to add to their wealth by receiving either regular

---

[139] Black, 'New Year ceremonies', 55.
[140] Thureau-Dangin, *Rituels*, 141-2, ll.368-84.
[141] ibid., 143-4, ll.404-14.
[142] cf. R.P. Dougherty, *The Shirkûtu of Babylonian Deities* (YOSR V/2, New Haven, 1923); Oelsner, 'Erwägungen', 138-9.
[143] Oelsner, 'Erwägungen', 139-40; Kümmel, *Familie*, 48ff.; 97ff.
[144] Postgate, 'Role of the temple'.

rations or else allotments, which they could divide, lease out, sell or leave to their descendants, provided that the duties connected with the particular income or holding were performed;[145] in other words, the owner was required to serve in the relevant position during a specified time, usually part of a month, or supply someone else to do so. The very alienability of shares in such offices and their accompanying income might indicate that temple and civic community were not easily separable entities. The temple with its landholdings was a resource to which a legally definable civic group had access. Investment in temple offices by members of this group further suggests that it was not the sole one at their disposal. Further, the king's personal involvement and close interest in the functioning of temples and, conversely, their dependence on him suggest that the temple represented one of the communal institutions by which royal control of city communities could be maintained. My contention in the context of this chapter would be that 'priests' as a distinct segment of the Babylonian population cannot be isolated in any clear or meaningful manner: the temple personnel were too diverse and were drawn from a specified group of the urban community, in an apparently independent and spontaneous fashion, sometimes dictated by economic exigencies; the group from which they came cannot be quantified, but may have been of considerable size and engaged in extensive commercial and/or industrial pursuits. Some support for this hypothesis – for that is what it must remain, given the one-sided documentation – is provided by the fact that members of the Egibi family were involved in administrative functions at the Eanna sanctuary at Uruk,[146] but are also known as one of the most important Babylonian business families, with extensive commercial connections.[147] Thus the only way in which a group could have been distinguished in the way that classical writers distinguished 'Chaldaeans = priests' in Babylonia, would be a juridical, and possibly socio-economic one, which defined who precisely might claim eligibility to hold shares in temple offices, whether through inheritance, gift or purchase.

Conclusions

It has proved extraordinarily difficult to demonstrate that there was any effective priestly opposition to the policies of Nabonidus. Apart from some understandable disturbances at the beginning of his reign, due to the mode of his accession, and some hostile judgments passed on

---

[145] Kümmel, *Familie*, 149; Oelsner, 'Erwägungen', 42-3 and nn.21 & 23; Doty, *Archives*, 119-21.

[146] Kümmel, *Familie*, 129-30.

[147] S. Weingort, *Das Haus Egibi in neubabylonischen Rechtsurkunden* (diss., Berlin, 1939); *RLA* I. 397.

him *after* Cyrus' conquest, nothing in the evidence as it stands allows one to accept the traditional explanation for his defeat by the Persians.

One important aspect that has emerged from this re-examination is the difficulties encountered when attempting to define 'priests' in the Babylonian context. At least in part, this problem derives from our modern Western assumptions about the role and functions of priesthood in society: the Babylonian evidence simply does not fit the pattern set by our cultural expectations. It may, however, be possible to look to different times or places and so find religious officials whose activities would provide a more apt source of comparison with the staffs of Babylonian temples. One good example might be the *'ulema* of the Islamic world, as described by Gilsenan:[148]

> Note that they (sc. the *'ulema*) are not what Westerners would call by the term *clergy*. The *'ulema* do not possess or monopolize a unique mediating role between the believer and God; they cannot promise or refuse salvation or grace, and the keys to hell or paradise are not in their hands. There is no mechanism of confession or penitence that they operate, and they are not God's substitute on earth. They are different, therefore, from a Christian hierarchy through which the believer must go to approach the Divinity.

Between the religious scholars of Islam and the Babylonian cultic personnel discussed in this chapter, there are of course great differences resulting not just from the political/historical circumstances of their times, but from the religious structures within which they operated; all the same, a number of features – such as their access to learning through training rather than personal sanctity,[149] the fact that almost all were prominent market traders,[150] and the impossibility of defining them as either a social class or a corporate group[151] – suggest some basic functional similarities. Further, such an analogy helps to illuminate a point of great importance to the historiography of this problem, namely that the conflict between king/state on the one hand and priests/church on the other, rather than being a pattern of events presented to us by the sources, may in fact be the creation of our own, necessarily European-centred, perspective.

---

[148] *Recognising Islam: an anthropologist's introduction* (London, 1982).
[149] ibid., 31-2.
[150] ibid., 48-9.
[151] ibid., 52-3.

6

Cult-Personnel in the Linear B Texts from Pylos

This chapter is concerned with the character of priesthood in the Mycenaean community at Pylos in the southern Peloponnese in the years down to 1200 BC. It necessarily adopts a different approach from all the others in this volume: the discussion sets out, not from historical problems, but from the documentary sources themselves. This approach is the only possible one, because our knowledge, or almost all of it, about Mycenaean civilization is derived either from archaeological remains or from a limited corpus of clay tablets, bearing writing in a script now called Linear B. For many years after the discovery of the tablets, they could not be read, nor was their language known. The decipherment of the script and the unexpected discovery that the language was an early form of Greek provide one of the most celebrated detective stories of modern scholarship, the hero being an amateur linguist, Michael Ventris. Only the achievement of this decipherment allows us to say anything at all about Mycenaean priesthood.

The search for Mycenaean civilization had originally been inspired by the belief that the poems of Homer – the *Iliad* and the *Odyssey* – reflected a poetic memory of a historical society; but the society that now emerged from the new written evidence seemed to be fundamentally different from any that would ever have been guessed at by the lovers of Homer. The documents that we have are lists, concerned for the most part with recording resources in the form of men, women, animals and crops and with the transfer of these resources for various purposes, including that of worshipping or honouring the gods and goddesses. It is not at all clear how this newly discovered world, based on palaces with developed record-keeping systems, related to the world of Homer's heroes. Perhaps, after all, Homer knew nothing about the Mycenaeans; the appearance at least is quite different.

Any hope of throwing light on the religious institutions of Pylos must, therefore, come from a meticulous examination of the few Linear B documents mentioning religious personnel; it is for this reason that the tablets are collected in an appendix at the end of this chapter (pp. 170ff.). This contribution exemplifies the difficulty of defining and identifying 'priests' in societies where we cannot apply our society's criteria; it is in fact the same problem as faces the other contributors, but for them it is relatively obscured by the greater wealth of evidence and tradition of interpretation available to them. Hooker's chapter brings out the issue of definition in its simplest form.

Cult-Personnel in the Linear B Texts from Pylos

James Hooker

The Mycenaean palace at Pylos, in the south-western Peloponnese, was destroyed by fire at a date close to 1200 BC. The ruins of the palace have yielded a considerable archive comprising clay tablets, labels and sealings written in the Linear B script. From these texts there can be constructed, though only in rather vague outlines, some account of religious practices and religious personnel in the state of Pylos shortly before the destruction of the palace.[1]

Severe limitations on our inquiry are imposed by the nature of the Linear B documents. The intention of the scribes was, for the most part, confined to the recording of numbers of persons or animals available for specific tasks and the amounts of commodities coming into, or dispensed from, the central store-places. Quite often the disbursement of commodities would be required for some religious purpose, such as sacrifice, anointing or the general maintenance of a cult-centre and its attendants. It may be convenient to consider here three types of inscriptions: first, those that mention actual offerings to named deities; secondly, those giving lists of commodities destined for religious functions; thirdly, miscellaneous texts that add to our knowledge of cult-personnel and their activities. The reader will find the most important of these texts reproduced in the Appendix to this chapter.

Offerings to deities

Among texts of the first type – those describing actual offerings – pride of place must be given to no. 1 in the Appendix (Tn 316). The importance of this tablet is matched by the difficulty of interpreting it in detail. Attention is drawn here only to a few salient facts.[2] The text records a number of valuable offerings made to a variety of divinities. It is uncertain whether it describes ceremonies that took place on the same occasion, or gives a consolidated account of different occasions.

---

[1] The evidence is presented by F.R. Adrados, 'Les institutions religieuses mycéniennes', *Acta Mycenaea* 1 (Salamanca, 1972) = *Minos* 11 (1970), 170-202. A. Brelich, 'Religione micenea: osservazioni metodologiche', *Atti e memorie del 1⁰ Congresso Internazionale di Micenologia* 1 (Rome, 1968), 919-28, contributes an important methodological essay.

[2] The rival interpretations are examined in my *Linear B: an introduction* (Bristol, 1980), 160-2.

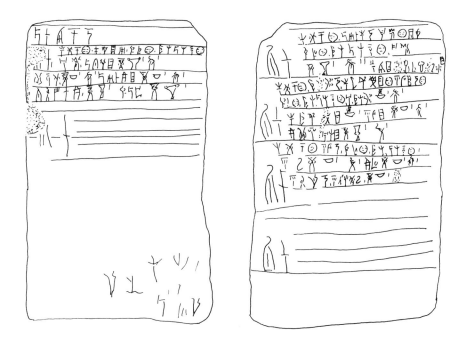

Fig. 20. Drawing of a clay tablet from Pylos recording various offerings (Tn 316, see Appendix, no. 1).

The word *pa-ki-ja-si* (line 2 of the recto) situates the ceremonies at a place named *pa-ki-ja-na*, which seems to have been a major cult-centre in the vicinity of the Pylian palace. The nature of the offerings is indicated by the logograms (conventionally transcribed in capital letters), which depict gold vessels and also, in some entries, men and women. The status of the human beings is disputed: they may be ritual victims, or simply persons dedicated to the service of the deity in question. Some of the deities are immediately identifiable, so far as their names go, with members of the Olympian pantheon; and, in particular, the occurrence in the dative case of Zeus (*di-we*) and of Hera (*e-ra*) in the same line (v. 9) suggests that these divinities were associated in cult as early as the Mycenaean period. Some other recipients of offerings are connected in some way with the Olympians: for instance, *po-si-da-e-ja* (r. 4) and *di-u-ja* (v. 4) are feminine formations of Poseidon and Zeus respectively. This tablet mentions not only divinities but also shrines, for example *po-si-da-i-jo* (v. 1), the shrine of Poseidon, the principal god of the place. Finally, we note with interest the *public* character of the ceremonies described. Although it has proved impossible to fit the word *wa-tu* (v. 1) into the syntactical structure of the whole inscription, there can be little doubt that it represents the Linear B spelling of ϝάστυ 'town' and that, in consequence, the 'town' (Pylos or Pakijana?) was in some fashion regarded as a participant in the rites.

The predominant place of Poseidon in Pylian cult is further exemplified by tablets that contain the noun *do-so-mo* 'offering'. Within the Es set there are numbered thirteen texts of very similar structure, of which we may consider two (646 = no. 2; 703 = no. 3).[3] No. 2 looks fairly straightforward: there is a man named *ko-pe-re-u* and an offering to Poseidon, whose name (predictably) occurs in the dative case – *po-se-da-o-ne*. The most obvious interpretation (not, as we shall see, necessarily the correct one) is that *ko-pe-re-u* is making, has made, or will be making an offering to the god consisting of the amount of wheat specified in the same line. Since, in each of the thirteen tablets, the amount in the first line is larger than that in any of the other lines, it is open to us to regard the persons named in lines 2-4 either as minor deities associated with Poseidon or as human cult-attendants.[4] It is more likely that they were in fact cult-attendants because the names in lines 3 and 4 occur also in other Pylos tablets, clearly referring to human beings. A problem arises over the distribution of the quantities of grain. In no. 2 (Es 646), and in each of the twelve parallel tablets, line 2 contains a dative plural word in *-si*, while lines 3 and 4 have the dative singular (in *-e-we*) of a *-εύς* noun. It is a curious fact that in each of the thirteen tablets, just as in this one, the same quantity of wheat is given in line 2, line 3 and line 4. The quantity varies from tablet to tablet, but within each tablet it remains constant. This fact raises a difficulty for the hypothesis that the wheat in lines 2-4 was intended for rations: for in that case, how could the ration for a multiplicity of persons be equated with that for a single person?

To attempt a comprehensive answer to this question would open up too large and complex a topic, that of land-holding in the Pylos tablets and specifically the way in which this is connected with cult. But a general indication of the problems may be given. It has long been recognized that the Linear B scribes designate plots of land not according to area but according to amounts of wheat. With this consideration in mind, we may approach two other texts in the Es set. These texts, 644 and 650 (= nos. 4 and 5), convey information about all thirteen men who are said to give offerings to Poseidon in the thirteen tablets already mentioned. No. 4 gives a list of the thirteen men, each named in the genitive case and each followed by *do-so-mo*. The term *we-te-i-we-te-i* comprises a reduplicated dative ϝέτει ϝέτει 'every year,

---

[3] cf. A. Heubeck, *Die Sprache* 4 (1958), 80-95 and De Fidio, *I dosmoi pilii*, 13-75.

[4] For the recipients in Es, see P.H. Ilievski, 'The recipients of the Es tablets', *Proceedings of the Cambridge Colloquium on Mycenaean Studies*, ed. L.R. Palmer and J. Chadwick (Cambridge, 1966), 238-44.

annually'. Once again, we have to resist the obvious interpretation of this tablet, namely that the thirteen men named are responsible for making an annual offering of the amount of wheat that appears by each name. This cannot be the meaning, since in each case the amount of the individual offering to Poseidon is larger, sometimes much larger, than the entire annual contribution of the person in question. Tablet no. 5 (Es 650) likewise gives a list of the thirteen men (with the inexplicable addition of a fourteenth). Each entry is formulated in a manner familiar from other land-tablets in the E series: for instance, line 1 gives *ko-pe-re-u e-ke to-so-de pe-mo* WHEAT 6, that is to say: 'Kopreus is in possession of so much seed-corn, namely six measures of wheat'. As already indicated, this amounts to a scribal shorthand to the effect that Kopreus holds land the area of which is indicated by the six measures of wheat. A comparison of these facts suggests that we are concerned not with a random collection of thirteen men who happen to have made certain offerings to Poseidon and to the god's cult-servants, but rather with plots of land together making up a kind of sacral estate. The thirteen men named *occupy* the plots (which vary considerably in size), but they do not own them; perhaps these plots are considered to be ownerless, or perhaps the god himself is regarded as their owner. Whether the size of offerings is related directly to the produce of the respective plots we cannot tell. It is preferable to think that the amounts of grain given in both nos. 4 and 5 are merely proportions. They perhaps indicate the fraction of the value of the plot which is expected to be set aside: in no. 4 for some general, unspecified annual offering; in the thirteen individual tablets for a specific offering to Poseidon and to the cult-servants.

Bringing to bear the slight evidence that is available, we can make some suggestions about the status of the land-holders and that of the cult-attendants. These land-holders seem, if anything, to occupy a lower social position than do the cult-servants. It would be quite wrong to regard these servants as acting in some menial capacity, as if the amounts of grain appended to their names represented their rations. A number of Pylos tablets (especially in the A series) do record the distribution of rations, but only to groups of workers who are not individually named. If the person named in line 4 of no. 2 (Es 646) is rightly equated with the *di-wi-je-u* in An 656, we can say with reasonable confidence that he occupied an elevated social position, since the latter tablet classed him as an *e-qe-ta* = (probably) ἑπέτας (retainer). To find an *e-qe-ta* officiating in the cult of Poseidon suggests that such service was honorific.[5] It may be that the enigmatic word in line 2 conceals the name of a family in the dative plural; that would be

[5] And in Ed 317 an unnamed *e-qe-ta* is included in a list with another man and two women, all of whom have sacral associations.

better than to interpret it as a generic term, as some have done. And the fact that, in any given tablet, exactly the same amount of grain is recorded in lines 2, 3 and 4 seems to emphasise the token character of these *do-so-mo*. The cult-attendants are named *honoris causa*, but the actual offerings (not necessarily in the form of grain) are intended for the upkeep of the shrine. There is, besides, the remarkable fact that one of the thirteen donors of a *do-so-mo* is referred to not by name but as *we-da-ne-wo do-e-ro* – 'the slave of Wedaneus' (Es 703). Whether or not this Wedaneus is the same man as the cult-attendant named in line 3, we have here a further indication that the thirteen land-holders have a lower status than that of the cult-servants.

A different type of offering to Poseidon is described in no. 6 (Un 718).[6] This tablet lists four distinct offerings, one to be given by an individual named *e-ke-ra₂-wo* (line 2), one by the *da-mo* (δᾶμος = 'local authority') (line 7), one by an official called the *ra-wa-ke-ta* (λαϝαγέτας) (line 9), and one by the *ka-ma* (line 11); this cannot be defined precisely, but, in view of other Pylos texts, should be some kind of guild closely associated with land-holdings. We learn more about *e-ka-ra₂-wo* from Er 880, where he is credited with a large holding of land at the very place, *sa-ra-pe-da*, which forms the first word in no. 6 (Un 718). *e-ke-ra₂-wo* thus seems to be the name of a local grandee whose offering is placed first and is, moreover, larger than any of the others. It is a source of difficulty in no. 6 that, after line 1 has provided a sort of 'heading' by stating the general subject-matter of the text (namely an offering to Poseidon at the place *sa-ra-pe-da*), line 2 should repeat the word *do-so-mo* and introduce the word *o-wi-de-ta-i*. The latter is not found elsewhere at Pylos, except on a clay label (Wa 731), which bears simply *do-so-mo* and *o-wi-de-ta-*. So it seems likely that the *o-wi-de-ta-i* ought to be taken as a dative plural and that, within the general context of ritual in honour of Poseidon, offerings are to be made to these *o-wi-de-ta-i*. No convincing analysis of this word has been forthcoming; but it may refer here to a society of cult-servants. The use of the future tense *do-se* (δώσει, he will give) in line 3 of no. 6 strongly implies that some religious obligation rested upon the various donors (whether they were individuals, like *e-ka-ra₂-wo* and the *ra-wa-ke-ta*, or the corporate entities *da-mo* and *ka-ma*) to make the offerings that are so precisely assessed.

Cult-goods

The second class of tablets includes those that refer to the disbursement of commodities for ritual purposes. Among such tablets

---

[6] See M. Lejeune, 'Le dossier *sa-ra-pe-da* du scribe 24 de Pylos', *Minos* 14 (1973), 60-76 and De Fidio, *I dosmoi pilii*, 77-129.

the most important are probably the Fr texts, recording amounts of olive oil dispatched to various gods and cult-places; but these texts make no certain reference to cult-personnel, and so they do not directly concern us at present. We may turn instead to two lists: no. 7 (Un 219), which records various amounts of several (unidentified) commodities, and no. 8 (Fn 187), recording amounts of barley and figs. It is uncertain whether the recipients have any close connection with one another; the respective scribes may simply have entered on the same tablet amounts of a commodity intended for miscellaneous destinations. The two texts have a number of elements in common that suggest that each is a coherent record of a specific consignment and that the consignments are intended to some extent for divinities, but more particularly for the maintenance of cult-places and of cult-personnel.

Looking first at no. 8, we are made aware of the distinction usually observed by Linear B scribes between personal recipients (indicated by the dative case) and places to which objects are consigned (indicated by means of the allative suffix -*de*). Thus line 2 contains a word which records the despatch of commodities to the shrine of Poseidon (*po-si-da-i-jo*) (cf. no. 1 v. 1), while in line 4 we find a reference to the cult-centre *pa-ki-ja-na*. All the other words are in the dative, and all are singular except the entries in lines 13, 15 and 18. The last-named entry, the dative plural of a derivative of the divine name Poseidon ending in -εύς, did not survive into later Greek, but it may be interpreted (especially in the light of line 2) as 'cult-attendants of Poseidon'.[7] The word denoting a class of persons in line 13 is of unknown meaning; but the word in line 15 is well attested in the A tablets of Pylos: it designates women engaged in the manufacture and decoration of cloth. It is not hard to see how such skilled workers might have had a place in a cult involving the dedication of pieces of cloth to divinities. More obscure is the part played by heralds, *ka-ru-ke* (which can hardly be anything other than the dative singular κᾱρύκει 'to a herald') occurs in lines 3, 5, 16 and 21. Why are four heralds recorded separately, and not grouped together like the workers in line 15 or the personnel of line 18? And what function did these heralds perform in the cult – if, indeed, they performed any? There are no wholly convincing answers to these questions. The four heralds may appear separately because only one belongs to each group; and they have, presumably, some ceremonial part to play in the cult-performance.[8]

---

[7] On the words for cult-servants. see especially J.-P. Olivier's dissertation *A propos d'une liste de desservants de sanctuaire dans les documents en linéaire B de Pylos* (Brussels, 1960).

[8] Some Classical inscriptions bring a herald into association with priests, priestesses and sacred embassies; cf. G. Daux, 'Un règlement cultuel d'Andros', *Hesperia* 18 (1949), 67.

However that may be, the dative singular of the 'herald' recurs in line 3 of no. 7. Line 4 shows further points of contact with no. 8: the *a-ke-ti-ri-ja-i* have already been mentioned, while *te-qi-jo-ne* is possibly a reduced spelling of the name *te-qi-ri-jo-ne* in line 12 of no. 8. The word *di-pte-ra-po-ro* contains a spelling of διφθερα- 'leather' in its first three syllables;[9] so once more we have a term indicating a craftsman who works in the cult-centre. In the dative plural *da-ko-ro-i* (line 5), the first element may continue syllabic *$\overset{o}{dm}$- (a development which would be in accordance with a well-known Greek sound-change). If we assume that this stem can mean 'temple' as well as 'house', then the whole word may be interpreted as 'shrine-attendants' of some kind.[10] The word *ra-wa-ke-ta* in line 10 reminds us that in no. 6 this functionary was charged with making an offering. If we may compare no. 7 with no. 6, in the latter text the *ra-wa-ke-ta* is seen in the role of donor, in the former he is the recipient of commodities, which will perhaps furnish the material of further offerings. But it is possible that no. 7 speaks of divinities alongside the human recipients. *e-ma-a₂* we have already encountered (no. 1 v. 7); this is probably, but not certainly, a spelling of the god's name which appears later as Hermes, *a-ti-mi-te* in line 5 is possibly the dative of the name Artemis. The status of *a-na-ka-te* and *po-ti-ni-ia* is uncertain. The first syllable of *a-na-ka-te* cannot be read with distinctness: if this reading were confirmed, it would represent the only spelling of the word in Linear B texts without initial digamma. The further question arises: if these two words are the dative of *anax* and *potnia* respectively, do they refer to a divine or to a human lord and lady?[11] Such a question is especially difficult to answer in respect of a text like this, in which both gods and human beings are found. If the lord and lady *are* human, they (like the *ra-wa-ke-ta*) may be seen as important participants in the cult; in Er 312 also the *wa-na-ka* and the *ra-wa-ke-ta* are brought into close association.

Cult-personnel and their activities

Finally, we must discuss some tablets in which persons are identified by terms which are undoubtedly of ritual significance. The short text no. 9 (Ae 303) is easy to understand as follows:

---

[9] cf. J.-P. Olivier, 'Étude d'un nom de métier mycénien: *di-pte-ra-po-ro*', *L'antiquité classique* 28 (1959), 165-85.

[10] The assumption that *$\overset{o}{dm}$-* can have these two senses, parallel to the two meanings of Latin *aedes*, runs counter to J. Chadwick's argument from the Of tablets at Thebes: *The Thebes Tablets* 2 (Salamanca, 1975), 89.

[11] A.M. Jasink Ticchioni expresses well-founded doubts about the divine character of any of the entries on this tablet: 'Contributi Micenei', *Studi micenei ed egeo-anatolici* 21 (1980), 227-8.

PYLOS [a place-name not connected grammatically with the remainder of the inscription]: slaves of the priestess on account of the sacred gold [namely] 14+ women.

The tablet is broken at the right, and it is possible that more than fourteen women were originally enumerated. It seems reasonable to conclude from this text that there existed at Pylos a shrine in the charge of a priestess and that in this shrine (according to a practice well known in later Greece) there was deposited a quantity of gold; but we cannot be certain whether this gold is called 'sacred' because it has been dedicated in some way or merely because it is kept in a sacred place. In any event, the quantity of gold must have been considerable, in view of the number of 'slaves of the priestess' connected with it.

To learn more about the status of these 'slaves of the priestess', and also of other cult-personnel, we have to consult further E tablets. We saw that some texts in the Es set seem to measure plots of land in terms of amounts of wheat. Other sets present a series of complex relationships among land-owners and land-holders; they sometimes refer, moreover, to rights and duties in some way connected with land-holdings.

In the list of land-holders in no. 10 (Ep 539), each (except the last) is identified both by name and by some descriptive word. In line 1 a woman named *pi-ro-na* is called *te-o-jo do-e-ra* (θεοῖο δούλα) 'slave of the god'.[12] She 'has, holds' (*e-ke*) a 'lease', as *o-na-to* is conventionally translated; and this 'lease' is held in respect of *ke-ke-me-na ko-to-na* – a technical term of the E series which means a plot of a strictly defined sort. Line 2 is closely parallel. In line 3, a male slave of the god (*te-o-jo do-e-ro*) is mentioned as a land-holder, and he holds his plot *pa-ra da-mo* 'from the local community, the δᾶμος'. A new element introduced in line 5: the dative singular participle *wo-zo-te*, possibly a spelling of ϝορζόντει or ϝροζόντει, in agreement with *ka-ma-e-we* (presumably a '*ka-ma*-holder'); the reference is obscure, but the performance of a duty seems to be involved. The list contains, as well as slaves of the god, slaves of the priestess (lines 7 and 8). In line 9 a land-holder is called 'slave of *ka-pa-ti-ja*': this woman is named in Un 443 as a donor of offerings; so once again we have a likely sacred connection. The following three lines name slaves of *a-pi-me-de* (i.e. Ἀμφιμήδης). A priest (*i-je-re-u* ἱερεύς) holds land in line 13. The name in the last line is that of *a-pi-me-de* himself, and (perhaps because he is so important) he receives no descriptive epithet; he is credited with a large holding, which is no mere *o-na-to* but an *e-to-ni-jo*. The precise

---

[12] The term is discussed by A. Tovar, 'Talleres y oficios en el palacio de Pylos: *teojo doero -ra* "domestico -a del rey" ', *Minos* 7 (1961), 101-22.

meaning of the latter word is unknown, but (as will be seen presently) it denotes a tenure superior to that indicated by *o-na-to*. If, as seems likely, this text refers to land-holdings at *pa-ki-ja-na*, we need feel no surprise that so many of the tenants have some connection with cult. Not all the tenants can have occupied a high social position, since the scribe appends the description 'priest' to one man as casually as he calls another an artificer or a shepherd. On the other hand, it is remarkable that persons called 'slaves of the priestess' or 'slaves of the god' are just as competent to hold interest in land as are the priests and priestesses themselves. It is not easy to determine the precise meaning of *do-e-ro* or *do-e-ra* in such contexts; but at least these words cannot here designate mere chattel-slaves. It might be a reasonable assumption that the appellation 'slave of the god' refers to a person of higher standing than does 'slave of the priestess'; but the texts themselves offer no support for such an assumption.

If asked to discuss the function, as distinct from the status, of an *i-je-re-u*, one would probably reply that he is a person who actually performs the sacrifice. It is therefore disconcerting to read on another Ep tablet, 613, the description of a *ka-ma-e-u* as *i-je-ro-wo-ko*, i.e. ἱεροϝοργός (sacrificer). In what way does he differ from an *i-je-re-u*? There can be no certain answer to this question; but it is worth recalling that in later Greek the neuter plural ἱερά means not only 'sacrificial victims', but also religious rites in a more general sense. Since, as we have seen, some tablets allude to religious rites not involving sacrifice, it is possible that the Mycenaean ἱερεύς referred to some broader class of religious officiant, while ἱεροϝοργός had the more specific sense.[13]

We have to turn to no. 11 (Ep 704) for information – meagre though it is – about the part played by the priesthood in contemporary society. Here again we find a list of personal names, each (except *ki-ri-te-wi-ja* in line 4) accompanied by a word denoting occupation or status. The meaning of *qe-ja-me-no* in line 1 is not known. In line 2 the female slave of the god is said to hold an *o-na-to*; the words in apposition to *o-na-to*, namely *i-je-re-ja ke-ra*, are usually understood as ἱερείας γέρας 'honorific gift of the priestess'. But to what type of genitive does ἱερείας belong? It could in theory imply that a gift had been conferred on the priestess; but, equally well, that *she* has made a gift to *Uwamia*. We know too little about the inter-relationships of the religious personnel to pronounce upon this matter. But, in any case, the unique comment made upon the priestess *e-ri-ta* in lines 5 and 6 is of greater

---

[13] On Mycenaean priests and priestesses, cf. M. Lejeune, 'Prêtres et prêtresses dans les documents mycéniens', in *Hommages à G. Dumézil* (Collection Latomus 45 (1960)), 129-39 = *Mémoires de philologie mycénienne* 2 (Rome, 1972), 83-93.

significance. We have already been told in line 3 that she holds an *o-na-to* of fairly modest size. But lines 5 and 6 speak of a much larger holding, in fact the largest holding mentioned in the Ep set of tablets. We are here afforded a rare and precious insight into the actual working of Mycenaean society and of its institutions. The meaning of these lines seems to be: Eritha the priestess holds (ἔχει) and claims (εὔχετοί τε) that the god (θεόν) holds (infinitive ἔχεεν) an *e-to-ni-jo*; but the *damos* says that he holds an *o-na-to* of *ko-to-na ke-ke-me-na*. Here is the justification for the statement made above, that an *etonijo* represents a tenure superior in some way to an *o-na-to*. The priestess is quite certainly cast in the role of an advocate, pressing the claims of religion against the secular *damos*.

Very often the Mycenaean documents seem to blur the dividing line between the religious sphere and the secular; or perhaps it would be better to say that the society that produced the documents did not generally distinguish between the two spheres.[14] But this text, if no other, makes a clear demarcation. The mention of two contending parties naturally implies the existence of some person, or body of persons, competent to resolve the dispute. The tablets themselves throw no light on their identity; but at least the present text indicates that a member of the Mycenaean priesthood might occupy a prominent place in society. It has still more to tell us. Lines 7 and 8 give information about the woman named *ka-pa-ti-ja*, described as a *ka-ra-wi-po-ro*. The latter word has been analysed, very ingeniously, as a spelling of κλαϝιφόρος 'key-bearer'. The syllables fit exactly, and the analysis is plausible in other respects, since Classical inscriptions refer to a key-bearer as a cult-official. Even if this analysis is not accepted, we cannot doubt that the *ka-ra-wi-po-ro* had connections with cult, since she figures in two other tablets (Ed 317, Un 6) in association with a priestess. This knowledge of the cult-connections of the *ka-ra-wi-po-ro* enables us to attempt an interpretation of lines 7 and 8. This woman holds two plots (*ke-ke-me-no*, dual); and, although obliged (*o-pe-ro-sa* = ὀφέλουσα) to work (*wo-ze-e* = ϝρόζεεν) with the two (*du-wo-u-pi*), she does not work (*o-u-wo-ze* = οὐ ϝρόζει). The syntax here is difficult; in particular, the presence of the instrumental ending *-pi* (= -φι) in *du-wo-u-pi* has not been explained satisfactorily.[15] But at least we may assume some connection between the numeral 'two' and the dual number of *ke-ke-me-no*. Hence this cult-official holds two plots on condition that she 'works'. But what is the precise signification of the

---

[14] L.R. Palmer refers to the 'pervading distinction made by the Palace between the royal branch and the divine branch of the economy': *Armées et fiscalité dans le monde antique* (Paris, 1977), 35-62, p. 40. But no such pervasive distinction can be elicited from the texts themselves: and in particular they give no hint of the 'collegiality' of *i-je-re-u* and *e-qe-ta* on the 'sacral estates', as claimed by Palmer.

[15] cf. A. Heubeck, 'Myk. *e- me* und *du-wo-u-pi*', *Živa antika* 19 (1969), 3-12.

verb 'works'? Does it refer to actual cultivation of the ground? Or ought we to think of the performance of some religious duty? The Greek could bear either meaning, and it is only by comparing other texts that a choice can be made. When we find in Ep 613 a *te-re-ta* (a person of high status, but without religious affiliations so far as we know) also having an obligation to 'work' but not 'working', and in the same text other persons who both 'hold' and 'work', we have to equate 'working' with cultivating and not with religious observance. The 'obligation' mentioned in such texts does not seem to constitute a kind of feudal duty to be performed in return for a grant of land; it is more likely that there were various contracts of holdings, some involving the land-holder in the actual cultivation of his plot, others not doing so. Whereas lines 5-6 of Ep 704 refer to the existence of a religious estate, in which the local community (*damos*) too has some interest, lines 7-8 envisage a cult-official who holds parcels of land on the same terms and subject to the same obligations that apply to secular tenants.

*

By way of summary, we can state that priests, priestesses and other cult-personnel are often mentioned in the Pylos tablets, and we may take it that, at least in *pa-ki-ja-na*, there was an elaborate organization of divine cult. The extant documents never display the personnel actually engaged in cult-activity; but the names or titles of the cult-personnel do occur in close proximity to divine names (especially that of Poseidon), and on one occasion they are apparently tending a shrine (no. 9). As well as those persons designated as priests, priestesses and so forth, certain high officials played a role in the cults, but an ambiguous role; we see, for instance, the *ra-wa-ke-ta* acting both as donor and as recipient of cult-offerings. The cult-servants properly so called are by no means set apart from the world; they are able to acquire the rights and obligations with respect to land that other persons acquire. Looking at the material as a whole, we may reasonably conclude that differing strata of society were involved in the cults in somewhat different ways. On one level, we have important land-owners maintaining estates at least partly for sacral purposes; on another, officials (perhaps state-officials) participate personally in the cults; on yet another, there is a whole array of cult-servants given the various designations described above – these do not, in their own right, occupy an outstanding place in society, although they belong to it; on a different level again, the local community (in its corporate capacity of *damos*) fulfils its religious obligations by making offerings to the gods but also maintains its rights against claims made by religious personnel. Such appear to be legitimate inferences from our material; it would be dangerous to go much beyond them.

Appendix: Linear B texts discussed

The words printed in capital letters in the texts below appear on the actual tablets as logograms; in the Mycenaean documents, logograms always stand for a certain quantity of some form of property (slaves, cereals, other food or valuables). In modern discussion, the tablets are referred to by a combination of letters and numbers; the letters indicate the series to which the document belongs, classified by the goods listed in it: thus, documents recording quantities of wheat have the initial capital letter E (e.g. nos. 2-5 below).

1. Tn 316
r. 1 po-ro-wi-to-jo
    2 i-je-to-qe pa-ki-ja-si do-ra-qe pe-re po-re-na-qe
    3 pu-ro a-ke po-ti-ni-ja GOLD GOBLET 1 WOMAN 1
    4 ma-na-sa GOLD GOBLET 1 WOMAN 1 po-si-da-e-ja GOLD GOBLET 1 WOMAN 1
    5 ti-ri-se-ro-e GOLD GOBLET 1 do-po-ta GOLD GOBLET 1
v. 1 i-je-to-qe po-si-da-i-jo a-ke-qe wa-tu
    2 do-ra-qe pe-re po-re-na-qe a-ke
    3 pu-ro GOLD GOBLET 1 WOMAN 2 qo-wi-ja na-[ ] ko-ma-we-te-ja
    4 i-je-to-qe pe-re-*82-jo i-pe-me-de-ja-qe di-u-ja-jo-qe
    5 do-ra-qe pe-re-po-re-na-qe a pe-re-*82 GOLD GOBLET 1 WOMAN 1
    6 i-pe-me-de-ja GOLD GOBLET 1 di-u-ja GOLD GOBLET 1 WOMAN 1
    7 pu-ro e-ma-a$_2$ a-re-ja GOLD GOBLET 1 MAN 1
    8 i-je-to-qe di-u-jo do-ra-qe pe-re po-re-na-qe a-ke
    9 di-we GOLD GOBLET 1 MAN 1 e-ra GOLD GOBLET 1 WOMAN 1
    10 di-ri-mi-jo di-wo i-je-we GOLD GOBLET 1
    11 pu-ro

This is the most important single tablet dealing with cult-observances, inscribed on both front (r(ecto)) and back (v(erso)). The details are much disputed. What seems to be certain is that the text records a series of offerings to various divinities at the cult centre of *pa-ki-ja-na*. The first word, *po-ro-wi-to-jo* (r. 1), is in the genitive case; it may be the name of the month in which the offerings were made. *pu-ro*, written four times at the left, is the capital Pylos: its occurrence in an inscription dealing with cult-operations at *pa-ki-ja-na* suggests that *pa-ki-ja-na* lay at no great distance from Pylos itself. The introductory formula *i-je-to-qe...a-ke* (r. 2-3 and v. 1-2, 4-5, 8) is obscure; it refers in some way to the bringing of the offerings. As examples of the offerings themselves, '*po-ti-ni-ja* GOLD GOBLET 1 WOMAN 1' (r. 3) is a statement that a precious vessel and a woman were offered 'to the Lady', i.e. πότνια (a generic term? or a specific goddess?); it is unknown whether the offering of a woman refers to a human sacrifice or to a dedication to the deity's service. Compare the offering (v. 9) of a gold vessel and a man to Zeus (*di-we*) and of a gold vessel and a woman to his consort Hera (*e-ra*).

2. Es 646
1 ko-pe-re-u po-se-da-o-ne do-so-mo	WHEAT 1 T 5
2 *34-ke-te-si do-so-mo	WHEAT T 1 V 4
3 we-da-ne-we do-so-mo	WHEAT T 1 V 4
4 di-wi-je-we do-so-mo	WHEAT T 1 V 4

The tablet records a 'gift, offering' (*do-so-mo*) of so much wheat made to Poseidon (*po-se-da-o-ne*) by Kopreus; also, offerings made to human recipients, presumably cult-servants.

3. Es 703

1 we-da-ne-wo do-e-ro po-se-da-o-ne	WHEAT T 3
2 *34-ke-te-si do-so-mo	WHEAT V 1
3 we-da-ne-wo do-so-mo	WHEAT V 1
4 di-wi-je-we do-so-mo	WHEAT V 1

Further offerings to Poseidon.

4. Es 644

1 ko-pe-re-wo do-so-mo we-te-i-we-te-i	WHEAT T 7
2 a-re-ku-tu-ru-wo-no we-te-i-we-te-i	WHEAT T 9 V 3
3 se-no do-so-mo we-te-i-we-te-i	WHEAT T 2
4 o-po-ro-me-no do-so-mo we-te-i-we-te-i	WHEAT T 1
5 ai-ki-wa-ro do-so-mo we-te-i-we-te-i	WHEAT T[
6 we-da-ne-wo do-e-ro do-so-mo we-te-i-we-te-i	WHEAT T 1 V 2
7 wo-ro-ti-ja-o do-so-mo we-te-i-we-te-i	WHEAT T 3 V 2
8 ka-ra-i do-so-mo we-te-i-we-te-i	WHEAT V 3
9 a-ne-o do-so-mo we-te-i-we-te-i	WHEAT T 2 V 3
10 ru-ko-u-ro do-so-mo we-te-i-we-te-i	WHEAT]V[
11 o-ka] do-so-mo we-te-i-we-te-i	WHEAT T 2 V 1
12 pi-ro-ta-wo do-so-mo we-te-i-we-te-i	WHEAT T 2 V[
13 ku-da-ma-ro do-so-mo we-te-i-we-te-i	WHEAT T 2 [

Further offerings of wheat (presumably to Poseidon) made *we-te-i-we-te-i*, i.e. annually; the names of the donors at the left are in the genitive.

5. Es 650

r. 1 ki-ri-ti-jo-jo ko-pe-re-u e-ke to-so-de pe-mo	WHEAT 6
2 a-re-ku-tu-ru-wo e-ke to-so-de pe-mo	WHEAT 7
3 se-no e-ke to-so-de pe-mo	WHEAT 1
4 o-po-ro-me-no e-ke to-so-de pe-mo	WHEAT 4
5 ai-ki-wa-ro a-te-mi-to do-e-ro e-ke to-so-de pe-mo	WHEAT 1
6 we-da-ne-wo do-e-ro e-ke to-so-de pe-mo	WHEAT T 4
7 wo-ro-ti-ja-o e-ke to-so-de pe-mo	WHEAT 2
8 ka-ra-i e-ke to-so-de pe-mo	WHEAT T 3
9 a-ne-o e-ke to-so-de pe-mo	WHEAT 1 T 5
v. 1 ru-ko-wo-ro e-ke to-so-de pe-mo	WHEAT 1 T 4
2 o-ka e-ke to-so-de pe-mo	WHEAT 1 T 2
3 pi-ro-ta-wo e-ke to-so-de pe-mo	WHEAT 1 T 2
4 ku-da-ma-ro e-ke to-so-de pe-mo	WHEAT 1 T 2
5 pi-ro-te-ko-to e-ke to-so-de pe-mo	WHEAT [ ]

This tablet is inscribed on both sides and records plots of land held by cult-servants of Poseidon: Kopreus (r. 1) etc. The first word may be a month-name in the genitive like *po-ro-wi-to-jo* at the beginning of no. 1 (Tn 316). The words *e-ke to-so-de pe-mo*, 'has so much seed(-corn)', amount to a recurrent formula in land-holding texts; after this formula, the actual quantity is specified. The quantity of wheat here registered is presumably what was needed to sow the plot in question.

6. Un 718

1 sa-ra-pe-da po-se-da-o-ni do-so-mo
2 o-wi-de-ta-i do-so-mo to-so e-ke-ra$_2$-wo
3 do-se WHEAT 4 WINE 3 OX 1
4 tu-ro$_2$ CHEESE 10 ko-wo *153 1
5 me-ri-to V 3
6
7 o-da-a$_2$ da-mo WHEAT 2 WINE 2
8 RAM 2 CHEESE 5 a-re-ro UNGUENT V 2 *153 1
9 to-so-de ra-wa-ke-ta do-se
10 RAM 2 me-re-u-ro FLOUR T 6
11 WINE S 2 o-da-a$_2$ wo-ro-ki-jo-ne-jo ka-ma
12 WHEAT T 6 WINE S 1 CHEESE 5 me-ri[

The text states that offerings are to be made to Poseidon by four parties: an important man named *e-ke-ra$_2$-wo* (2); the *da-mo*, that is the local community (7); a well-attested functionary known as the *ra-wa-ke-ta* (9); and the *ka-ma* (apparently a kind of guild of land-holders) (11).

7. Un 219

1 e-ke-ra-ne tu-wo 2 O 1[
2 pa-de-we O 1 pa-de-we O 1
3 ka-ru-ke PE 2 KA 1 O 6
4 te-qi-jo-ne O 1 a-ke-ti-ri-ja-i KA 1
5 a-ti-mi-te O 1 da-ko-ro-i E 1
6 di-pte-ra-po-ro RA 1 O 3 ko-ro[ ] 1
7 a-na-ka-te TE 1 po-ti-ni-ja[
8 e-[ ] U 1 e-ma-a$_2$ U 1 pe-[
9 a-ka-wo-ne MA 1 pa-ra-[ ] 2
10 ra-wa-ke-ta MA 1 KO 1 [ ] ME 1 O 1 WI 1

These are items of produce given to a mixed list of divinities (e.g. to *e-ma-a$_2$*, i.e. Hermes, 8) and to human recipients (e.g. *ra-wa-ke-ta*, 10).

8. Fn 187

1	a-pi-te-ja	BARLEY[ ] FIGS 2
2	po-si-da-i-jo-de	BARLEY[ ] FIGS T 1
3	ka-ru-ke	BARLEY[ ] FLOUR
4	pa-ki-ja-na-de	BARLEY T 1[ ] FIGS T 1
5	ka-ru-ke	BARLEY T 1 V 3 FIGS T 1 V 3
6	de-do-wa-re-we	BARLEY T 1
7	ku-ri-na-ze-ja	BARLEY T 2 FIGS T 2
8	u-po-jo-po-ti-ni-ja	BARLEY T 5 FIGS T 4
9	o-pi-tu-ra-jo	BARLEY T 3
10	au-to-*34-ta-ra	BARLEY T 1
11	a-ma-tu-na	BARLEY T 1
12	te-qi-ri-jo-ne	BARLEY V 3
13	u-do-no-o-i	BARLEY T 3
14	po-te-re-we	BARLEY T 4 FIGS T 4

15 a-ke-ti-ri-ja-i BARLEY T 1 V 3
16 ka-ru-ke BARLEY T 1 V 3
17 i-so-e-ko BARLEY T 2
18 po-si-da-i-je-u-si BARLEY T 1 V 3
19 *34-ke-ja BARLEY T 1 V 3 FIGS[
20 a-ro-ja BARLEY V 3
21 ka-ru-ke BARLEY T 1 V 3

This text records the consignment of barley, flour and figs to human beings (e.g. *ka-ru-ke*, 'herald', 3) and to places (e.g. *po-si-da-i-jo-de*, 'shrine of Poseidon', 2)

9. Ae 303
pu-ro i-je-re-ja do-e-ra e-ne-ka i-je-ro-jo ku-ru-so-jo WOMAN 14[

This records at least fourteen women in charge of the sacred gold at Pylos; these were presumably temple-servants.

10. Ep 539
 1 pi-ro-na te-o-jo do-e-ra o-na-to e-ke ke-ke-me-na ko-to-na
 2 e-ri-qi-ja te-o-jo do-e-ra o-na-to e-ke ke-ke-me-na ko-to-na
 3 i-na te-o-jo do-e-ro o-na-to e-ke ke-ke-me-na ko-to-na pa-ro da-mo
 4 po-so-re-ja te-o-jo do-e-ra o-na-to e-ke ke-ke-me-na ko-to-na
 5 po-so-re-ja te-o-jo do-e-ra o-na-to e-ke pa-ro da-mo ka-ma-e-we
   wo-zo-te to-so pe-mo WHEAT
 6 te-qa-ja te-o-jo do-e-ra o-na-to e-ke ke-ke-me-na ko-to-na pa-ro
   da-mo to-so pe-mo WHEAT T 2
 7 me-re-u i-je-re-ja do-e-ro o-na-to e-ke pa-ro [ ]ma-ta
   ka-ma-e-we o-u-qe wo-ze to-so pe-mo WHEAT V 2
 8 te-te-re-u i-je-re-ja do-e-ro o-na-to e-ke ke-ke-me-na ko-to-na
   pa-ro da-mo to-so pe-mo WHEAT V 3
 9 pu-[ ]-da-ka ka-pa-ti-ja do-e-ro o-na-to e-ke ke-ke-me-na ko-to-na
   pa-ro da-mo to-so pe-mo WHEAT T 3 V 3
10 e-ni-to-wo a-pi-me-de-o do-e-ro o-na-to e-ke ke-ke-me-na ko-to-na
   pa-ro da-mo to-so pe-mo WHEAT T 1
11 to-wa-te-u a-pi-me-de-o do-e-ro o-na-to e-ke ke-ke-me-na ko-to-na
   pa-ro da-mo to-so pe-mo WHEAT T 8
12 wi-dwo-i-jo a-pi-me-de-o do-e-ro o-na-to e-ke ke-ke-me-na ko-to-na
   pa-ro da-mo to-so pe-mo WHEAT T 2
13 we-te-re-u i-je-re-u o-na-to e-ke ke-ke-me-na ko-to-na pa-ro da-mo
   to-so pe-mo WHEAT 2 T 3
14 a-pi-me-de e-ke e-to-ni-jo ke-ke-me-na-o ko-to-na-o to-so pe-mo
   WHEAT 4 T 6

This is a 'land-holding' tablet, giving a list of persons (whose names occur in the nominative case at the beginning of each line) holding an *o-na-to* (i.e. a kind of beneficial interest in land). This particular *o-na-to* consists of a special sort of plot known as *ke-ke-me-na ko-to-na*, the exact meaning of which is not known but which must refer to something like 'common land', since in many instances the plot is said to be held *pa-ro da-mo*, 'from the local community'. The *e-to-ni-jo* mentioned in line 14 seems (especially on the evidence of no. 11 (Ep 704)) to be an interest in land superior in status to an *o-na-to*. The relevance of the text for the student of cult lies in the fact that many of the land-holders have cultic connections, suggesting that the lands in question are estates of Poseidon: e.g. *pi-ro-na* in line 1 is stated to be *te-o-jo do-e-ra*, 'female slave of the god', *i-na* in line 3 a male slave of the god, *me-re-u* in line 7 a male slave of the priestess, while *we-te-re-u* in line 13 is himself an *i-je-re-u* ('priest').

11. Ep 704

1 o-pe-to-re-u qe-ja-me-no e-ke ke-ke-me-na ko-to-na to-so pe-mo
                WHEAT 2 T 5
2 u-wa-mi-ja te-o-jo do-e-ra o-na-to e-ke-qe i-je-re-ja ke-ra
                to-so pe-mo WHEAT T 1 V 3
3 e-ri-ta i-je-re-ja o-na-to e-ke ke-ke-me-na ko-to-na pa-ro da-mo
                to-so pe-mo WHEAT T 4
4 ki-ri-te-wi-wa o-na-to e-ko-si ke-ke-me-na ko-to-na pa-ro da-mo
                to-so pe-mo WHEAT 1 T 9
5 e-ri-ta i-je-re-ja e-ke e-u-ke-to-qe e-to-ni-jo e-ke-e te-o
                da-mo-de-mi pa-si ko-to-na-o
6 ke-ke-me-na-o o-na-to e-ke-e to-so- pe-mo WHEAT 3 T 9
7 ka-pa-ti-ja ka-ra-wi-po-ro e-ke ke-ke-me-no o-pe-ro-sa du-wo-u-pi
                wo-ze-e o-u-wo-ze
8 to-so pe-mo WHEAT 4

This is a further list of holders of *ke-ke-me-na* land, with a reference to a dispute between the priestess *e-ri-ta* and the local community over a title to land in lines 5-6: Eritha the priestess holds and claims (*e-ke e-u-ke-to-qe* = ἔχει εὔχετοί τε) that the god holds (*e-ke-e te-o* = ἔχεεν θεόν) an *e-to-ni-jo*; but the local community says that he holds an interest consisting in a *ko-to-na ke-ke-me-na* (*da-mo-de-mi pa-si...e-ke-e* = δᾶμος δέ μίν φασι...ἔχεεν).

PART III

The Roman Empire

7

From Republic to Principate:
priesthood, religion and ideology

This chapter, like the two that follow, is concerned with religion and priesthood in the Roman Empire. The term 'Roman Empire' is used, confusingly, in three distinct senses in modern discussions: first, it refers to the monarchic political regime established by the first emperor Augustus, following the downfall of the Republican constitution; secondly, it indicates the chronological period during which the Roman world was governed by emperors; thirdly, it refers to the vast geographical area over which Rome had direct control. Paradoxically, a large part of this area had come under Roman control (by conquest or other means) during the period of the Republic, long before the advent of Empire in its chronological sense.

The new political regime (also known as the 'Principate') did not represent a complete break with the Republican constitution that had gone before: members of the élite continued to hold the traditional offices of state; the titles of *consul*, *praetor* and so forth remained; the senate continued to sit and even had some of its legal powers increased; the emperor himself, at least in part, defined his powers in terms of the traditional magistracies and honours of the Republic. But, despite these elements of continuity, the position of the monarch was in practice dominant: he monopolized military force; he largely controlled access to political office; his wishes were elaborately respected by the senate; it was assumed, almost from the very start of the Principate, that he would have a successor on the throne.

Richard Gordon's first chapter is concerned with the period of transition between Republic and Empire (or Principate) – from the time of civil wars in the middle years of the first century BC (the effective end of the Republican constitution), through the dictatorship of Julius Caesar (whose dominance in the state made him almost first emperor), to the establishment of the new regime under Augustus and his successors. In part this goes back to the themes of the first two papers in this volume, as Gordon starts from a discussion of the role of priesthoods (particularly the major priestly colleges) in the closing years of the Roman Republic. But he moves on to consider how those traditional priesthoods, with their traditional titles and many of their traditional duties, functioned in the new regime of the Principate; and then to explore the monopolization of priestly honours by the emperor himself and the contribution of this pre-eminent priestly role to the political power of the new monarch.

From Republic to Principate:
priesthood, religion and ideology*
Richard Gordon

Priestly colleges and the creation of the Principate

We have no term which accurately represents the institutions and attitudes characteristic of Roman religion. Cicero would have been surprised to discover that we refer to the religion of the late Republic as 'polytheism', thus emphasising the fact, of interest only in a Christian context, that numerous divinities received worship. By contrast, when C. Aurelius Cotta, the Academic spokesman in Cicero's dialogue *De Natura Deorum* (*On the Nature of the Gods*), describes Roman religion, he does not, in fact, mention gods, whether few or many. He says, 'As a whole, the *religio* of the Roman people is divided into *sacra* and *auspicia* – a third additional heading being the warnings produced concerning the future from portents and prodigies by the interpreters of the Sibyl (that is, the *XVviri sacris faciundis*) and the *haruspices*'. And he goes on – speaking expressly as a priest as well as a philosopher – to lay emphasis on the political character of Roman religion: 'Romulus, by founding the ritual of taking the auspices, and Numa, by founding the *sacra*, laid the foundations of our state, which assuredly would never have been able to become so great without our having taken the greatest care to placate the immortal gods.'[1] What is significant for Cotta about Roman religion is not so much the objects of worship but the institutions which made possible Rome's greatness, among them the two key sacerdotal colleges, the *pontifices*, who supervised the *sacra*, the ensemble of rules and rituals which we loosely group under the word 'religion', and the *augures*, who had responsibility for the *auspicia*, a major axis of communication between men and gods.

* Much of the work on this chapter (and the two that follow) was done at the British School at Rome; and it was finished at the Fondation Hardt, with financial assistance from the British Academy. I would like to thank all three institutions, and especially Amanda Claridge, for their kindness. The editors, and Robin Cormack, have been over indulgent to a slothful contributor.

[1] Cicero, *Nat. D.* 3, 2, 5. This threefold division reappears in Cicero's thinking. See, for example, *Leg.* 2, 8, 20 & 12, 30-1: also *Har. Resp.* 9, 18 (where the *haruspices*, however, appear to form an independent category of a fourfold division of priesthoods). For other ancient attempts to classify traditional priesthoods, see M. Beard, pp. 44-7 above.

This emphasis upon the importance of the priestly colleges to the maintenance of Roman religion and so of the Roman state reappears elsewhere in the late Republic and early Empire. For example, we may instructively compare the organization of the greatest modern book on Roman religion, the second edition of Georg Wissowa's *Religion und Kultus der Römer* (1912), with that of Varro's *Antiquitates Rerum Divinarum (Religious Antiquities)* which appeared in 47/46 BC, and of which we have a good general knowledge through its extensive quotation by Augustine in Books 4 to 7 of *De Civitate Dei (City of God)*.[2] Wissowa, after devoting eighty pages to a historical narrative divided into four periods, chose to describe the gods next, a subject to which he devoted 280 pages, about half his space. The third part, about 200 pages, deals with sacral law, rituals, festivals, games, sacred places and the various priestly colleges. Finally, there are two useful appendices on the calendar and the list of temples officially accorded space by the Roman people. By contrast, Varro omits history almost entirely as a possible means of organizing his knowledge of Roman religion, although some consciousness of historical decay seems clearly to have been central to his purpose in writing the book in the first place.[3] In keeping with his basic assumption that, though a God of some sort truly pre-exists, civic religion is a thoroughly human creation,[4] Varro devotes the three books after the general introduction to an account of the three major sacerdotal colleges.[5] There follow three books on shrines and sacred places; three on festivals and three on rituals public and private. Only then does Varro turn to discuss the divinities of the Roman people.[6] Moreover, there is no evidence that he emphasised what is for us one of the most striking features of Roman religious organization, its control by the Senate, for which in a sense the sacerdotal colleges acted as committees.[7] Rather, the scope and minuteness of the authority of the *pontifical* college were stressed, as well as the antiquity of priestly institutions at Rome. For although the

[2] See Cardauns (ed.), *Varros Antiquitates RD* with his more general discussion, 'Varro und die Römische Religion, zur Theologie, Wirkungsgeschichte and Leistung der *Antiquitates Rerum Divinarum*', *ANRW* II, 16.1, 80-103.

[3] See, for example, *RD* fr. 2a and 12.

[4] Fr. 20; 22; 35-7; 39.

[5] Cardauns (ed.), *Varros Antiquitates RD*, 39-46. Unfortunately almost nothing survives of these books. Cardauns allows only five, mostly single-sentence, fragments on the pontifical college; the longest surviving fragment, under the *XVviri s. f.*, is really about the Sibylline books and oracles.

[6] For the organization of *RD*, see fr. 4, which establishes the division into four sections of three books each (omitting Book 1). On the principles of this division (found elsewhere in Varro's work), see J.E. Skydsgaard, *Varro the Scholar* (Analecta Romana, Instituti Danici Suppl. 4, Copenhagen, 1968), 10-37.

[7] See M. Beard, pp. 31-4 above; with Wissowa, *RK*[2] 394-8; Mommsen, *Staatsrecht*[3] 1, 312-13; 2, 20-4; G.J. Szemler, 'Religio, priests and magistrates in the Roman Republic', *Numen* 18 (1971), 103-31.

historical tradition ascribed the institution of eight sorts of priestly authority to Numa (described in great detail by Dionysius of Halicarnassus), Varro specifically stressed the extraordinary number of 'priests and servants of the gods' appointed by Romulus: 'No one could name any other newly-founded city in which so many priests and servants of gods were appointed from the beginning.'[8]

Although from a modern point of view the various priestly organizations of Rome may be of interest in tracing the historical development of her composite religion, by the late Republic they had mostly become more or less quaint survivals. The massive political and social changes which accompanied Roman imperial expansion led to an effective simplification of religious organization. The chief beneficiaries of these pressures towards simplification were the three major sacerdotal colleges. This is well illustrated by Book 2 of Cicero's *De Legibus (On Laws)* in which he attempted a theoretical and systematic description of an ideal religion which is at least convergent with (if not based upon) Varro's analysis of Roman religion.[9] Few of the great variety of Roman priests are mentioned. Greatest stress is laid on the three major colleges, represented as important integrative institutions in the Roman state. The pontiffs not only organize the calendar and the ritual aspects of religion, they provide a crucial bridge between the public world and the private world through their supervision of funerary and tomb law (to which Cicero devotes a surprising amount of space). The augurs have the task of integrating the public life of Rome with the signs sent by the gods through *signa* and *auspicia*. The *XVviri* (who however hardly feature in Cicero's account) integrate the prophecies of those outside priestly circles who nevertheless may have insight into the will of the gods, the *fatidici* and *vates*, with the public procedures of the state.[10]

[8] Dionysius of Halicarnassus, *Ant. Rom.* 2, 64-73 and 2, 21, 1 = Cardauns (ed.), *Varros Antiquitates RD* 62, Appendix ad librum XIII, b.

[9] It is commonly argued that Cicero owed no intellectual debt to Varro. See, for example, J.M. André, 'La philosophie religieuse de Cicéron', in A. Michel and R. Verdière (eds.), *Ciceroniana (Mélanges Kumaniecki)* (Leiden, 1975), 11-21, esp. 19-20; E. Rawson, 'The interpretation of Cicero's "De Legibus" ', *ANRW* I, 4, 334-56, esp. 342-9. But this view is surely untenable. Cicero and Varro had known each other since at least 59 BC and it is positively attested that, while working on *De Republica* (to which *De Legibus* is a companion piece), Cicero obtained some books by Varro (Cicero, *Att.* 4, 14, 1; 16, 2). Note also several striking similarities between Cicero's and Varro's ideas on religion (compare *Leg.* 2, 19 with *RD* fr. 32 and *Ling.* 5, 86; *Leg.* 2, 22 and *RD* fr. 32 and *Ling.* 5, 86; *Leg.* 2, 22 and *RD* fr. 18). Of course, it is not simply a matter of Cicero copying Varro, but rather of his use of Varronian themes.

[10] See, for tomb law, *Leg.* 2, 25, 45-37, 62; for signs 2, 11, 21; 17, 31; for prophecies 10, 20; 16, 30. Cicero is attempting here (as elsewhere) to impose some coherence on the complex organizational structure of Roman priesthoods – an attempt which leads to some strange oversimplifications (such as his notion that the *XVviri* were solely concerned with prophecy) and awkward divisions (such as that between *flamines* as priests of individual gods and *pontifices* as priests of all the gods). For a rather different attempt at organizing

If we ask the reason for the late Republican stress upon the priestly colleges, two answers occur. The first arises from the very emergence of theoretical enquiry into the Roman state and its functions. This made necessary an attempt to make explicit the function of institutions hitherto embedded in unselfconscious practice. We may urge that the three major priestly colleges offered a conceptual framework within which the extreme complexity of Roman public religion could be represented both to outsiders and to the élite itself. They could be used to represent Roman religion as divided into three aspects: rituals (*sacra*); the official sacralization of places and moments (augury); exceptional interventions by divine powers (prodigies and portents). Nor is it difficult to understand why it is that, of these, augury, and to a lesser extent the interpretation of prophecies and omens, dominate the historical record, and the iconography of coinage in particular, in the late Republic. Though the Romans liked to think of themselves as concerned with piety for its own sake, the really interesting facts of a religious kind were those which directly affected political careers and success. Augural symbols appear with increasing frequency on late Republican coins because, as Cicero stresses in *De Legibus*, the priesthood offered a degree of personal authority: augurs did not in general act as a college but as individuals.[11] Moreover, the *auctoritas* (prestige) possessed by a member of a sacerdotal college helped one to maintain a political presence of an official kind even when one did not enjoy *imperium* (formal magisterial power). The second reason for the stress upon the sacerdotal colleges is aristocratic competition for membership in them.

There were therefore conceptual and pragmatic reasons for the breaking by Julius Caesar of what had since the death in 180 BC of C. Servilius Geminus (both *pontifex maximus* and *Xvir s.f.*), been one of the rules of the senatorial élite: that even its most prominent members should hold only one priestly office. Caesar, already *pontifex maximus* since 63 BC, was elected *augur* and *XVvir* in 47 BC; and perhaps in compensation, added one member to each of these three colleges and possibly three to the *VIIviri epulonum*.[12] Octavian, as his heir, rapidly

and hierarchizing Roman priesthoods, see Livy's account of Numa's priestly organization – culminating (as Cicero) with the college of *pontifices*, but laying most stress on the position of the single *pontifex* (*maximus*) (Livy 1, 20).

[11] For augurs and augural law, see Linderski, 'Augural law' (esp. 2190-225 on the operation of individual augurs). Augural symbolism on coins is discussed by J.R. Fears, *Princeps a diis electus* (*MAAR* 26, Rome, 1977), 99-111 – though he pushes his case much too far. The first coin of the series, that of C. Minucius Augurinus (135 BC) is discussed by M. Crawford, *RRC* no. 242, with pp. 273-5; n.242²⁻⁵; and by T. Hölscher, 'Die Anfänge römischer Repräsentationskunst', *RhM* 85 (1978), 315-57.

[12] Dio 42, 51, 4 with Hoffmann Lewis, *Official Priests*, 22 and Scheid, 'Prêtres', 621. J.A. North, 'Religion and politics from Republic to Principate', *JRS* 76 (1986), 251-8 (esp. 257-8) rightly stresses these moments.

accumulated the pontificate, the augurate and the quindecimvirate; and finally, maybe sometime later, became *VIIvir*.[13] And, as all Italy witnessed, on 6 March 12 BC as Augustus he was elected *pontifex maximus* on the death of the aged former triumvir, M. Aemilius Lepidus, who had been elected immediately after Caesar's death in 44 BC.[14] This cumulation of priesthoods, and the associated attention paid to the sacerdotal colleges, is certainly parallel to the familiar non-Republican cumulation of traditional magistracies and pro-magisterial *imperium* by Augustus and his successors, and at one level simply marks the exceptional success of Octavian in the deadly game of late-Republican competition for power. But it should also be seen as the institutional expression of several other convergent pressures which are my subject in this paper.[15] My question is this: what are the most appropriate contexts for understanding the cumulation of sacerdotal roles by the Roman emperors?

Augustus' assumption of the office of *pontifex maximus* and his involvement in the priestly colleges acted also to underpin and legitimate his 'revival' of Roman public religion. This revival was both eclectic and self-serving, conservative and radical. The first shrines to be restored by the new régime were not, it seems, the most important but some of the oldest – the temples of Jupiter Feretrius, Victoria and Saturnus, among others; if the choice is significant, there are evocations of Romulus and perhaps even earlier heroes.[16] The revival of the priesthood of Jupiter (*flamen Dialis*) in 11 BC, the closure of the temple of Janus on 11 January 29 BC, the foundation of the temple of Mars Ultor in the Forum Augustum, all evoked the religious activity of Numa.[17] And it is in relation to Numa that Livy comments upon the moral and regulatory functions of religion: '[The Romans'] constant preoccupation with the gods ... had so imbued all their hearts with piety that it was regard for promises and oaths by which the state was governed in place of fear of the laws and punishment.'[18] In the next

[13] The office of *pontifex maximus* was decreed in 44 BC to be hereditary in Caesar's family (Dio 44, 5, 3). Octavian become *pontifex* in 47 BC, *augur* in 42, *XVvir* in c. 37. That he was *VIIvir* by 16 BC may perhaps be inferred from a coin of that year which includes a representation of the emblems of all four major priestly colleges (*RIC* I, 74, no. 150).

[14] Augustus, *Res Gestae* 10, 2; Degrassi, *Inscriptiones Italiae* XIII, 420-1.

[15] See W. Speyer, 'Das Verhältnis des Augustus zur Religion', *ANRW* II, 16 1. 3, 1777-805, esp. 1794-5.

[16] Gros, *Aurea Templa*, 26 (though I would stress *if* the choice is significant; it would be easy to exaggerate the implication of such facts).

[17] *Flamen Dialis*: Suetonius, *Aug.* 31, 4; Tacitus, *Ann.* 3, 58, 5; Dio 54, 36, 1 (for the foundation by Numa, see, for example, Livy 1, 20, 1 – though a different version is offered by Plutarch, *Num.* 7, who ascribes the *flamen Dialis* to an earlier period). Janus: Livy 1, 19, 2-3, with specific allusion to Octavian's closure of the gates in 29 BC. Numa and the cult of Mars: Livy 1, 20, 3.

[18] Livy 1, 21, 1. See K. Gläser, *PW* s.v. Numa, col. 1249 and W. Kunkel, 'Über das Wesen des augusteischen Prinzipats', *Gymnasium* 68 (1961), 353-70, esp. 357-8 (= W. Schmitthenner (ed.), *Augustus* (Darmstadt, 1969), 311-35).

sentence the point is made clear: the moral superiority brought about by Numa's religious innovations justifies Rome's authority and universal hegemony.[19] Ideologically, Numa's religious reforms made it possible for Rome to secure the fruits of the military conquests implicit in Romulus' organization of a military society. As Velleius Paterculus observed, fate, 'preserver of the State and the World', provided in Augustus 'a founder and preserver of the name of Rome' at the conclusion of the civil war – a neat blend, in other words, of Romulus and Numa.[20]

The evident calculation in Augustus' 'revival' of Roman religion marks just one step, albeit an important one, in an already old process, the appropriation by the Roman élite of the religious institutions of the Roman people.[21] What should be emphasised here is not the direct dependence of the state upon lavish gifts for the building of temples by individuals victorious in war nor the control by the senate of religious matters so much as the insidious changes which accompanied the expansion of Rome. The first of these changes which I propose to discuss here – and one that relates to priestly operations – is the role of writing in the development of Roman religion.

Religion and writing

The numerous calendars surviving from the late Republic and early Empire in whole or part are familiar as 'sources' for the historian of Roman religion.[22] But they are also interesting evidence of the degree to which the complexity of Roman religion was linked to the institution of literacy. The form of the list is here crucial. Even more than in a modern diary (which may include such diverse pieces of information as public holidays, phases of the moon and the birthdays of the royal family), we find in these Roman calendars an enormous amount of information, neatly registered under different categories, information which, if it were stored simply in human memories, could never be presented in such a form. A rational and articulate process of selection

---

[19] Livy 1, 21, 2 says explicitly only that the neighbours of Rome considered it *nefas* (impious) to offer violence to a state entirely devoted to worship of the gods; but this piety lies behind the successful expansion under Tullus Hostilius (the next king). For late Republican religious justifications of imperialism, see P. Brunt, 'Laus imperii', in P. Garnsey and C.R. Whittaker (eds.), *Imperialism in the Ancient World* (Cambridge, 1979), 159-91.

[20] Velleius Paterculus 2, 60, 1. See E. Cizek, 'L'image de renouvellement historique chez Velleius Paterculus', *StudClas* 14 (1972), 85-92, esp. 89-92.

[21] John Scheid has recently addressed this problem in relation to the election of priests and the *Lex Domitia* of 104 BC; see Scheid, 'Prêtre'.

[22] For full information on the surviving calendars from Italy (including drawings and photographs), see Degrassi, *Inscriptiones Italiae* XIII; more briefly Wissowa, *RK*[2], 2-4; Latte, *RRG*, 1-3.

and allocation of information has taken place. We may note, for example, (1) the letters marking the *nundinae* ('market days'); (2) letters marking the legal status of each day of the year; (3) each of the three fixed days each month, the Kalends, Nones and Ides; (4) the relation of each day to the fixed days; (5) the dates of all the forty-five traditional public holidays; (6) new holidays and anniversaries of the late Republic and Empire; (7) information about holidays, notices of games, feasts and market-days, and notes on their significance; (8) notes on the foundation dates of important temples (*dies natales*), their locations and the gods they are dedicated to; (9) some astronomical information; (10) notes on the significance of certain festivals etc.

Some of the information given in the calendars is certainly 'practical', but it would be a mistake to assume that the rash of late Republican and early imperial examples is due to a new interest in practical information. For in fact a great deal of the information is quite gratuitous, merely 'interesting', as well as highly unsystematic.[23] Rather, Roman calendars are an excellent illustration of one of the consequences of literacy to which Professor Goody has drawn attention. Writing provides not merely the obvious opportunity of recording great bodies of material (which can be, and frequently has been, achieved by illiterate societies by use of mnemonic devices or systems) but also of organizing it in many different ways and from many points of view.[24] The very existence of calendars produced in turn a considerable body of commentary and exegesis, by prompting newly obvious questions concerning the meaning of this or that item of information, or the story 'behind' a given fact – questions which frequently required lengthy descriptive answers which consequently appeared together in the same volume without any coherent connection: the only connection lay in the original list, the calendar. Immediate personal involvement in religious acts could hardly compete with the privilege of this new kind of representation of the religious system. The most famous of these commentaries based on calendars is Ovid's *Fasti*, an incomplete long poem probably based on an earlier prose commentary by Verrius Flaccus.[25] But we know also of Varro's work in the *Antiquitates* on festivals (indeed, that work is, in a sense, as a whole a commentary on the calendar), of Suetonius' *De Anno Romanorum* (*On the Year of the Romans*), and of the sources that

[23] A. Kirsopp Michels, *The Calendar of the Roman Republic* (Princeton, 1967), 3-15; 22-30; Bömer (ed.), *Fasten* 1, 33-44.

[24] Goody, *Domestication of the Savage Mind*; cf. B. Stock, *The Implications of Literacy* (Princeton, 1978). One must, of course, be cautious here: G. Gossen, *Chamulas in the World of the Sun* (Cambridge, Mass., 1974), 27 emphasises the complex knowledge of their calendars possessed by the peasants of Chamula (Mexico), without recourse to graphic representations.

[25] See W. Fauth, 'Römische Religion im Spiegel der "Fasti" des Ovid', *ANRW* II, 16. 1, 104-86, esp. 113-22. For discussion of Ovid's sources, see Bömer (ed.), *Fasten* 1, 22-8.

The Roman Calendar

The conventions of the calendar (see also pp. 184-5):

1. The letters marking the *nundinae* ('market days') are those in the left-hand column – here, B, C, D, E etc.

2. The letters marking the legal status of each day of the year are in the furthest right-hand column.

N = *nefastus* (a day on which no assembly was permitted and no formal procedures at civil law could be initiated)

F = *fastus* (a day on which procedures at civil law *could* be initiated)

C = *comitialis* (a day on which assemblies could be held or procedures at civil law initiated)

NP = ?*nefastus publicus* (perhaps a day of public festival, as well as one on which the other restrictions of *nefasti* applied)

EN = *endotercisus* (a day which counted as *nefastus* in the morning or evening, but *fastus* in between)

3. The three fixed days each month, the Kalends, Nones and Ides are marked here as K (1 Oct), NON (7 Oct) and EID (15 Oct) (central column)

4. The relation of each day to the fixed days is marked by the number (VI, V, IV etc) in the central column, indicating the place of each day in relation to the next Kalends, Nones or Ides.

5. The dates of the traditional public holidays are marked by an abbreviated title of the festival in large capitals (here, for example, MED for Meditrinalia, 11 Oct).

6. New holidays are here marked also by an abbreviated title in large capitals. So, for example, AUG (12 Oct) indicates the Augustalia, a festival founded in 19 BC.

7. Particular information on holidays, games etc is included in small capitals. In the entry on the Augustalia, the calendar notes 'Fer(iae) ex s(enatus) c(onsulto), q(uod) e(o) d(ie) Imp. Caes(ar] Aug(ustus) ex transmarin(is) provinc(iis) Urbem intravit araq(ue) Fort(unae) Reduci constit(uta)' ('Festival established by decree of the senate, because on that day the Emperor Caesar Augustus returned from overseas territory and entered the city, and an altar was set up to Fortuna Redux (Fortune who "leads back")')

8. Notes on the foundation dates and location dates of temples are also given in small capitals. Here, for example, on 18 October, record is made of the anniversary of the temple of Janus near the theatre of Marcellus (refounded by Tiberius in AD 17).

9. Astronomical information is not included in this calendar. Other calendars mark, for example, the entry of the sun into the different astrological signs.

Opposite: The surviving part of the month of October – from the *Fasti Amiternini*, an inscribed stone calendar (AD 20) from central Italy (adapted from *Inscriptiones Italiae*, XIII²).

Date		Expansion
1 Oct	B K· OCT N FIDEI IN CAPITOLIO	B k(alendae) Oct(obres), n(efastus). Fidei in Capitolio
2 Oct	C VI F	C VI f(astus)
3 Oct	D V C	D V c(omitialis)
4 Oct	E IV C IEIVNIVM CERERIS	E IV c(omitialis). Ieiunium Cereris
5 Oct	F III C LVDI DIVO AVGVSTO ET FORT REDVCI COMMITT	F III c(omitialis). Ludi divo Augusto et Fort(unae) Reduci committ(untur)
6 Oct	G PR C LVDI	G pr(idie) c(omitialis). Ludi
7 Oct	H NON F LVDI	H non(ae) f(astus). Ludi
8 Oct	A VIII F LVDI	A VIII f(astus). Ludi
9 Oct	B VII C GENIO PVBLIC FAVSTAE FELICITATI VENER VICTR IN CAPITOL APOL IN PALL LVDI	B VII c(omitialis). Genio public(o), Faustae Felicitati, Vener(i) Victr(ici) in Capitolio, Apol(lini) in Pal(atio). Ludi
10 Oct	C VI C LVDI	C VI c(omitialis). Ludi
11 Oct	D V MED N·P LVDI FER IOVI	D V Med(itrinalia), np. Ludi. Fer(iae) Iovi
12 Oct	E IV AVG N·P LVDI IN CIRC FER··· Q·E·D IMP CAES AVG EX TRANSMARIN PROVIN VRBEM INTRAVIT ARAQ FORT REDVCI CONSTIT	E IV Aug(ustalia), np. Lud(i) in Circ(o). Fer(iae) ex s(enatus) c(onsulto), q(uod) e(o) d(ie) Imp. Caes(ar) Aug(ustus) etc … (see facing page)
13 Oct	F III FONT N·P FERIAE FONTI	F III Font(inalia), np. Feriae Fonti
14 Oct	G PR EN	G pr(idie) en(dotercisus)
15 Oct	H EID N·P	H eid(us) np
16 Oct	A XVII F	A XVII f(astus)
17 Oct	B XVI C	B XVI c(omitialis)
18 Oct	C XV C IANO AD TEATHR MARCELLI	C XV c(omitialis). Iano ad theatr(um) Marcelli
19 Oct	D XIV ARM N·P	D XIV Arm(ilustrium), np
20 Oct	E XIII C	E XIII c(omitialis)
21 Oct	F XII C	F XII c(omitialis)

lie behind Book 4 of Johannes Lydus' compilation *On the months*.[26] In the case of the calendar, the development of an ingenious instrument for organizing in tabular form large quantities of information in turn prompted the further development of new kinds of information about the religious system, which re-presented that system in unfamiliar and indeed traditionally unthinkable ways.

A second area in which writing was indispensable to the growth of complexity in the Roman religious system is the pontifical rules: a compilation of precedents, explanations and formulae developed within (and known only to) the pontifical college. According to Livy, these had originally been drawn up by Numa; but they had increased to an enormous extent, and unsystematically, in the post-regal period.[27] The significance of this area of writing was twofold. In the first place, just as with Roman law with which it is intimately connected, the writing down of the pontifical rules – particularly the recording of precedents – provided the basis for the growth of a cumulative body of decisions and of a higher system of rules for interpreting them. (The consequence of an objective, and increasing, set of precedents, is the need for higher level rules for deciding between competing precedents, just as in law.) The existence of writing both increased the number of precedents that could be discovered and made necessary the formalization of the rules governing the selection and adaptation of precedents. The larger the group of precedents, the more complex these 'secondary' rules; and writing made it more difficult to suppress or forget 'outmoded' precedents, which would have happened more easily in a purely memorized system. Writing here does not so much change the basis of rule-bound argument within the college, as allow much greater sophistication and complexity – in short, the elements of a bureaucratic system of religious adminstration.[28]

Thirdly, writing made it possible to maintain a large mass of what we may term 'obsolescent religious categories', terms for religious institutions, concepts and physical objects which no longer, or perhaps

[26] Varro's eighth book was on festivals (Cardauns (ed.), *Varros Antiquitates RD*, 53-6); for fragments of Suetonius' work, see fr. 113*-123* and pp. 177-92 (Reifferscheid). Note also Th. Köves-Zulauf, 'Plinius d. Ä. und die römische Religion', *ANRW* II, 16. 1, 187-288, esp. 230-2.

[27] Livy 1, 20, 5-7. For the general character of these pontifical rules, see G. Rohde, *Die Kultsatzungen der römischen Pontifices* (*RGVV* 25, Berlin, 1936).

[28] Latte, *RRG*, 205-6 has a section in his chapter on pontifical religion headed 'Kasuistische Differenzierung', but he does not connect the use of complex argument with any concrete social processes. Search of F.P. Bremer (ed.), *Iurisprudentiae antehadrianiae quae supersunt* (Leipzig, 1896-98) reveals the names of eleven men (prior to the emperor Claudius) who as *pontifices* or even *iurisprudentes* are known to have commented in writing on the pontifical rules – that is, were in some way involved in their systematization; many others must have been involved, but did not write books. In the Principate there was a department of the imperial *familia* with responsibility for such matters (see *CIL* VI, 8878 = *ILS* 1685, with Wissowa, *RK*², 497 n.2).

never, had any general acceptance or understanding. In effect, writing offered a sovereign means of institutionalizing unintelligibility. If the *locus classicus* of unintelligible categories in Roman religion is Arnobius' famous chapter in *Adversus nationes* (*Against the Gentiles*), where he makes such devastating fun of the mumbo-jumbo of the pontifical vocabulary, by the late Republic there were numerous books on various religious topics, of which the earliest known is the commentary on the hymn of the Salii by L. Aelius Stilo Praeconus.[29] What should be stressed is that these commentaries did not remove the unintelligibility of obsolete categories or bizarre rules; they simply compounded it by pseudo-explanations, imaginary etymologies, arbitrary references to 'historical' events and energetic use of all the other weapons in the armoury of obscurantism. As for the significance of such unintelligibility, we may note the comments of Ernest Gellner: 'Unintelligibility leaves the disciple with a secret guilt of not understanding or not avowing it, or both, which binds him to the master who is both responsible for it and seems untainted by it. The belief that the naked emperor is clothed is better social cement than that a naked one is naked – or even that a clothed one is clothed.'[30] As Gellner points out in another essay, we may, by 'excessive indulgence in contextual charity' – that is, by too readily assuming that because it was 'their religion' the Romans necessarily understood it – neglect the possibility of 'social controls through the employment of absurd, ambiguous, inconsistent or unintelligible doctrines' (or, we may add, institutions or practices).[31]

Yet another contribution of literacy to the development of Roman religion can be found in the new possibilities opened up for 'primitive intellectuals'. All so-called traditional societies produce individuals whose self-appointed task it is to think through religious difficulties or to construct their own cosmologies. In the absence of writing, however, their thoughts are doomed to perish except insofar as individual scraps are appropriated into the generally accepted body of religious meaning. But their historical origin in an individual's thought is then

[29] Arnobius, *Adv. Nat.* 7, 24. See Varro's comments on the learnedness of Stilo – *Ling.* 7, 2. In the first century we know of several similar (non-legal) attempts to write on such specifically religious topics. Note, for example, Granius Flaccus, *De Indigitamentis* (*On Religious Formulae*), *De Ritu Sacrorum* (*On Ritual*), *De Sacerdotibus* (*On Priests*); Gavius Bassus, *De Diis* (*on Gods*); Cornificius Longus, *De Etymis Deorum* (*On the Derivation of the Names of the Gods*); C. Iulius Hyginus, *De Diis Penatibus* (*On Household Gods*), *De Proprietatibus Deorum* (*On the Characteristics of the Gods*). For further details, see Rawson, *Intellectual Life*, esp. 298-316.
[30] Gellner, 'Is belief really necessary?', 55.
[31] 'Concepts and society', in *Cause and Meaning in the Social Sciences* (London, 1973), 39. I do not intend to imply that there were not other important social pressures involved in the evolution of legal rules; see, especially, R. Bauman, *Lawyers in Roman Republican Politics: a study of the Roman jurists 316-82 BC* (Münchener Beiträger 75, Munich, 1983).

lost for ever. In the absence of literacy, this process of absorption of new thinking is unproblematic and unselfconscious, but its long-term effect is to permit a religious system slowly to change, to remain adequate to the cognitive and interpretative demands made upon the system by the members of the society. Literacy provides remarkable opportunities to such people (Hesiod is an excellent example, in Archaic Greece), not only in saving their thoughts from erosion but in permitting a higher degree of systematization and consistency in their thinking.[32] But this advantage for the individuals is more problematic for the system as a whole, and tends to lead directly to mere reduplication of separate systems of thought which can only be coped with by a process of what we might call 'anarchic syncretism': 'Where all ideas are composible, where anything goes and can be joined with anything else, no exchange, or replacement, no progress will arise: at best, an amorphous accretion, an unselective and uncritical syncretism'.[33] The social production of full-time intellectual specialists which literacy makes possible may be directly contrary to the long-term interests of the religious system even while individual systems of thinking may reach new levels of sophistication (and thus modern approval). The system may be faced with an increasingly large number of unassimilable interpretations, which leads to cognitive despair and hence the demotion of the system as a source of authoritative collective meanings. If it survives, it does so more as cultural quotation, as 'tradition', than as a cognitive system. The intellectual specialists of course imagine they are being helpful: Varro, believing Roman religion to have lost numerous traditional deities 'not by enemy invasion but by the citizens' neglect', actually hoped that his *Antiquitates* would be the contemporary equivalent of Aeneas' saving of the Trojan gods or Caecilius Metellus' rescue in 241 BC of the sacred objects from the temple of Vesta in the Forum.[34] But the erosion of the cognitive adequacy of the system that stems from this intellectual activity encourages rather the growth of specialist, 'pragmatic' cults (especially healing cults), and then the emergence of a sharp gulf between the religious beliefs of the élite and the mass of the illiterate population.

It is of course extremely difficult to separate the effects of literacy

---

[32] cf. Goody, *Domestication of the Savage Mind*, ch. 5. An example from Rome might be the cosmogony elaborated by M. Valerius Messalla Rufus (cos. 53 BC), 55 years an augur (see Macrobius, *Sat.* 1, 9, 14).

[33] Gellner, 'Is belief really necessary?', 54. One thinks, in the case of Rome, of Nigidius Figulus; see now D. Liuzzi (ed.), *Nigidio Figulo, astrologo e mago* (Lecce, 1983), esp. the fragments of his *De Diis (On Gods)*, from at least nineteen books.

[34] See Varro, *RD*, fr. 2a and 12. Cf. C. Koch, 'Der altrömische Staatskult im Spiegel augusteischer und spätrepublikanischer Apologetik', in *Religio* (Nuremburg, 1960), 176-204, esp. 199-200; Rawson, *Intellectual Life*, 312-13; Cardauns (ed.), *Varros Antiquitates RD*, 94-6.

from the effects of other social changes which have historically accompanied it. That is certainly the case in the Roman Republic. But we may at least argue that the appropriation by the Roman élite of control over the religious system – not merely the obvious control, which existed from earliest times, over the detailed rules of ritual, but control over the major emphases of the system and over the sorts of meanings it was able to generate – was enormously furthered by the development of literacy among that élite and its application as a technique to aspects of the religious system. In itself, the technique of writing might have led to a greater openness, and indeed to some extent that did happen;[35] but it also provided the means for further mystification and appropriation. The process can be understood as one which transformed an originally common cognitive project into an essentially arbitrary set of rules whose primary effect was to perpetuate élite control over the system. In short, the growing significance of writing in Roman religion was one of the most important means of turning that religion into ideology, into a means of maintaining the social domination of the élite. But there were other means too of achieving this end.

Religion and ideology

The process of Roman expansion under the Republic produced a familiar series of social changes, above all the extraordinary increase in the scale of wealth and power controlled by the élite organized in the Senate and equestrian orders. The unstable competitive ethic of this élite, especially the senatorial élite, led directly to an insatiable demand for additional resources once the critical destabilization of the Hannibalic war (218-292 BC) had taken place. This more or less uncontrolled imperialism led in turn to class, or quasi-class, formation. 'While the social strength of values in simple societies lacking great concentrations of power will usually rest on value commitment, in

---

[35] The classic examples of writing and publication being perceived as a step towards openness are Papirius' publication of the laws of the kings at the time of Tarquinius Superbus, the codification and publication of law in the XII tables in the early years of the Republic and Cn. Flavius' publication in the fourth century both of the correct legal formulae for bringing a case and of the calendar (which marked the days on which an action could be brought) – see H.F. Jolowicz and B. Nicholas, *Historical Introduction to the Study of Roman Law*³ (Cambridge, 1972) 13; 86 n. 2; 91 and A. Watson, 'Roman private law and the *Leges Regiae*', *JRS* 62 (1972), 100-5, esp. 103-4. But it is a recurrent theme in the record of the early history of Rome – see Livy 1, 32, 2 on the 'publication' by Ancus Marcius (the fourth king of Rome) of Numa's commentaries on religious rites (destroyed, according to the tradition, and later re-copied by Papirius). These stories correspond to the ideal of an integrated society which shares religious and other values. The opposite, 'political' project is legitimated by the famous story of the burning of Numa's secret books by the urban praetor Q. Petillius Spurinus in 181 BC (see, for example, Livy 40, 29, 9-14); religious knowledge is dangerous and must be controlled, especially when written.

modern societies, rich in institutions, institutional power, rather than
disembodied commitment, becomes of paramount importance.'[36] While
of course late Republican or early Imperial Rome was not a 'modern
society', it was certainly not 'simple': indeed, one of the theoretical
reasons for studying such an empire is the encouragement it offers us
to create special 'intermediate' models replacing the insidious
bipolarity of the dichotomy 'archaic' versus 'modern'. At any rate, one
interesting feature of the middle and late Republic is its development
of ideological representations whose function was to sublimate the
interests of the dominant land-owning élite (above all as organized
institutionally in the senate) into a justificatory set of ideals.[37] It was
precisely the rapidity and the scale of the transformation of Roman
society which created the need for such ideological representations, as
the socially-distorting effects of uncontrolled imperialism traced
themselves not merely upon the peasantry but upon the élite itself.

The main role of a legitimating ideology is not primarily as a mask
consciously employed to deceive social subordinates, even if we can
find traces of such an attitude in relation to religion in the Republic.[38]
Rather ideology acts as an 'unconscious veil distorting the image of
social reality within [a] class and sublimating its interest basis'.[39] The
familiar rhetoric of divinely-sanctioned imperialism summarized in
Horace's Roman Odes and in Vergil's *Aeneid* Book 8 is an obviously
relevant ideological production, since it served to re-present, in the
guise of fate and piety, a social fact – that is, imperialism – driven by
entirely different social forces. Those real-world forces themselves
inexorably threatened the ideological veil which concealed them, when
they produced the intestine savagery of the civil wars of the first
century BC. But the civil wars themselves were in turn veiled,

[36] Merquior, *Veil and Mask*, 24.

[37] 'Ideological thinking is always *sectional*; it is to be predicated of groups (mainly
classes), not of society as a whole' (Merquior, *Veil and Mask*, 34).

[38] e.g. Varro, *RD* fr. 20; 21; 22; Cicero. *Nat. D.* fr. 1; *Dom.* 1, 1-2; cf. H.W. Attridge, 'The
philosophical critique of religion under the early empire', *ANRW* II, 16. 1, 45-78, esp. 46-12.
9-11, but it is generally confused with the question of élite belief in the late Republic. For
me, the production, both in Greece and in the later Republic, of a two-tiered (at least)
religious system, with 'intellectuals' (i.e. self-selected members of the civic élites)
distancing themselves from 'normal' practice of civic or traditional religion, is an excellent
example of the 'veil' at work. The 'intellectuals' perceive the impossibility of defending
'normal' religion, but produce as an alternative a more sophisticated version of the same
basic system, which is much less challengeable (cf. N. Denyer, 'The case against divination:
an examination of Cicero's *De Divinatione*', *PCPhS* n.s. 31 (1985), 1-10) – but still perfectly
appropriate to their interests as members of an élite. It is also true, and interesting, that
the intellectuals generally adopt such critical positions in only one of their roles: 'It is of the
essence of social roles that they never demand total involvement by the actors, but only
segmental and partial involvement' (A. Gouldner, *For Sociology: renewal and critique in
sociology today* (London, 1973), 210).

[39] Merquior, *Veil and Mask*, 24-34

understood as the punishment of the Romans through their greed for excessive wealth, indifference to natural limitations or boundaries, lack of piety towards the gods. The central cause, the competitive ethic of the élite, could not be admitted.[40] In effect, the response to the civil war was simply the inverse of the earlier ideological representation of imperial success, and in no sense a breaking through the veil.

One of the characteristic features of the Roman religious system is the effort expended, partly in writing, to fix its forms and usages. The Roman élite came to pride itself on its 'absurd' readiness to repeat ceremonies *ad infinitum* until the performance should be entirely free from fault. Careful record was made of priests forced to quit because they had neglected the rites; one, Q. Sulpicius, because his hat fell off while he was sacrificing.[41] The justification is made clear by Valerius Maximus: 'For our state has always considered that everything should be secondary to *religio*.'[42] Consciousness that the suppliers of sacrificial animals and other 'invisible' interested parties might make thereby untoward profits was not permitted to outweigh the value of sticking rigidly to the rules.[43] This attachment to forms is usually taken as a characteristic of Roman religion from the beginning, and then made into a token of sincerity of belief and commitment. Rather, the attention devoted to formal ritual should be understood as exemplary of a much more extensively operative social good in Roman society, action inspired by pure respect for the customs and conventions recognized by the social group.[44] Even in a period when attention to forms was under threat because of changed life-styles, the appearance of 'greed' and of naked self-interest, one area more than any other could be made to express the attention ideally lavished upon the presentation of social forms. Religious action, and above all sacrifice, could be made into aesthetic action, action for itself, free of self interest. In other words, formulaic religious action represented the pure accumulation of 'symbolic capital'. 'Wealth, the ultimate basis of power, can exert power, and exert it durably, only in the form of symbolic capital; in other words, economic capital can be accumulated only in the form of symbolic capital, the unrecognizable, and hence

---

[40] See P. Jal, 'Les dieux et les guerres civiles dans la Rome de la fin de la République', *REL* 40 (1962), 170-200.

[41] Valerius Maximus 1, 4-5, with various incidents. On the rules, see J. Scheid, 'Le délit religieux dans la Rome tardo-républicaine', in *Le délit religieux dans la cité antique* (CEFR 48, Rome, 1981), esp. 121-6.

[42] 1, 1, 9.

[43] See, for example, the interesting account of Dio 60, 6, 4-5 (AD 41): fraud and accident meant that even as many as ten repetitions were sometimes necessary, 'generally by those who benefited from these repetitions'. So Claudius had a law passed to shorten the *ludi* to one day only, which in practice prevented repetition.

[44] Bourdieu, *Outline*, 194.

socially recognizable, form of the other kinds of capital.'[45] The sacerdotal colleges of Rome can be seen as the guardians of the alchemical transmutation of base wealth into inexhaustible prestige, through the insistence upon the minutely exact performance of forms; and part of the ideological value of the religious system to the élite can be seen as its being the purest case of this 'disinterested' action.

Priesthood and magistracy: the civic compromise

There is no reason to halt the analysis here. The notion of symbolic capital can help us to recognize the ideological importance of two other important features of religious action, not merely in the Roman Republic but also more generally in the Hellenistic and Imperial periods. The first feature is the association between priesthood and generosity. Generosity, institutionalized in the various forms of 'voluntary' payments (*summa honoraria*), in practice obligatory for priests on election, should be seen primarily neither as redistribution nor as social insurance.[46] Rather, generosity is one of the most subtle means of maintaining lasting asymmetrical relationships between social unequals. The priest or magistrate, in principle a member of a central or provincial élite group, obtains what is for the most part a symbolic good (the priesthood). In return he (or she) dispossesses him/herself of frequently enormous amounts of real goods, including the provision of games, feasts, monetary distributions and dispensations of oil or wine, help to the poor or orphaned, the construction of useful or prestigious civic buildings.[47] What he or she finally accumulates, however, is symbolic capital, the most durable form of wealth, in the form of 'obligation, gratitude, prestige, personal loyalty'.[48] The civic magistracy of the Graeco-Roman world, of which priesthood is a sub-class, should be understood as a routinized system for the creation of symbolic capital in a context in which the modern means of institutionalizing such capital, above all through education systems, the art market in all its international forms, and the entertainment industry were developed to only a very limited degree (but nevertheless clearly present). On the other hand, the élites of the

---

[45] *Outline*, 195. Bourdieu has since ceased to employ the notion of 'symbolic capital', but it serves my purpose here quite adequately.

[46] Redistribution: Debord, *Aspects sociaux*, 74; 346, n. 205. Social insurance: Broughton, Roman Asia Minor', esp. 810-12. In other words I subscribe to a version of P. Veyne's 'political' argument (*Le pain et le cirque* (Paris, 1976), 298-327).

[47] A.R. Hands, *Charities and Social Aid in Greece and Rome* (London 1968), 62-115; cf. Bourdieu, *Outline*, 189: 'The greater the extent to which the task of reproducing the relations of domination is taken over by objective mechanisms, which serve the interest of the dominant group without any conscious effort on the latter's part, the more indirect and, in a sense, impersonal become the strategies objectively oriented towards reproduction.'

[48] Bourdieu, *Outline*, 192.

Empire did not have to maintain their domination by a constant personal effort of creating or restoring social relations, as they would have had to do in a simpler society. The maintenance of domination could be achieved by discontinuous and routinized means, above all by the holding of public office.

The second feature of Graeco-Roman religious systems of interest in connection with accumulation of symbolic capital is the elusive relationship between civic and religious office. No single formulation of this can be satisfactory; but it can be illustrated by reference to two insignificant but telling mythical incidents. The first concerns the history of Athens under its early kings, and in particular the hero Boutes, the ancestor of the aristocratic family of Eteoboutadae which provided the hereditary priests of Poseidon-Erechtheus. A version known to Hesiod named Boutes as a son of Poseidon; but once the historiographers got to work he was made the son of King Pandion and brother of Erechtheus. Apollodorus continues the story: 'When Pandion died, his sons divided their father's inheritance between them, and Erechtheus got the throne (*basileia*) and Boutes got the priesthood of Athena and Poseidon-Erechtheus.'[49] On the one hand, the elder brother obtains the kingship; but the longer lasting and more prestigious post – surviving for centuries when the kingship was merely a memory of the remote past – turns out to be the priesthood.

The second illustration has already been alluded to: the ambiguous relationship between Romulus and Numa, which with regard to religion is presented now as one of polarity, now as that between a whole entity and its supplement. Livy, in keeping with the first view, makes Romulus the founder of the political system of Rome and the begetter of its military tradition; Numa is the effective organizer of the religious system.[50] Dionysius, however, while insisting that Numa did not alter any of the religious institutions of Romulus, who 'established the principal rites of (Roman) religion', saw his work as one of adding 'whatever he thought had been overlooked by Romulus, consecrating many shrines to gods who had not yet received honours, setting up numerous altars and temples, founding festivals for each of them, appointing priests to take care of them and making rules for rituals and cult, purifications and very many other ceremonies and honours, such as no Greek or barbarian city has, even those who have now or in the past plumed themselves most upon their piety'.[51] As so often, the

---

[49] See Plutarch, *X Orat.* 7, 843 b-c; Hesiod, fr. 223 (Merkelbach-West); Apollodorus 3, 15, 1.

[50] Most explicitly, Livy 1, 21,6; cf. 1, 10, 1-11, 4; 15, 6-8; 17, 4; 19, 1-2; 21, 1-2.

[51] Dionysius of Halicarnassus, *Ant. Rom.* 2, 23, 6; 2, 63, 2. For the emphasis on the role of Romulus in Dionysius, see C.J. Classen, 'Romulus in der römischen Republik', *Philologus* 106 (1962), 174-204, esp. 192-6.

supplement bids fair to overwhelm the original; but the point to stress here is the manner in which this uncertainty over the founding facts of Rome replicates a deeper, non-trivial uncertainty over the place of religion, and priesthood, in the Roman scheme of things. Is it religion which is really distinctive of Rome; or its military power?

The crucial point about the Roman (and Greek) distinction between civic magistracy and priesthood is its elusiveness, the sheer impossibility of definitional clarity. The fate of any attempt to impose clarity is illustrated by the following quotation: 'In the senate, just as in all public affairs, separation in priestly and political functions was carefully maintained, although the line of separation was merely a legal technicality if and when the senator or the magistrate was a priest. The fact that most priests were members of the senate by virtue of political magistracies created the conditions in which priestly prestige and senatorial pre-eminence were interwoven.'[52] It has been generally agreed that Roman priests were not magistrates; yet they wore the same robe, the *toga praetexta*, during the performance of their functions; the *pontifices* had extensive powers of interference in private lives; and augurs had the right to cause the discontinuation of public business. Priesthood had, as it were, plagiarized the rules for magistracy.[53] Inversely, it is not difficult to find evidence that priesthoods were conceived in a purely instrumental manner: throughout the Principate, as in the Republic, the Senate, or sometimes the emperor alone, took final decisions with or without the advice of the priestly colleges on matters of religious concern; Pliny the Younger, writing to Trajan in AD 101-2 to ask for preferment to one of the colleges, treats them as though they were exactly like other desirable political fruits; Cicero refers blatantly to the good sense of the *maiores* (ancestors) 'in choosing the most distinguished men for sacerdotal office' to provide ballast for the ship of state.[54] Yet special rules remained to make priests different: they had to be and to remain unmaimed; augurs could not lose their power of augury, even if they were stripped of membership of the college; Augustus, at the funeral of M. Agrippa, and Tiberius at Drusus' funeral, as pontifices were not allowed to see the corpse, and delivered the *elogium* (funeral oration) separated from the corpse by a hanging.[55]

[52] G.J. Szemler, *Priests of the Roman Republic*, 58; cf. Scheid, 'Prêtre', 268-9.

[53] Bleicken, 'Oberpontifex und Pontifikalkollegium'; while Scheid, 'Prêtre', 248-66 re-emphasises the well-known fact that not all priests on cooptation were even senators.

[54] On decision-making on religious matters in the Principate, see F. Millar, *The Emperor in the Roman World* (London, 1977), 355-61; Pliny's requests, *Ep*. 2, 1, 8; 4, 8; 10, 13; Hoffman Lewis, *Official Priests*, 14-16 (on the practice of election). For the 'good sense' (*consilium*) of the *maiores*, see Cicero, *Dom*. 1, 1, 2.

[55] Unmaimed: Dionysus of Halicarnassus, *Ant. Rom*. 2, 21, 3; augural powers: Plutarch, *Quaest. Rom*. 99. There is conflicting evidence on the precise details of pontifical purity in relation to corpses. Dio, describing Agrippa's funeral (54, 28, 2-5), cannot understand the

There is a thorough muddle then (and the muddle in the Greek world is even more complete). But it is a muddle with a purpose. The indeterminacy can be linked with the process of ideological domination. On the one hand, the religious system must be represented as an autonomous set of rules, issuing from the past and empirically competent to maintain proper relations with the gods. Neither the set of divinities to whom cult was offered by the state nor the rules under which they were placated could be admitted to be produced directly by a socially-interested dominant group under its own authority. The objectivity, the otherness, of the rules which constitute religion was at least partly guaranteed by the existence of a separate priesthood. At Rome, the type of the priest was the priest of Jupiter, the *flamen Dialis*, who epitomized the ideal separateness of the world of religion from the world of politics and the struggle for power. The more outlandish the rules which separated him, and his wife, from the world (lovingly detailed in the second century AD by Aulus Gellius), the more perfectly the objective existence of the religious rules, and, further back, the divinities they conjure into existence, was confirmed.[56] On the other hand, the ideological benefits of the religious system, above all its exemplification of the purest forms of disinterested action, could not be obtained if there were not close links between the 'executive' (the élite in active politics) and priesthood.

Historically, whether in fact or fiction, what we may call the Graeco-Roman 'civic compromise' – the lack of clear distinction between magistracy and priesthood – derived from the victory in the early Archaic period in Greece and in Rome of the aristocracy over the kings and the absorption by the aristocracy of the kings' religious offices and functions. At the end of a long political evolution, the 'civic compromise' produced its logical culmination, the Roman emperor. The *princeps* fused permanent multiple magistracy with permanent multiple priesthood. He poured out wealth in return for these symbolic goods. And so he accumulated the kind of symbolic capital that only gods, perpetual givers and perpetual receivers, could aspire to.

*

My argument, then, is that priesthood is by no means as invisible in the late Republic as is normally supposed. The prominence of

presence of a hanging between Augustus and the corpse; presumably the rule did not still apply in his day. It seems most likely that *pontifices* were forbidden to see (Dio 54, 35, 4; Seneca, *Ad Marc*. 15, 3) and so, *a fortiori*, to touch (Dio 56, 31, 3) corpses. A similar rule seems to have applied to augurs (Tacitus, *Ann*. 1, 62).

[56] Aulus Gellius, *NA* 10, 15; Plutarch, *Quaest. Rom*. 40. See also Pötscher, 'Flamen Dialis'; Boels, 'Flaminica Dialis'.

priesthood (the sacerdotal colleges) can be understood in two complementary contexts, both of which concern the process of transforming Roman religion into a component of a larger ideological structure which directly served the interests of the ruling élite. At the conscious level, it is plain that (1) priesthood was of intellectual value in the process – a lengthy one – of the appropriation of the religious system by the group most interested in perpetuating it; (2) it was understood to be one of the guarantors of the changelessness and permanence of the 'essence' of Rome conceived as fixed right from the early days of the kings; (3) it was represented as a special form of disinterested authority in the factional conflict of the civil war. The cumulation by Octavian/Augustus of membership in all four of the *amplissima collegia* ('most distinguished colleges') should be seen as motivated, in a quite unspecific way, by all these considerations. But there were also less conscious, less 'mask-like', ideological pressures at work. If we place the transition from Republic to Principate in historical context, it becomes plausible to argue that the inclusion among his roles by the *princeps* of membership in the colleges was a logical consequence of a process of 'veiling', whereby the élite concealed from itself the reality of its domination. The crucial consideration is that of symbolic capital, built up both by the particular form of Graeco-Roman priesthood, which involved prestation on a massive scale, and by an increasingly mystified, but of course wholly objective, system of religious rules and practices.

8

The Veil of Power:
emperors, sacrificers and benefactors

The life of the Roman Empire in the first two centuries AD depended very heavily, both at the local and at the imperial level, on the expectation of generosity to the community by individual members of the élite; this phenomenon of civic life is today called 'euergetism', after the figure of the *euergetês*, the benefactor. We know the system best from the Greek-speaking cities of the eastern half of the Empire, where the tradition was well-established within the Hellenistic kingdoms set up by the successors of Alexander the Great. When the Romans arrived, they established at first only a very loose protectorate of the area; city institutions were left much as they had been and continued to provide the basis of the administrative system. But euergetism, whether or not specifically Greek, was not by any means confined to the East: the Emperor himself, the members of the Roman senate and the local men of power in their own cities over the whole empire – all were expected to spend money for the welfare of their fellow citizens, on the financing of building projects, on paying for elaborate festivals or games, or on providing benefits for their poorer fellow-citizens. Their achievements are recorded and honoured in inscriptions put up in their thousands throughout the Mediterranean world and the results of their donations are still to be seen in the remains of public buildings, temples and aqueducts in all the provinces of the Empire. This aspect of ancient life has received a great deal of attention from historians in recent years, notably in Paul Veyne's *Le pain et le cirque* (1976).

In the second of his three chapters, Gordon argues that we should see a precise association between the practice of euergetism and the position of sacrificer or priest. So the most familiar presentation of the emperor as sacrificer, from which this study begins, provides a key image: disseminated throughout the Roman world, it almost appropriated for the emperor the central ritual act of pagan religion, but at the same time evoked the *euergetês*. It thus provided for the citizens of the empire a summary or model of two of the most powerful influences for creating coherence of outlook and practice. It is a remarkable fact that the Romans contrived during this period to maintain peace and unity through most of Europe, North Africa and the Near East, at a period when communications were slow and dangerous, without creating any kind of elaborate administrative structure and without any considerable military presence, except on the frontier zones. To understand how that happened, we have to look not to military or administrative forms only, but to the common interests and ideas shared by Roman aristocrats and the local notables, who kept the cities working and collected the taxes to send to Rome. Gordon's account of priesthood is to be understood in the context of this complicity.

The Veil of Power:
emperors, sacrificers and benefactors
Richard Gordon

To construct a history of religion in the Roman Empire is a well-nigh impossible task: there are topics but no subject, quantities of information but little sense to be made of it. The difficulties that beset the historian of the religion of archaic and classical Greece reappear, still more intractable. One of the reasons for this is the assumption that the proper study of the history of religions is divinity and beliefs about divinity: and no one has ever succeeded in counting the number of divinities worshipped in the Roman Empire. A book dedicated to the study of priesthood in the ancient world provides an excellent opportunity to move away from divinities towards fundamental institutions of the religious system, above all the practice of sacrifice, and the group which controlled public sacrifice, the emperor and the élites, both in the centre and in each locality. Sacrifice was a 'natural' institution in the ancient world, but that does not mean that it has no history or that its relation to the political order did not change.

To study only those who received some sort of title of priesthood – *hiereus, neokoros, kosmeteira, pontifex, praefectus sacrorum, flamen, antistes, sacerdos*, and many more – would be to miss the point, since one of the bases of the Graeco-Roman system was to link official titles of priesthood with social status on the one hand, and with civic magistracy on the other. Like the spelling of words in English, these titles tell one something of the history of each community in the empire, but little else. The system as a whole can be understood only by tracing the relationship between the *princeps*, the crucial figure in the centre, and those in Rome and in the provinces who found in him support for their own social and political status. Of course the Roman Empire was not in the ordinary sense a society, rather a congeries of settlements only loosely integrated with one another. In such circumstances, most of the links they had with each other and with the centre were symbolic, above all religious. But these religious links were at the same time an essential part of the domination enjoyed by the élites of the empire.

This paper considers first the sacrificial or 'priestly' role of the *princeps*, starting from the visual representations of sacrifice on major monuments of 'official' Roman art. It argues that the emperor's sacrificial role cannot be divorced from his role as benefactor or

Fig. 21. Sacrificial relief from the passage through Trajan's Arch at Beneventum (South Italy), dedicated in AD 114. Trajan himself is on the right of the altar, his head covered and wearing a wreath.

euergete on a massive scale; but rather that these roles *together* (and I stress *together*) provided a model for the élite more generally, both in Rome and in the provinces. The second part of the paper focusses particularly on the élite itself. It explores the nature of the 'civic compromise' – that is the failure within traditional Graeco-Roman cult to differentiate sharply between magistracy and priesthood; and it suggests that this refusal is not just a curious 'fact' about the Roman system but a central mode of domination.

The emperor as priest and sacrificer

On the left of the archway of Trajan's Arch at Beneventum (modern Benevento, in South Italy), dedicated by the Senate in AD 114 to Trajan as *pontifex maximus*, is set a relief representing an ordinary sacrificial scene (Fig. 21).[1] Trajan is shown with his toga partly draped over his head (*capite velato*) – the iconographical mark of a sacrificant presiding over a specifically Roman ritual[2] – and wearing a wreath. He pours an offering, probably of wine, onto a small, flaming, portable altar. The offering-dish, the *patera*, is lost, but would have largely concealed one

[1] Ryberg, *Rites*, 154-6; pl. LV, fig. 83. Note also the commentary by E. Simon, *Die Götter am Trajansbogen zu Benevent* (Trierer Winckelmannsprogramm 1, Mainz, 1981) pl. IV, 2, with the full photographic record of M. Rotili, *L'arco di Traiano a Benevento* (Rome, 1972).
[2] For the use of *caput velare* as a technical term in relation to sacrifice, see H. Freier, *Caput Velare* (Diss. Tübingen, 1966), 26-9.

of the two assistants, *camilli*, who carries a small box, *acerra*, from which the chief sacrificant took the incense which was also burnt on the altar prior to the actual killing of the victim. The insignificant *camilli* are placed at the very centre of the relief, with the altar, the principal mediatory point between this world and the other world, slightly off-centre to the right. Had the offering-dish survived, it would have directed the eyes of a spectator to that point, and so up the arm of the chief sacrificant (Trajan) to his face. One would then become aware that all the wreathed, toga-clad participants in the sacrifice in the centre are looking right, towards the emperor. The emperor himself, together with a small number of participants immediately behind him, is looking somewhere to the observer's left, in such a way as to direct attention, finally, towards the victim. The victim's forequarters have been crammed behind the bulky figure of the *Genius* of the senate and it is surrounded by *victimarii*, whose task it was to manage the victim during the ritual. One of these kneels to twist the animal's head down and round so as to expose the nape of the neck to the stunning axe; another raises his axe for the kill. The status of the *victimarii* as public slaves is indicated by the fact that they are naked to the waist, thus contrasting sharply with the emphatic 'togation' of their social superiors clustered around the emperor. Behind loom the *fasces* (bundles of rods), signs of legitimate authority within the state.

A very ordinary sacrificial scene, then. Its banality is what should interest us, its naturalization of numerous ideological assumptions. In the present connection, two are of particular interest. First, the relief presents what at first glance looks like a coherent, lifelike image: the passionate attention to details, the curls of the hair, the leaves of the wreaths, the triple cutting-knives in their sheaths on the waist-bands of the *victimarii*, the metallic legs of the tripod ending in lion's claws – all help to sustain this first impression. But on inspection it turns out that the relief represents a highly coded narrative of an ideal-typical event.[3] No real historical event could possibly bear more than a faint similarity to this one. Such a partial narrative is forced, by sheer limitation of space, into making choices. And choices reveal values. The main emphasis here is not upon the ostensible theme, the offering of a victim to the gods, but upon the sacrificant, the emperor. An original iconographic scheme which, so far as our evidence goes, did indeed concentrate upon the death of the animal (or rather upon the moment before it was stunned: a point of dramatic silence) has been abbreviated, resumed, in order to concentrate upon a present political fact, the sacrificial role of the *princeps*.

---

[3] This is intended as a partial disagreement with the opinion, powerfully argued by Scott Ryberg in her justly famous *Rites of State Religion*, and now commonplace, that Roman historical reliefs constitute an extreme form of documentary realism.

Fig. 22. Two coins illustrating the theme of the emperor's piety in sacrifice. On the left a gold coin of Hadrian (BMC, III, 337:776, 134-8 AD) shows the emperor pouring a libation over a tripod, while the victim is slaughtered on the left. On the right a bronze coin of Marcus Aurelius (BMC, IV.1, 619:1400, 170-1 AD) shows a similar scene, but the victim itself is now barely visible slumped behind the tripod (see p. 205).

Secondly, the relief fuses representations of two different constituents of the series of actions we refer to as 'sacrifice', which did not in fact occur at the same time: the preliminary offering by the chief sacrificant, which is allocated a great deal of space and visual interest; and a sort of non-event or hiatus, the moment before the hammer or axe was brought down onto the cervical vertebrae, the victim fell partly paralysed and the carotids were opened with the *cultres* (knives), here safely in their sheaths. In effect, what we might have thought to be *the* meaning or emphasis of Roman state sacrifice, communication with the other world through the death of a victim, has been elided. Moreover, this scene-type is the closest approach of Roman iconographical convention to the moment of death. Usually, the animal is represented led in procession, though the sacrificant is already at work over the altar.[4] Only one surviving official relief shows the dead victim with its liver being cut out for inspection by the *haruspices*, although this was one of the principal overt purposes of state sacrifice (Fig. 4). No representation at all shows the ritual consumption of the *exta* (the noble internal organs) by the participant members of the sacerdotal colleges.

We should conclude from these points that Roman official 'sacrificial reliefs' are only about sacrifice in a very peculiar sense. They allude to a familiar public event in a schematic fashion which enables them to

---

[4] Brendel, 'Immolatio', 196-7

highlight the role of the sacrificant, not the communicative function of the ceremony (as earlier Greek reliefs had done, and even one or two Roman imitations in the Republic).[5] And taken as a whole, one of the peculiarities of Roman sacrificial iconography is the massive domination of the emperor. In actuality, there must have been very large numbers of official sacrifices of one sort or another performed by magistrates, especially consuls, ordinary and suffect, by the Arval Brethren, by provincial governors, by army and legionary commanders, which were not even notionally conducted by the emperor. But one would not suspect this from the iconographic record.[6] The only Italian reliefs showing sacrificial scenes without the emperor are those set up by *vicomagistri* (ward-officials) and *VIviri Augustales* (local officials concerned with the cult of the emperor), that is, essentially by freedman aping their social superiors.[7] And the ideal monopoly by emperors of sacrificial iconography is confirmed by the coin-series, beginning with Trajan, but particularly important in the reigns of Antoninus Pius and Marcus Aurelius, which make use of the *immolatio boum* stereotype in connection with the legend VOTA PUBLICA, referring to the discharge by the emperor of a past undertaking to make a votive offering in the public interest.[8] These coins, being forced to make even more stringent choices than reliefs, frequently limit the sacrifical scene still further, showing the emperor, alone, offering the preliminary libation, and with a minute victim slumped obscurely in the background.[9]

[5] See Ryberg, *Rites*, 22. Characteristic of the Greek choice (which, of course, is not *normative*) are some fourth-century BC reliefs at Brauron showing the divinity/divinities on one side of the altar, the human beings on the other in procession – see, e.g., *BCH* 83 (1959) Chron. 589, fig. 26.

[6] This extraordinary dominance is fully documented by Ryberg, *Rites*. Of the few (surviving) representations of an official other than the emperor sacrificing, note the *praefectus praetorio* T. Flavius Constans, whose altar to the German goddess Vagdavercustis (*c.* AD 164) was found in Cologne (*CIL* XIII, 12057 = *ILS* 9000) – though there is no indication whatever that this is anything other than a private dedication; the city official (perhaps) shown sacrificing beside the emperor in a relief from Sabratha (Ryberg, *Rites*, 136 n. 52; G. Caputo, *Il teatro di Sabratha e l'archittetura africana* (Rome, 1959), 19-20, pl. 40, fig. 71); L. Calpurnius Piso represented in the imperial cycle at Velleia (*CIL* XI, 1182 = *ILS* 900) – though he is perceptibly smaller than the female imperial statues around him (See K.-P. Goethert, 'Zur Einheitlichkeit der Statuengruppe aus der Basilika von Velleia', *RhM* 79 (1972), 235-47, esp. 239 n. 19); and M. Julius Cottius (see n. 36 below). In addition some coins from the earliest years of the Principate depict men other than Augustus sacrificing – e.g. *BMC* I, 19, no. 97f; 76, no. 161.

[7] The best known is the altar showing the four *magistri* of the *vicus Aes(c)leti* sacrificing a bull and a boar (*CIL* VI, 30957 = Ryberg, *Rites*, 59-60; pl. XVI, fig. 30). There is a convenient list in C. Pietrangeli, 'L'ara dei Lari di Soriano nel Cimino', *BCAR* 64 (1936), 13-17, esp. 14-16.

[8] For example, Hadrian: *BMC* III, 337, no. 776; Antoninus Pius: *BMC* IV. 1, 282, no. 1745-47; Aurelius: *BMC* IV.1, 619, no. 1400-401.

[9] For the process of eliminating unnecessary elements, compare *BMC* IV, 282, no. 1745 (Antoninius Pius sacrificing out of a patera, *capite velato*, with a bull fallen by the tripod) with ibid. no. 1746 (the same, but no bull).

To be sacrificant in this type of sacrifice is not to labour. Just as the Roman élite owned slaves to perform the labour required to produce their lives of spectacular idleness, so 'sacrificing' meant to introduce the ceremony by making the preliminary offerings. To be sure, the *pontifices* had to carry a special type of knife, the *secespita*, rather like a stage dagger, which at some remote period had been used by them to free the *exta* once the animal's abdomen had been opened and the rib-cage cut through. But so far as we know it was in the historical period entirely ornamental.[10] Indeed, in what is virtually the only literary reference to it, it must have been ornamental: Tiberius, by way of droll gesture when fearful of a conspiracy, caused the *secespita*-blades of his fellow *pontifices* to be replaced with leaden ones.[11] The labour involved in sacrifice is, in the visual record, vividly performed by only muscular slaves; the social status of the sacrificant is marked by his separation from that labour.

The visual representation of public sacrifice at Rome thus summarily reproduces key aspects of the social and political system: one could hardly wish for a more direct, if unconscious, testimony to the relationship between religion and the social order. But it is the control by the *princeps* over the visual representation of sacrifice which demands our attention. Why should it be so? There is, of course, no ready made answer to this question, waiting to be plucked from the ancient sources. Although modern scholars may construct an explanation of Roman sacrifice by putting into modern words themes and associations which were almost entirely implicit and unspoken for the actors, the system itself produced no theological account of the meaning and purpose of sacrifice.[12] That certainly does not imply that it was meaningless; but it does imply that new meanings could very easily be attached to it. To a degree, sacrifice was a 'vacant sign'. And I wish to suggest that one of the important new uses of sacrificial imagery by the emperors was in response to a difficult and indeed intractable problem, the character of the relationship between the 'religion of Rome' and the 'religion of the Roman Empire'.

It is clear that one of the roles of the *princeps* as *pontifex maximus* was to safeguard the integrity and continuity of the traditional public rituals of Rome.[13] But at the same time it is obvious that by far the greater number of innovations in the ritual calendar of Rome was in

[10] For *Sescepita*, see Festus, *Gloss. Lat.* p. 472.

[11] Suetonius, *Tib.* 25, 3.

[12] For ancient intellectuals' (feeble) attempts at theorizing on the purpose of sacrifice, see W. Pötscher (ed.), *Theophrastus, peri eusebeias* (Leiden, 1964); J. Rudhardt, 'Les mythes grecs relatifs à l'instauration du sacrifice', *MH* 27 (1970), 1-15.

[13] W. Speyer, 'Das Verhältnis des Augustus zur Religion', *ANRW* II, 16. 3, 1777-805, esp. 1779-82; D. Little, 'Politics in Augustan Poetry', *ANRW* II, 30. 1, 254-370, esp. 260-71 & 277-8b.

connection with the imperial house. Our surviving early imperial calendars, to say nothing of a mid-third-century military calendar such as the *Feriale Duranum*, are full of ceremonies in honour of emperors, past and present, their wives and children, nephews and nieces, birthdays, victories, accessions to office, deaths and ascensions.[14] The artificiality of Augustus' revival made this consumption of Roman religion by imperial festivals entirely plausible. For during the last two centuries of the Republic Roman religion had increasingly depended upon the conflicts of the élite for its ability to continue to generate meanings. The removal of those conflicts by Octavian/Augustus removed the argument from religion, turning it into a naked instrument of ideological domination. And one of its ideological functions in the early Principate was to insulate Rome from the cultural consequence of her own imperialism: the religion of Rome became a guarantee not merely of her supremacy but also of her freedom from contamination by her subjects. As we shall see, the attitude of successive emperors towards the priesthoods of Rome suggests that this notion was to a degree maintained to the very end of the Principate: Rome was different from her Empire and her religion was an emblem of that difference. The so-called tolerance of the indigenous religions of the provinces is rather to be understood as a consequence of this colonial attitude.

But the historical choices made by successive emperors eroded this difference continually. Without constant repression, with all its impossible costs, the provinces had to be induced to love their servitude. If that meant above all the recruitment of local aristocracies into the central élite, it also meant the widening of the citizen base (culminating in the universal extension of citizenship to all free inhabitants of the Empire in 213-214), the army as an agent of acculturation, the mobility of shippers, craftsmen, tourists and slaves, the manipulation of their imperial masters by provincial élites, the spread of the cult of Jupiter and above all that of the emperors. All these developments meant that the desire to maintain a symbolic distance between centre and periphery was doomed to ineffectiveness. And it seems to me that the institution of sacrifice was one of the key means whereby some kind of synthesis was effected between the religion of Rome, in the narrow sense, and the religion of the Empire taken very broadly. It became a sort of code for membership in this unwieldy congeries of disparate cultures.

To a very considerable degree we are dealing with processes that were scarcely conscious, as so often with religious developments. But

---

[14] See P. Herz, 'Kaiserfeste der Prinzipatszeit', *ANRW* II, 16, 2, 1135-200. The same volume contains a reprint of the Hoey-Fink-Schneider edition of the *Feriale Duranum*: J. Helgeland, 'Roman army religion', 1481-6 (*YClS* 7 (1940), 1-222).

during the course of the Principate sacrifices by emperors seem to have lost their implication in particular rituals of the traditional religion of Rome (above all triumphs and public *vota*) and to have become symbols of a very generalized conception of 'piety' sustained by the emperors in the name not of the *Senate and People of Rome* but of the Empire as a whole. I would go further and claim that sacrifices by emperors also became paradigms or exemplars of public sacrifice throughout the empire, ideal and grandiloquent versions of the proper means of communication with the other world. There was an elective affinity between this symbolic paradigm and the real-world changes also encouraged by the imperial system, the absorption of more and more wealth by small numbers of the élite in each locality. Just as the emperor's symbolic capital was bound up with his acquisition of offices as well as his vast euergetism, so the same system, allying office to prestation, was encouraged in imitation all over the Empire: one of the interesting developments of the Principate is the restriction in fact but not in theory of office, including priesthood, to a smaller and smaller circle of gilded families in each locality. The Principate also encouraged further changes: the massive extension of cities on a Graeco-Roman model through the Empire and the corresponding religious changes; the extension of the Roman model of office-holding and priesthood to areas not controlled by cities, for example in Egypt and in the great temple-states of Asia Minor, and more generally into 'villages'; the transformation of existing native priesthoods into Graeco-Roman priests. Moreover, since these processes depended entirely upon the maintenance, and further development, of an already enormously unequal and steeply stratified society, symbolic means of integration were invaluable. The paradigmatic quality of the emperor's sacrificial activity encouraged the spontaneous demand for access to public sacrificial positions such as those of the *vicomagistri* and *VIviri Augustales*, and beyond that for access to quasi-public positions, such as priesthoods of *collegia* (local or trade associations), and in the cults of the Magna Mater and of Isis. If small numbers of the very rich in each town monopolized official sacrificial positions, the Empire was sufficiently differentiated to provide alternatives.

Diverse as it was, the Roman Empire had particular need of symbols of unity. One of the images already present in the political language of the Republic, that of the body, could be easily adapted.[15] In these terms, the emperor would represent the head, the directing intelligence of the whole body; his power and authority would be the sinews of coherence. Without him, the body is useless.[16] Connected

[15] See J. Béranger, *Recherches sur l'aspect idéologique du Principat* (Basel, 1953), 218-52.
[16] ibid., 231-6; note esp. Seneca, *Clem.* 1, 5, 1 (addressing Nero): 'animus reipublicae tuae es, illa corpus tuum' ('you are the soul of the state and the state your body').

with this imagery of unity is the idea of the emperor as affording an example to the rest of the empire, just as he was 'regulator of the world and father of the earth'.[17] It has been well observed that the title *optimus* (best) implies that the emperor had a paradigmatic role, and the clearest expression of the idea duly turns up in Pliny's Panegyric of Trajan: 'We do not need strict rule so much as an example.'[18] But the idea was already 'a regular topos in panegyric or in other writings about the *princeps*'.[19] Augustus already implies his own function as a model in *Res Gestae*: 'By introducing new laws I have reintroduced numerous traditional *exempla* which had already begun to disappear from our age, and have myself left *exempla* in many things to be handed down to our descendants'; and he is said by Suetonius to have been fully conscious of his own imitation of great men of the past and of the exemplary role of the *princeps*.[20] Velleius Paterculus, for whom the *religio* of Tiberius was an important part of his moral claim to authority, asserts: 'for the best of emperors (*princeps optimus*) teaches his fellow citizens to do right by doing so himself, and though he is the greatest in authority, he is still greater in the examples which he sets'; while Quintilian observes that it is characteristic of Romans to work by example.[21]

Augustus' revival of religion was intended to exemplify the *pietas* of his rule. One of the best illustrations of the role of example in that revival is to be found in the right-hand front panel of the Ara Pacis.[22] The scene (Fig. 23) shows the famous sacrifice at Lanuvium of the sow with the thirty piglets by Aeneas on his arrival from Sicily, and is surely intended to prefigure the main sacrifice which is represented on the two outer faces of the monument by the well-known processions of the imperial family, priests and other dignitaries. In other words, Aeneas' sacrifice is the type of Roman sacrifice. And there are excellent reasons for thinking so. Aeneas, a Trojan, is represented as wearing a

[17] Martial, 7, 7, 5 (AD 92); cf. 9, 6, 1. On this theme in general, see J. Vogt, *Orbis Romanus: zur Terminologie des römischen Imperialismus* (Philosophie und Geschichte 22, Tübingen, 1929), 18-22.

[18] *Pan.* 45, 6, with the entire section; also Ovid, *Met.* 15, 833-4 and *Fast.* 6, 647-8. Seneca, *Clem.* 2, 2, 1 offers the idea of the diffusion of the quality of *mansuetudo* throughout the Empire thanks to the display of it. For *optimus* implying example, Ch. Wirszubski, *Libertas as a political idea at Rome during the late Republic and early Principate* (Cambridge, 1950), 153-4.

[19] A. Woodman (ed.), *Velleius Paterculus, The Tiberian narrative (2, 94-131)* (Cambridge, 1977), 245.

[20] *Res Gestae* 2, 12-13. See also Suetonius, *Aug.* 31, 5 and 89 (one of his most boring habits, no doubt).

[21] Velleius Paterculus 2, 126, 5; Quintilian 12, 2, 30.

[22] The best brief discussion is Simon, *Ara Pacis.* For the whole complex of buildings around Augustus' massive sundial, of which the Ara Pacis was a part, see E. Buchner, *Die Sonnenuhr des Augustus* (Mainz, 1982) and (for a brief English discussion) N. Horsfall, 'Augustus' sundial: architecture, astronomy and propaganda', *Omnibus* 9 (1985), 5-7.

Fig. 23. Relief panel from the Augustan Altar of Peace (Ara Pacis) in Rome; see also Fig. 1. The scene depicted is Aeneas' sacrifice on landing in Italy. Aeneas, on the right, holds his hand out over an altar of turfs, now partly damaged. At the bottom left is the sow to be sacrificed.

toga without a tunic, which corresponds to the oldest form of Roman dress, and *capite velato*, the specifically Roman (and perhaps Etruscan) mark of a sacrificant, clearly distinct from the Greek style of sacrifice, with head bare.[23] The lance in his left arm denotes high social status, and is one among several allusions to Augustus himself. The most important of these is the illustration in the top left-hand corner of a small temple, showing two male gods sitting on thrones. These are generally identified with the household gods of Aeneas, which he saved from Troy; and so it can plausibly be linked with the occasion of the erection of the Ara Pacis – that is the celebration of Augustus' return home from abroad, to his own household gods. Finally, the sacrificial activity of *pius* Aeneas (who followed the sow faithfully, even when she stopped in a most unpromising spot) exemplifies the piety of the Roman sacrificant, Augustus above all.

[23] Oldest form of Roman dress: Aulus Gellius, *NA* 6, 12. Opposition between Roman and Greek styles of sacrificing: Festus, *Gloss. Lat.* pp. 431-2; 462; Macrobius, *Sat.* 1, 8, 2. For the adoption of sacrifice *Graeco ritu* at Rome, see, for example, the coins commemorating Domitian's Secular Games (AD 88): *BMC* II, 390, no. 411; 393, no. 425. etc.

The motif of Augustus' piety represented by the image of a sacrificant appears in other contexts too. There are three major types of imperial statues created in Augustus' reign, and dominant throughout the Principate: the togate, the cuirassed (loricate) and the idealizing.[24] Of the several togate types the one which here concerns us is the representation of the emperor, or a member of his house, in the manner of a Roman magistrate sacrificing, that is *capite velato*. This type has been thought to represent the emperor as *pontifex maximus* or even the *genius* of the emperor, but neither hypothesis is convincing.[25] While the other major types represent the emperor in military roles or allude to heroic or divine status, the togate types refer to his civic roles, recently highlighted in an outstanding study by Wallace-Hadrill.[26] They are the least differentiated of the emperor's roles, the least exclusive, the least inaccessible.[27] The reference of the veiled togate statues is to the role of the emperor in maintaining the *pax deorum* as sacrificant – a public role which is in principle no different from the role of every *paterfamilias* who sacrifices to the Lares in his own house.

Very little is known of the motivation of decisions to erect statues of emperors, especially in so-called cycles – and it is certain that a very large number have disappeared, particularly those made of precious metal. To all intents our evidence is confined to a small selection of the cheapest and most insignificant examples.[28] We know that there were about 80 statues of Octavian made of (presumably solid) silver scattered about Rome before 29/28 BC; and there must have been hundreds of bronze and marble ones in the city during his lifetime, and several thousand all over the Empire.[29] Of these only about 230

[24] H.G. Niemayer, *Studien zur statuarischen Darstellung der römischen Kaiser* (Mon. Artis Romanae 7, Berlin, 1968), 38-9.

[25] See, for example, K. Fittschen, review of Niemayer (n. 24), *BJ* 170 (1970), 541-52, who dismisses the argument that the emperor is seen in these statues as *pontifex maximus*, but argues (unnecessarily) that they are connected iconographically with images of the Genius of the emperor. P. Zanker has dated the earliest veiled statues of Octavian/Augustus as one of the first of his so-called 'Actium-type' – thus preceding Augustus' election as *pontifex maximus*; see P. Zanker, *Studien zu den Augustus-Porträts, 1: Der Actium Typus* (Abh. Akad. Wiss. zu Göttingen, Phil-hist. Klasse, 3 Folge, 85, 1973), esp. 13-14; 40.

[26] 'Civilis princeps; between citizen and king', *JRS* 72 (1982), 32-48.

[27] I. Lana, 'Civilis, civiliter, civilitas in Tacito e Suetonio: contributi alla storia del lessico politico-romano nell'età imperiale', *AAT* 106 (1972), 465-87.

[28] Hence the massively larger representation of mostly dreadful provincial copies by local craftsmen than copies known from Rome or even Italy. It is often quite doubtful whether a given head is of a particular emperor: P. Zanker, *Provinzielle Kaiserporträts: zur Rezeption der Selbstdarsellung des Princeps* (Bayerische Akad. der Wiss., Phil-hist. Kl. Abh, NF 90, Munich, 1983), 7-9 and the excellent pictures of heads of Hadrian (11-20).

[29] The Pekáry, 'Statuae meae ... argenteae steterunt in urbe XXC circiter, quas ipse sustuli: Interpretationen zu Res Gestae Divi Augusti 24', in E. Lefèvre (ed.), *Monumentum Chiloniense: Festschrift E. Burck* (Amsterdam, 1975), 96-108.

Fig. 24. The northern frieze of the arch set up by M. Julius Cottius at Susa (Segusio) in the Italian Alps in 9/8 BC. The altar is only partly visible on the extreme left; in the centre is a large boar being led to sacrifice.

survive, including posthumous heads; and of these, about twenty represent Augustus as sacrificant. Only one – that of the Via Labicana – certainly comes from Rome; all the others from Italy or the provinces.[30] And although some of the latter group derive from *coloniae* (settlements of veteran soldiers), petty Rome abroad, several do not.[31] We can surely argue from this fact that as early as the reign of Augustus (or Tiberius, since some of them may be posthumous) images that might seem to refer to a specifically Roman type of sacrifice were being set up outside the area where the 'religion of Rome' could have been the norm, and are therefore presumably tokens of a looser

[30] K. Vierniesel, P. Zanker, *Die Bildnisse des Augustus: Herrscherbild und Politik in kaiserlichen Rom* (Glyptothek, Munich, 1979), 48 (with map, pp. 58-9). For the Via Labicana statue, see L. Mariani, *BCAR* 38 (1910), 97-117.

[31] The list can be reconstructed from: I. Montini, *Il Ritratto di Augusto* (Mostra Augustea della Romanità: Civiltà Romana 5, Rome, 1938), 61-70 (listing 12-13); B. Freyer-Schauenburg, 'Augustus capite velatus: zu einer unpublizierten Porträtbüste von Samos', in E. Lefèvre (ed.), *Monumentum Chiloniense: Festschrift E. Burck* (Amsterdam, 1975), 3-4 (I owe this reference to K. Dunbabin); U. Haussmann, 'Zur Typologie und Ideologie des Augustusporträts', *ANRW* II, 12.2 (1981), 513-98. The following places outside Italy, which were not *coloniae* in the Julio-Claudian period, have produced statues *capite velato*; Tigani, Samos; Pollentia, Mallorca; Gigthis; Cyme; Athribis, near Alexandria.

Fig. 25. Panel from the arch of Septimius Severus at Lepcis in North Africa, AD 203. The figure of Septimius himself is lost, but the female figure (extreme left) is his wife, Julia Domna, who makes an offering at an altar with her right hand (see p. 214).

meaning of sacrifice than a reference to a specific ritual at Rome.

After the death of Augustus, veiled heads of emperors, even Julio-Claudians, are extremely uncommon (only three known veiled heads of Hadrian out of *c*. 134 accepted likeness, for example), though sporadic examples have been claimed even in the late third.[32] The obvious explanation is that the *civilian* roles of the emperors became less typical for those ordering new statues: and Tonio Hölscher has argued that in the third century the emperors actually cease to offer sacrifice for victory in the iconography – they became themselves the recipients of worship.[33] But the example of imperial sacrifice could be exported to the provinces by other means than imperial statues. The most striking examples are provided by the illustrations on commemorative arches set up all over the Empire both by rulers and by subjects. We may take a small selection scattered widely in space and time. The first is the arch at Susa (Segusio) set up in 9-8 BC by M. Iulius Cottius, the *praefectus* of a number of North Italian Celtic tribes in the Cottian Alps.[34] The north frieze of this arch represents a

[32] J. and J.-C. Balty, 'Notes d'iconographie romaine, II', *RhM* 86 (1976), 175-93 (identifying a *velatus* from Ephesos as Claudius Gothicus). The editors of *Römische Herrscherbild* are not impressed.
[33] *Victoria Romana* (Mainz, 1967), 118. This is only a tendency, of course. The Decennalia base in the Forum (celebrating the ten-year anniversary of the Tetrarchs in AD 303) is sufficient to remind us that the iconographic tradition of sacrifice continued into the Tetrarchy: Scott Ryberg, *Rites*, 117-19; pl. XLI, fig. 61.
[34] Ryberg, *Rites*, 104-6; pl. XXXIV; and, in greater detail, J. Prieur, 'Les arcs monumentaux dans les Alpes occidentales: Aoste, Suse, Aix-les-Bains', *ANRW* II, 12. 1, 442-75, esp. 451-9, pl. IV-XX.

characteristic Roman ritual, the *suovetaurilia* (the sacrifice of a bull, ram and boar) in confirmation of a treaty-agreement, with a procession accompanied by lictors, and the animals, hugely exaggerated in size to stress the political importance of the event.[35] In the centre is an altar, with a veiled figure standing to the left facing another on the other side. They are generally identified with Cottius and his son and heir Vestalis; but one would certainly expect a representative of the emperor if the arch commemorates a treaty.[36] Whatever the identification, a Roman ritual is represented far from the limits of Italia and the writ of pontifical rules; a client king dedicates an arch to Augustus by making use of symbols whose value is necessarily different from their value at Rome itself.

The second example is the main sacrificial scene from the arch of Septimius Severus at Lepcis in North Africa, probably dating from AD 203.[37] Unfortunately the central slab of the left-hand portion is missing; but it must have shown the altar more or less central, with Septimius Severus, standing on its left, offering the preliminary libation. To the right of the altar Julia Domna (his wife) survives; she holds an *acerra* in her left hand and offers incense with her right. Next to her is a flute player, behind her the figure of the goddess Roma. Behind and alongside these major figures are thirty-five others, men in civilian dress clustered towards the right, military officers on the left. This is emphatically a social occasion. And at each extreme appears a victim: on the left, a *victimarius* guides a decorated 'ox' by the horn, while to the right a quite insignificant little animal – possibly a cow – is simultaneously about to be stunned and having its throat cut.[38] But no one is concerned with this: all eyes are directed towards the figures in the centre. In the context of the other scenes on the arch, especially the figure of Concordia (Concord) arranged between Caracalla and Geta (the sons of Septimius), it seems evident that the dominant meaning of the sacrificial scene is to preserve the imperial house, to maintain the continuity of key imperial institutions and to bring these iconographically into relation with the social hierarchy in Lepcis. Apart from the figure of Roma, the religion of Rome in a narrow sense no longer signifies. It is through the emperor and his family that the periphery is

[35] Prieur (ibid., 456-7) thinks the frieze probably marks the submission of the Alpine people to Rome.

[36] Prieur (ibid., 457) identifies the *velatus* as Augustus, the figure on the right as Cottius. Cottius and Vestalis: B.M. Fellati-Maj, 'Il fregio commemorativo dell'arco di Susa', *RPAA* 33 (1960-61), 129-53.

[37] Ryberg, *Rites*, 134-6, pl. XLVIII, fig. 73. The fullest illustrations are (still) in the rather inaccurate publication of R. Bartoccini, 'L'arco quadrifronte dei Severi a Lepcis', *Africa Italiana* 4 (1931), 32-152, esp. 130, fig. 95; 133, fig. 97. See also J.B. Ward-Perkins, 'Severan art and architecture at Lepcis Magna', *JRS* 38 (1948), 59-80, esp. 75-7 (whose date I follow).

[38] On this section, see Brendel, 'Immolatio', 204; 208, pl. 79.

connected with the centre, and one of the crucial means of integration is sacrifice.

A similar observation can be made about the third example, the sacrifice scene on the south-east face of the south-west pylon of Galerius' massive arch at Thessaloniki (begun AD 298/9), which has aptly been described as 'strident imperial propaganda'.[39] The victim has virtually disappeared, being added almost as an afterthought on the extreme right. The centre is occupied by an altar on which pine cones are blazing. On the left is Diocletian, wearing a fringed chlamys and holding some sacrificial instrument in his right hand. On the right of the altar is Galerius, in military costume. They are surrounded by a bevy of ideal figures. Behind Diocletian is Jupiter, wearing a fragmentary zodiac; behind the altar are two female figures, Oikoumene (The Inhabited World) in a pose of mourning, comforted by Homonoia(?) (Harmony); behind Galerius is Eirene (Peace). The only 'real' figures are two *camilli* holding sacrificial instruments. The loss of interest in documentary relief goes hand in hand with the appropriation of the meaning of sacrifice by the imperial power: Jupiter is not the recipient of the offering so much as a reminder of Diocletian's paraded association with the god (which extended even to adding the title 'Iovius' – belonging to Jupiter – to his imperial nomenclature); and the same point is made by the small sculptures of Jupiter and Hercules on the two faces of the altar which are presented to the spectator.[40] As Aelius Aristides claimed more than a century earlier, the Empire has become a single city.[41]

Finally, coinage also provides important images of imperial sacrificial activity. The evidence is too large to be dealt with in detail here, but some basic points may be made. Sacrificial implements occur commonly on coins from imperial mints.It is generally agreed that they register a non-specific message of the piety of the emperors rather than particular priesthoods or events.[42] Indeed when PIETAS AVG ('piety of the emperor') is the legend of the coin, it is commonly illustrated by an act of sacrifice, either by Pietas herself or by the emperor. Such scenes continue to the very end of the Principate.[43] It is as if the exemplary

[39] M.S. Pond Rothman, *AJA* 80 (1976), reviewing the fundamental publication of the arch – H.-P. Laubscher, *Der Reliefschmuck des Galeriusbogens in Thessaloniki* (AF 1, Berlin, 1975). Note also (briefly) Ryberg, *Rites*, 139-40, pl. XLIX, fig. 76. and the old photographs in K.F. Kinch, *L'arc de triomphe de Salonique* (Paris, 1890); they are not only more picturesque, they reveal a monument less abraded than now.

[40] See W. Seston, 'Jovius et Herculius ou l' "epiphanie" des Tétrarqes', *Historia* 1 (1950), 257-66 = *Scripta Varia* (CEFR, Rome, 1980), 441-50; Liebeschuetz, *Continuity and Change*, 235-45.

[41] Aelius Aristides, *Roman Oration* 61.

[42] H. Mattingly, *BMC* III, xl-xliii is the best brief discussion.

[43] For *Pietas Aug*, see J. Beaujeu, *La religion romaine à l'apogée de l'Empire* (Paris, 1955), 280-91.

Fig. 26. Sacrificial scene from Galerius' arch at Thessaloniki, North Greece, begun in AD 298/9 (see p. 215).

piety of the emperor was best imaged by displaying him (as on commemorative arches) in a sacrificial context. Moreover, this iconographic pattern is found throughout the Roman world. From the late second century on, coins minted locally in Asia Minor include types showing emperors in sacrificial roles, perhaps commemorating an imperial visit.[44] While a third-century 'medallion' struck at Rome clearly alludes to the emperor's role as sacrificer in the east. It was struck during Gordian III's Persian campaign (AD 242-Spring 244) and shows a sacrifice in front of a domed round pedimental temple with four steps. This temple (perhaps to be identified as that at Antioch) is marked out as Eastern by the Greek inscription on its architrave – *Nike hoplophoros*, translated into Latin as *Victoria Augusti* ('Victory of the Emperor'). Behind the emperor, who is pouring a libation onto a small round altar as a *popa* (the *victimarius* who actually kills the animal) swings the mallet onto the victim's neck, are two *fasces*.[45] Once more, the 'religion of Rome' is now seen to be conducted wherever the Princeps happens to be, and in relation to the central political and military needs of each successive régime.

[44] For example, *Sammlung v. Aulock* 1, nos. 33; 36; 311; 811; 1277 etc.
[45] *RIC* IV. 3, 51, n. 324 (see also p. 11).

Fig. 27. Detail of Fig. 26. the figures on either side of the central altar are Diocletian (in the fringed robe) and Galerius (in military dress) (see p. 215).

What we witness is the universal quality of imperial sacrifice, its disengagements from the narrow world of the City of Rome, and its paradigmatic, exemplary intention. This can hardly be better illustrated than by the survival of odd examples of what must have been extremely common moulds for making the special cakes that were distributed to the population after sacrifices.[46] Some of these are in the form of sacrificial animals and gods' attributes; but for my purposes here the most interesting were found at Sirmium in Pannonia and at Silchester in Britain. The first shows the Genius of an emperor sacrificing at a round altar, holding a cornucopia; the second Septimius Severus in the act of sacrifice, with three military standards in the background.[47] George Boon, who published the British example, observes: 'Like their modern counterparts, the chocolate medallions on sale at jubilee- or coronation-time, cakes moulded (to represent

[46] They are generally called 'crustulum moulds'. See briefly, A. Alföldi, 'Tonmodel und relief medaillons aus den Donauländern', *Mélanges Kuszinsky* (Diss. Pann., Ser, 2, X, 1938), 312-14. On such cakes at sacrifice, see Varro, *Ling.* 5, 107; *Rust.* 2, 8, 1.

[47] Sirmium: E. Thomas, 'Religion', in A. Lengyel and G.T.B. Radan (eds.), *The Archaeology of Roman Pannonia* (Lexington-Budapest, 1980), 177-206. Silchester: G.C. Boon, 'A Roman pastry-cook's mould from Silchester', *AntJ* 38 (1958), 237-40 (quote, p. 237).

Fig. 28. Coin commemorating the piety (*pietas*) of the emperor, issued under Gaius (Caligula), AD 37-8 (BMC I, 153:41). On the obverse (left), the goddess Pietas (Piety) is shown, with the titles of the emperor on the border. On the reverse (right) Gaius is represented sacrificing in memory of the deified Augustus. The large letters SC stand for 'Senatus Consulto' ('by decree of the senate'), which implies that, at least formally, the coin was issued under the authority of the senate.

Fig. 29. A medallion struck at Rome to commemorate the Persian campaign of Gordian III in AD 242-4. The emperor stands on the right of the temple, with covered head; while the victim is being killed on the left (see p. 216).

emperors or religious scenes) were prepared for particular occasions of public festivity.' To be sure, Graeco-Roman sacrifice involved having a party as well as communicating with the divine. But there is more to it than that. To think of the participants at festivals as far from Rome as Britain or Pannonia nibbling the head of the sacrificant emperor on their way home suggests a quite extraordinary degree of banalization of what in the time of Augustus had been a solemn, original and difficult motif, mediating the centre and periphery of the Roman world through the image of the emperor engaged in an (erstwhile) peculiarly Roman ritual: what had been a new image of domination is here seen not only as *accepted*, but also as *banal*. But for the historian of mentalité such banality is always interesting. 'Every established order tends to produce ... the naturalization of its own arbitrariness.'[48]

Priesthood and euergetism at Rome

The sacrificial role of the *princeps* is not, of course, to be understood in isolation: it is inextricably linked with his *philanthropia* (benevolence), his *liberalitas* (generosity), and so with his accumulation of symbolic capital. In that respect, his sacrificial activity serves as an example to all the élites in the Empire. Overtly, sacrificial activity fulfils a specific duty, to maintain satisfactory relations with the gods; but it is never clear whether this duty is allocated to the élite or appropriated by it. What is clear is the way in which the visual record of sacrificial activity of a public kind in the Principate is virtually monopolized, in several modes, by the imperial system; and also how local religious life in the Empire became suffused with references to the emperor and in a sense dependent upon his presence.[49] It is as though the nexus, evident to the modern historian, between (a) the political structure of the Empire (summarized in the emperor's relations with both centre and periphery), (b) the use of inequality of wealth to perpetuate structures of dependence more effective than those based on mere violence, and (c) the sacrificial system, could not be fully veiled, but found expression in the dynamic extension of a particular kind of civic priesthood. It is to this matter that we must now turn.

By far the most active agent of change, social, economic and symbolic, in the Roman Empire was the institution of the Principate itself. As often, of course, the intended changes were either illusory or ineffective; of far greater importance were unintended changes that resulted from long-term or invisible forces. Inversely, it sometimes served the purpose of emperors to attempt to resist change. One of the clearest examples of such resistance is provided by the emperors' attempts to use the Roman priesthoods as guarantors of the changelessness of Roman religion, emblems of the claimed continuity between the *principes*, especially the first *princeps* and the earliest history of Rome. How conscious individual emperors were of this function of the priesthoods of Rome is uncertain: once Caesar had added small numbers of extra priests in 47 BC and Augustus had been

---

[48] Bourdieu, *Outline*, 164. This is the experience Bourdieu refers to as 'doxa', so as to distinguish it from an orthodox or heterodox *belief* implying awareness and recognition of the possibility of different or antagonistic beliefs.

[49] For the East, see, especially, Price, *Rituals and Power*.

given the right to choose additional priests *supra numerum* without limit in 29 BC, there was no need for elaborate change. Elections for priesthoods from 17 of the tribes under the Lex Labiena of 63 BC probably continued under Augustus, as did popular elections for magistracies; and even after Tiberius' abolition of the latter in AD 14 'popular' assemblies formally to elect both magistrates and priests continued to be held.[50] What we might note as innovations – the inclusions of honorific phrases about the emperors and their relatives in the song of the Salii, the reorganization of the Arval Brethren between 30 and 27 BC as (in effect) imperial priests, the flaminate in honour of Julius Caesar – may perhaps have been seen as improvements in the spirit of antiquity: we know that the *sodales Augustales* were later modelled upon the existing *sodales Titii*.[51] Certainly the determination displayed both by Caesar and by Augustus to increase the patriciate (patricians were essential to maintain the authentic links of priesthood with early Rome: once upon a time, it was believed, all priests had been patricians) suggests a deliberate policy with regard to priesthood.[52] More explicit is Tiberius' refusal to accept the proposal by L. Apronius in AD 22 to include the *fetiales* among the existing four *amplissima* or *summa collegia* because such a change was not in accord with tradition.[53] 'Tradition' was a useful instrument to wheel out when a proposed change did not stem from the needs of the imperial house; but of course that is not to suggest that Tiberius' response was in any overt way cynical. If the main function of the priestly colleges under the Principate was to emblematize the underlying or real continuity between Principate and early Rome, an appeal to 'tradition' was entirely appropriate.

There are other reasons to believe that the ideological function of the sacerdotal colleges taken as a whole was at least partly conscious. It has been shown by John Scheid that despite the emperors' theoretical right to increase the number of priests in any college this was not generally done in practice except to find places for princes of the imperial house.[54] Besides the emperors demonstrated a clear desire for continuity by permitting roughly a third of all holders of major priesthoods to 'inherit' them from their fathers or a close relative: there was even talk of a right to such priesthoods.[55] Thirdly, the emperors

---

[50] For increase in priestly numbers, see Dio, 42, 51, 4-5; 43, 51, 9; 51, 20, 3; for the practice of election, Hoffmann Lewis, *Official Priests*, 12-23 and Schumacher, 'Vier Kollegien', 665-6.

[51] Song of Salii: Dio 51, 20,1 (Octavian's name); Tacitus, *Ann.* 2, 83, 1 (Germanicus); SHA, *Marc.* (son of Marcus Aurelius). Arvals: Scheid, *Arvales*, 344. *Sodales Aug.*: Tacitus, *Ann.* 1, 54, 1; *Hist.* 2, 95, 1.

[52] See Livy 6, 41, 4-9; cf. Hoffmann Lewis, *Official Priests*, 23.

[53] Tacitus, *Ann.* 3, 6, 4.

[54] Scheid, 'Prêtres', 617-22, cf. 646-54; Hoffmann Lewis, *Official Priests*, 12.

[55] For example, Tacitus, *Hist.* 3, 86; *Ann.* 6, 40, 3.

practised a deliberate restriction upon the distribution of priesthoods by enforcing cumulation. There were roughly 620 places available in the priestly colleges: in theory every senator might have one (to say nothing of the equestrian priesthoods). Instead, we find it normal for a relatively few individuals to cumulate membership in one major college and several minor ones: as a reward for his achievements in Africa and in Germany, the future emperor Galba, among other honours, was co-opted into three priestly colleges, the *XVviri sacris faciundis*, the *sodales Titii* and the *sodales Augustales Claudiales*.[56] Between 29 BC and AD 37, 23 priests occupied 50 priestly offices to our certain knowledge – our almost total ignorance of the membership of minor priestly colleges means that the true figure must have been much higher.[57]

On the other hand, along with the perception of continuity with the remote past went recognition of the instrumental value of sacerdotal offices. So evident is it that successive emperors used the appointments as instruments of patronage that the study of the priesthoods of the Principate has usually been seen as an aspect not of Roman religion but of the history of the senatorial élite.[58] Calculations have been made of the proportions of men who entered priesthoods at different points in their careers; of the proportions of consuls, praetors, quaestors, and even more junior magistrates, who might expect, if they were not already appointed, to enter a college. Almost endless inferences can be drawn about the status of individuals in relation to the emperor, the standing of families and the workings of the patronage system. Moreover the symbolic advantages of priesthood to members of the senatorial élite were considerable, and assisted them in their own extension of their patronage-networks (the equivalent of politics in the imperial system). We have already seen that members of the pontifical college could approach so close to the emperor that one of them might easily assassinate him; several Roman historical reliefs show priests beside the emperor; on the Ara Pacis procession, the four *flamines*, Dialis, Quirinalis, Martialis and Iulialis, follow on immediately behind Augustus as sacrificant, quaint in their *apices* (their distinctive pointed hats) – one of them even holds a *commetaculum*, the sacred wand used by flamines to clear away the crowds from their path: the only known illustration of this item of

---

[56] Suetonius, *Galba* 8, 1. On cumulation in general, see Schumacher, 'Vier Kollegien', 1795-804. Note that Scheid (*Arvales*, 376) questions the meaningfulness of the distinction between 'major' and 'minor' as the empire wore on – certainly the *sodales* of *divi* came to be recruited from the most eminent imperial families.

[57] Scheid, 'Prêtres', 629.

[58] Hoffmann Lewis, *Official Priests*, 2; Schumacher, 'Vier Kollegien', 665-6; 768. Scheid, 'Prêtres', 611 questions this assumption, but in effect does the same thing.

ceremonial equipment.[59] It is not at all surprising to find Pliny the
Younger rather desperately pushing himself forward in search of an
appointment by Trajan 'to an augurate, or membership of the *VIIviri
epulonum*'; or to find that others invariably got there first until his own
patron, Julius Frontinus, finally by dying left a gap in the augural
college, into which Pliny gratefully slipped.[60] Because they had this
double quality – collectively symbols of continuity and changelessness,
as well as day to day instruments of imperial patronage – it was
inevitable that the 'reality' of the latter role was much more significant
to ordinary ambitious senators that the symbolic function. But it is
only a very partial truth to claim that under the Principate priesthoods
were the equivalent of the modern British honours system.[61]

But even the emperors could not resist the changes which they
themselves had brought about. The legitimating role of the sacerdotal
colleges gradually faded, as the emperor's own religious role vastly
increased. The imperial system was itself responsible for the elision of
the significance of the sacerdotal colleges. The changes imposed by the
intrusion of a Princeps, wielding increasingly institutionalized and
formal authority, upon the competitive political system of the Republic
deeply influenced the functioning of the religious system. One of the
critical functions of the priestly colleges in the Republic had been their
'ring-holding' role, their right to invoke sacral law in the face of
violations, or attempted manipulations, of the rules by individual
aristocrats. Under the Principate that role was valueless. The ring was
now held by the emperor, and far more effectively than the colleges
could hope to do, constrained as they were by their members' own
participation in the competitive system (whence the constant cries of
'foul' when religion was invoked to halt individual ambitions).[62] The
emperors' innovations in the religious system could hardly be sensibly,
let alone critically, discussed.[63] Those aspects of the priesthood which
had always existed, the honorific and symbolic aspects, duly came to
the fore; it became precious as a mark of one's relation to the emperor
rather than as a mark of respect from one's peers, the more valuable
because fought for in public. It hardly mattered to decide issues that

[59] Simon, *Ara Pacis*, 17, Hoffmann Lewis, *Official Priests*, 19-21. For the *commetaculum*
see Paul (Festus), *Gloss. Lat.* p. 56.

[60] Pliny, *Ep.* 2, 1, 8; 4, 8; 10, 13.

[61] As does, for example, A.N. Sherwin-White (ed.), *The Letters of Pliny* (Oxford, 1966),
272.

[62] cf. C.R. Phillips, 'The sociology of religious knowledge in the Empire to 284 AD', *ANRW*
II, 16, 3, 2677-773, esp. 2692, n. 43.

[63] Note Dio's remark on Octavian's consultation (in 38 BC) of the *pontifices* over his
proposed marriage to Livia (while pregnant): 'Perhaps they really found (their answer)
among the *patria*, but certainly they would have said (what they said), even had they not
found it' (48, 44, 2).

might affect the *pax deorum*, because no career, no ambition could be affected. As far as we know, the pontifical college was officially consulted only twice in the entire century of Julio-Claudian rule; the XVviral college once.[64] The unintended changes were directly contrary to the emperors' aim of using the sacerdotal colleges as elements in a strategy of legitimation; but they faithfully reflected the logic of the imperial system. It is a truism that at Rome religion and politics were inextricably intertwined; but the converse is also true: the abolition of politics involved also the break-down of the Republican religious synthesis predicated upon the appropriation of religious authority by the political élite. The emperors took over the religion of Rome.

But in one area tradition could be built upon. In the Republic, it seems, it had been customary for a priest on election to provide some expensive public entertainment, and the cost of the sumptuous feast he had to give to his new colleagues.[65] Though the sources are virtually silent, there is casual evidence for more or less compulsory payments, *summa honoraria*, in respect of membership of the Roman sacerdotal colleges in the Principate. One incident, related by both Suetonius and Dio Cassius, makes this extremely likely; it concerns the emperor Gaius, who, it is said, in AD 40 forced members of his household, including his wife and Claudius the future emperor, to pay for the privilege of holding a newly-instituted priesthood of himself as Jupiter Latiaris. Dio puts the price of this at 10 million HS (that is, ten times the minimum wealth census for a senator). Suetonius, in a more circumstantial passage, puts the sum at 8 million sesterces (that is, eight times the minimum wealth census of a senator), a demand which forced Claudius to mortgage his property. When he was unable to meet the debt, 'his property was advertised for sale to meet the deficiency in accordance with the law regulating confiscations' (tr. Rolfe).[66]

The Roman senatorial élite treated the acquisition of priesthoods in the Roman sacerdotal colleges as symbolic but highly desirable goods. The emperors used these posts just as they used their other means of patronage, as means of creating an enduring relation of dependence, gratitude and respect towards themselves, in short to create symbolic capital. But priesthood had another facet, as the *summa honoraria*

---

[64] *Pontifices*: Tacitus, *Ann.* 11, 15, 3; 12, 8, 2. *XVviri: ILS* 5050 = Riccobono, *FIRA* 1², no. 57. Of course, regular committee work persisted throughout the Principate, above all for the pontifical college in relation to private graves (e.g. *CIL* VI, 1884 = *ILS* 1792); and it was as *pontifex maximus* that Domitian condemned the unfortunate Vestal, Cornelia (Suetonius, *Dom.* 8, 4; Pliny, *Ep.* 4, 11, 6-9).

[65] 'Yet the *cena aditialis* has often cost a most careful man a cool million HS' (Seneca, *Ep.* 95, 41). See also the augural dinner given before 67 BC by Q. Hortensius Hortalus, mentioned by Varro, *Rust.* 3, 6, 6; Pliny, *HN* 10, 23, 45; Macrobius, *Sat.* 3, 13, 1; and Cicero's excuses for being absent from M. Apulleius' feast, *Att.* 12, 13, 2; 14, 1; 15, 1.

[66] Suetonius, *Claud.* 9, 2; Dio 59, 28, 5. Sensible doubts about other aspects of Gaius' religious mania need not extend to the principle of these *honoraria*.

show, as a vehicle for the institutionalization of euergetism towards the people of Rome, as a means of compelling the senatorial élite to imitate the emperor's generosity. Their generosity is no longer overtly political, as in the Republic, but it serves a social purpose none the less in displaying as spectacularly as possible the social inequality which enabled them to give so generously and forced the recipients gratefully to receive. If the emperor alone gives, he makes impossibly wide the gulf which separates him from all others – he becomes as it were an evident *god*;[67] if the leading members of the senatorial order also give, euergetism becomes a sign of the social responsibility of an entire order. And that they give in consideration of a non-political good, a priesthood, a purely symbolic good, makes it clear that the euergetic system is for the good of the people, who receive real benefits in return for giving honour. Mask and veil here coincide: for the true purpose of giving is not to receive honour, but to maintain the power and wealth of the élite. It cannot be sufficiently emphasised that the relative 'success' of the Roman Empire, by comparison with other much more violently extractive, and unstable, pre-industrial empires, lay largely in the extension of the euergetic system of unequal exchange very widely through the Empire.[68]

Priesthood and euergetism among the provincial élite

The same pattern can be perceived throughout the Roman Empire. In the Western half of the Empire, as the Romans built new cities or changed the status of existing towns so as to make them subject to Roman municipal rules, so along with those rules the Roman type of civic priesthood spread. The surviving charter granted by Caesar to the town of Urso in Southern Spain (the so-called 'Lex Julia Coloniae Genetivae') shows clearly how the local institutions could be modelled on those of the centre. 'As respecting pontiffs and augurs created out of the Colonia Genetiva Iulia by C. Caesar or the persons who by his command established the colony, such persons shall be pontiffs and augurs of this Colonia Genetiva Iulia and shall have their place in the college of pontiffs and augurs within the said colony, under all the conditions and with all the rights appertaining to pontiffs and augurs of every colony. And the said pontiffs and augurs, having places in their several colleges, and also their children, shall have exemption from military service and public duties solemnly guaranteed, in such

---

[67] Note S. Martin's comment, 'The senate (better "senators") seems to have provided an important link between the emperor and his subjects. As emperors became more elevated and more remote figures – they had to rely more, not less, on the mediation of their own dependants' (*JRS* 75 (1985), 225).

[68] The concealed 'bottom line' means that: giving + gratitude/honour = power for the élite.

Fig. 30. Roman ritual in some of its aspects could be mirrored outside Rome. This coin (issued for Octavian, BMC I, 104:638, 29-27 BC) shows on the obverse (right) the ritual of the foundation of a colony – modelled on the legend of the foundation of Rome, in which Romulus ploughed a symbolic furrow round the site of his new city. On the reverse (left) is the head of Apollo.

wise as a pontiff in Rome has or shall have the same, and all their military campaigns shall be accounted as discharged ...'[69] So the spread of city formation involved also the spread of the particular Roman type of priesthood.

The Roman forms of local government also brought with them the institution of the *summum honorarium*, civil as well as religious: it was not merely the forms and names of central priesthoods that were imposed. The key associations between wealth, public office, beneficence and the religious system could thus be disseminated throughout the Roman world. This complex relationship is unselfconsciously evidenced by thousands of honorific inscriptions and statues set up as marks of these transactions. Two inscriptions, recently discovered in Nîmes, illustrate the point well. The first records the erection of a statue to a priestess of the imperial cult, who had been made exempt from payment of the *summum honorarium*, in recognition of her father's generous benefactions: 'To Attia Patercla, daughter of Lucius, perpetual priestess (of the emperor) without payment of the *summum* by order of the most sacred town council, because of the generous gifts of her father who, in addition to all other things, left in his will 300,000 sesterces to the public fund of the VIviri (?), so that the VIviral games may be held for ever; Daphnion her freedman (put this up) the spot being granted by decree of the

---

[69] Riccobono, *FIRA* 1², no. 21, section 66, translated in E.G. Hardy (ed.), *Three Spanish Charters* (Oxford, 1912), 28-9.

decurions.' Here private gratitude and obligation on the part of a freedman are matched by the city council's grant of land to receive the statue.[70]

The second example records the generosity of another imperial priestess who not only made a lavish gift to her town on entry to her priesthood, but also paid for the statue which the town council voted to her in gratitude: 'To Indelvia Valerilla, daughter of Titus, perpetual priestess (to the emperor), who, in return for the honour (of being appointed) set up a silver statue with its base in the law-courts costing 50,000 HS. In return for that example of her munificence, the most sacred council decreed that a statue should be set up for her at public expense. Gratified by the gesture, she bore the cost herself.' One could want no clearer illustration of the elaborate way in which any vestige of an interested contract, a forced payment, is concealed beneath the ever more emphatic concern solely with 'empty' honour.[71]

But it is the East, and particularly Asia Minor, that provides the most striking examples of priestly generosity, as of generosity on appointment to an ordinary magistracy. I propose to consider in some detail two examples of this – so as to explore different facets of the connection between euergetism and local civic priesthood.

The first is that of Cleanax, son of Sarapion, of Cyme in the Aeolid. He is known only from a fragmentary stele, now in the J. Paul Getty Museum in Malibu, erected on the occasion of his quitting the office of *prytanis* (a local magistracy in Cyme).[72] It probably dates from the period 2 BC – AD 2, and documents in exhaustive detail the fact that Cleanax has never lost any opportunity to bestow his beneficence upon the council, the Roman community, and the people of Cyme (ll. 7-8). Only those which concern his priesthood are of relevance here. As priest of Dionysus Pandamos, 'he celebrated the mysteries founded by the city, and paid all the expenses necessary for the five-yearly celebration of the mysteries, at which time the magnitude of the sums involved ... displayed his *philodoxia* (love of honour, i.e. reputation for munificence) and *eusebeia* (respect for the worship of the gods), sums he alone paid and which he was the first to engage to pay...' (ll. 12-16). He also invited by public proclamation the citizens, the Roman (Italian) community, the *paroikoi* (the dependent population that worked the land) and the foreigners to a feast in the sanctuary of

[70] *AE* 1982, 68 10. The editors date the inscription between M. Aurelius and *c*. AD 200.

[71] *AE* 1982, 682 (dated AD 161-200). On such gestures, D. Ladage, *Städtische Priester und Kultämter im Lateinischen West des Imperium Romanum zur Kaiserzeit* (Diss. Köln, 1971), 114-20; A. Hands, *Charities and Social Aid in Greece and Rome* (London, 1968), 50-1.

[72] P. Hodot, 'Décret de Kymè en l'honneur du prytane Kleanax', *The J. Paul Getty Museum Journal* 10 (1982), 165-80. J. and L. Robert, *Bulletin Epigraphique* 1983, no. 323 is an essential addendum, whose interpretation I have generally followed.

Dionysus and 'entertained them magnificently; and he did this every year' (ll. 16-19). In other words, Cleanax has invented a new kind of charge upon himself (and doubtless his successors) by putting on a public festival entirely at his own expense (l. 16); by putting up posters, he attempts to ensure the largest possible attendance, but he also objectifies his munificence in the litter of the placards making the announcement, which are a physical sign of the generation of that hidden gratitude which is to become his symbolic capital. More important, however, is Cleanax's transformation of the cult of the gods into an opportunity to accumulate symbolic capital for himself: a delicate boundary, between use of the religious system by the élite and its usurpation, has been crossed; and such gestures become increasingly common in the Principate.[73]

The list of Cleanax's benefits during his subsequent magistracy illustrates the closeness of the relation between civic office and religious function in the Graeco-Roman city. For as *prytanis* Cleanax, on entry into office on the first day of the year (probably Augustus' birthday, 23 September), 'performed the sacrifices to the gods according to custom, distributed sweet wine to all the inhabitants of the city (without restriction of category), offered splendid entertainments for the goddesses and performed the (annual) vows for a prosperous new year and sacrifices according to custom, and entertained many citizens and Romans for several days in the *prytaneum* (civic hall)' (ll. 30-4). On the usual day for celebrating the festival of the dead, 'he performed the customary sacrifices, and had the *chondrogala*[74] distributed to all the inhabitants of the city, slave and free'; there followed another festival, in the month of Corydon: 'On his own initiative, he invited by verbal proclamation the citizens, the Romans, the *paroikoi* and the foreigners to banquet in the *prytaneum*, and gave out portions to the people in the same way as the other *prytaneis*; he provided laurel for the processions (the *daphnephoria* in honour of Apollo) and gave a feast for the priests, for the victors in the sacred games, to the magistrates and many citizens' (ll. 36-40). Finally, during an imperial festival celebrated by the province of Asia, 'he offered the sacrifices and the banquets at which the meat is consumed, as he had promised, first of all sacrificing a bull to Caesar Augustus, his sons (Caius and Lucius Caesar) and to the other gods, sacrifices with which he entertained in (?) the market-place the Greeks, the

---

[73] Schmitt-Pantel, 'Festin' points out that this process begins already in the second century BC. See also P. Schmitt-Pantel, 'Euergétisme et mémoires du mort', in G. Gnoli and J-P. Vernant (eds.), *Le mort, les morts dans les sociétés anciennes* (Cambridge and Paris, 1982), 177-88.

[74] The *chondrogala* seems to have been a sort of milk soup made from coarse ground flour.

Romans, the *paroikoi* and the foreigners, by proclamation on posters ...' (ll. 40-5).

The inseparability of civic and religious functions is abundantly plain: the generosity of Cleanax expresses itself in the manner most directly and concretely advantageous to his fellow-citizens, in feasts, meat-eating and the distribution of wine. We hardly need to note the way in which such social occasions, both the rituals themselves and the organized feasting in and out of *prytaneum*, recapitulate an ideal version of the local social hierarchy.[75] Religious celebrations provide a privileged context within which a certain notion of community can be evoked: all are united in gratitude to the generosity of Cleanax. The actual, and fundamental, divisions of the local society are repeatedly rehearsed, in an almost incantatory manner, reminding us that the wealth of Cleanax almost certainly derived from his dominant roles in reproducing the very social relations that his activity as euergete serves to veil. And finally the insertion into the text of the shadowy figures of the emperor Augustus and his two adoptive sons (Gaius and Lucius) neatly demonstrates the Chinese-box structure of the Roman Empire: as one penetrates further down the social hierarchy and out towards the periphery, one finds systems of relationship which recapitulate on a smaller, local, scale the pattern of domination which enabled the personal rule of Octavian to be transformed into the institution of the Principate.[76]

The second illustration concerns the gifts of an exceptionally wealthy woman, Menodora daughter of Megacles from Sillyon in Pamphylia. Three inscriptions relating to this woman were found at Assar Koy in Southern Turkey in the 1880s.[77] She came from a line of wealthy landowners, 'one of the grandest and richest of Sillyon'.[78] During the early third century Menodora held many offices, 'religious' and 'civil': she was high priestess of the Augusti (presumably the emperors Septimius Severus and Caracalla), priestess of Demeter and of 'all the gods', hierophant for life of the city's gods, *dekaprotos*, *demiourgos* and *gymnasiarch*. Her daughter (whose name is not mentioned) was *gymnasiarch*, and her son Megacles was *demiourgos*. As in the case of Cleanax, priesthoods and civic offices are listed together as though there were virtually no distinction between them. As holder of these positions, Menodora made three different kinds of gifts to the people of Sillyon: (a) distribution of money and corn to the

[75] Schmitt-Pantel, 'Festin', 93.

[76] Price, *Rituals and Power*, ch. 9, denies 'that the imperial cult was part of the ideological superstructure (or) that it legitimated political power'. This seems plain daft: to deny the relationship is in fact to undo the good done by his earlier analyses.

[77] G. Radot – P. Paris, 'Inscriptions de Syllion [*sic*] en Pamphylie', *BCH* 13 (1889), 486-97 = *IGR* III, 800-2 (statue bases).

[78] ibid., 90. The editors provide a conjectural genealogical table on p. 489.

entire people (b) 300,000 drachmae to aid orphans and children (c) 304,000 drachmae for building a temple, three silver statues inside it, a gilt and ivory statue of Tyche together with the ornamentation of its base, a silver sacrificial table and the coffering of the ceiling.

The first point to make about Menodora's gifts, apart from their sheer size and the minute attention to detail, is that the hierarchy of the city is given a monetary expression. The first inscription includes the following list (ll. 16-22):

bouleutês (councillor)	86 dr.
geraios (elder)	80 "
ecclêsiastês (member of the assembly)	77 "
the wives of each of these	3 "
citizen	9 "
vindictarius (freed slave)	3 "
apeleutheros (freed slave)	3 "
paroikos ('serf')	3 "

It is evident that the major purpose of this philanthropy is not to relieve poverty. Part of the function of philanthropic gestures is to register and naturalize the inequalities of the social system in each community, just as the emperors' patronage and generosity marshals and orchestrates the overall hierarchy of the system as a whole. The gifts objectify the relations of respect, dependence, authority and power upon which the entire euergetic system rests. Moreover, the fusion of the euergetic system with the sacrificial system in civic priesthood evokes both the divine necessity and the social responsibility of the existing social order. The relationship proposed by the sacrificial system between god and man (inferiority; reciprocity between unequals; providential beneficence; changelessness) is implicitly offered as a model of the relationship between the élite and the rest of the community. On the one hand, the Roman Empire institutionalized the figure of the *princeps* who, if he were not a god, was certainly not a man; on the other, by imitating the *princeps'* genial fusions of sacrificial activity with euergetism on a grand scale, the élite at every level, even in the miserable town of Pamphylian Sillyon, by the subtle alchemy of symbolic capital, forged its own subordinate legitimacy.

Secondly, the nature of what is given, the distribution of food, wine, oil and money; the buildings, the art products, the silver goods for rituals; the foundations and orphanages, construct an image of what is needful to the community, an idea constructed by the élite in terms of its own judgments of value.[79] Lavish goods for the gods are set side by

---

[79] P. Debord, *Aspects*, 74-5; cf. J. Andreau, 'Fondations privées et rapports sociaux en Italie romaine, Ier – IIIe s. ap. J.C.', *Ktema* 2 (1977), 157-209.

side with necessaries for orphans. Just as the élite takes responsibility for the community it takes responsibility for the gods. It thus sets itself up as the major carrier of central values in the community. At the same time, the community becomes dependent upon the élite for the means of worshipping 'piously', that is, equipped with suitably lavish items of religious paraphernalia: the élite inserts itself surreptitiously into the communication between here and the other world, not by claiming some special mediatory status but by means of the provision of the agencies of worship.[80]

Finally, women appear here, as frequently in the Principate (and earlier, to some extent), not merely as occupants of priesthoods, which had always been possible, but in the role of *euergetês*, that is, as honorary men. The dynamic of the euergetic system gradually erodes one of the principles of the traditional political systems of the Greek cities: these euergetic women are symptoms of changes in local inheritance systems and of the pressure of Roman law upon them; and also of the pressure which the obligation to give puts upon all wealthy families in a locality. They do not mark any particular shift in the social power of women in general, as Menodora's gifts to the wives of the local élite – and the complete absence of the women lower down the social scale – testify.[81]

Patriotism and piety are fused in these inscriptions. To what end? What is the ideological value of this odd fusion? A hint at the answer is provided by one of the inscriptions from the sanctuary of Leto in the city of Xanthos in Lycia, in honour of Q. Veranius Tlepolemus, high priest of the emperor in AD 149.[82] The inscription describes him as 'gentlemanly, honourable, patriotic, noble, notable for his moral character, his conversation and his lack of excessive display'. The most interesting feature of this description is its praise of restraint in self-display, in a context in which quite evidently enormous amounts of money and energy were expended in display. The fusion between patriotism and piety ensures that the social functions of 'philanthropy' can be veiled: the object of erecting inscriptions and statues can be suppressed in consideration of the true disinterestedness of generosity, In giving one seeks literally for nothing, as true piety does not look for a reward. Duty is the most delicious disguise of self-interest. And the very fact of the continuity of many of these élite families was sufficient

---

[80] Schmitt-Pantel, 'Festin', 89: the banquets of benefactors create new religious feasts in the city, constructed entirely around their own social and political concerns.

[81] For a full discussion of these women commanding wealth, see R. van Bremen, 'Women and wealth' in A. Cameron and A. Kuhrt (eds.), *Images of Women in Antiquity* (London, 1983), 223-42. P. Veyne, *Le pain et le cirque* (Paris, 1976), 276; 357, n. 261, classes magistracies held by women with those held by children, dead persons and gods (though this list is not, as it stands, without difficulties).

[82] *TAM* II. 1, no. 288 = *IGR* III, 6286-98.

proof of the pleasure the gods took in their piety.[83]

*

Insofar as there is an overall development discernible in the complex history of civic priesthood in the Principate, its rationale surely lies in this fusion of the religious system with the socio-political system, a fusion which served to veil from the central and local élites the true character of their domination. There is a consistent set of attitudes throughout the Empire, despite numerous institutional and detailed differences. The sacrificial system is one of the key links between the imperial system organized at the centre and the local control exercised by the local élites at the periphery. Euergetism is the socially responsible use of wealth, and so, as a system, proclaims the necessity of social inequality; the existence of social inequality is a natural phenomenon, because it is based on the distinction, entirely natural, between this world and the other world. Moreover, sacrificial euergetism contributes powerfully to a remodelling of the notion of community in the absence of political structures through which the aspirations of the mass of the population might have been articulated. This process is dynamic: the potentially disruptive consequence of new forms of social power achieved through the wealth (whose accumulation was encouraged by the fiscal system of the Empire) could be absorbed into the status quo through the sacrificial system.[84] The profusion of priestly roles amongst the non-élite and upwardly mobile – the *vicomagistri*, the *VIviri Augustales* and the innumerable collegiate organizations – may be seen as so many testimonies to the ideological effectiveness of the sacrificial system. In its turn, the part played by the élites, central and local, in the maintenance of the sacrificial system was not disinterested but rather a crucial element in their domination.

[83] A clear example of a family dominant (and holding priesthoods) in generation after generation is provided by the Claudii of Panamara in Caria. These generations can be traced in A. Laumonier, 'Recherches sur la chronologie des prêtres de Panamara', *BCH* 61 (1937), 236-98 and *I. Stratonikeia* I, 67; 76; 90.

[84] For the important economic role of the fiscal system, see K. Hopkins, 'Taxes and trade in the Roman Empire', *JRS* 70 (1980), 101-25. I broadly support this account, without necessarily believing in the details.

9

Religion in the Roman Empire:
the civic compromise and its limits

The Romanization of the Mediterranean world during the first centuries of the Christian era provides the historical context for this final chapter on priesthood and religious authority in the Roman empire. In its geographical sense, that Empire included a vast number of formerly independent local communities, with their systems of government and their own languages. These communities, particularly in the Western half of the Empire, gradually assimilated Roman language, artistic and architectural forms and religious practice – by a process of 'Romanization' that has often been remarked upon, but which is difficult to interpret.

It is, perhaps, all too easy to imagine the Romans operating (as they themselves sometimes claimed) with a civilizing zeal – bringing the comforts of high culture and literate sophistication to the benighted barbarians. This is, no doubt, part of the story, but only part. As some Roman writers recognized, Romanization was closely linked to domination. Tacitus, for example, writing in the second century AD, tells of the eager adoption of Roman habits by the native élite in the newly conquered province of Britain:

> The natives, who used to reject the Latin tongue, now aspired to rhetoric; even the wearing of our dress became a distinction and the toga came into fashion and, little by little, the Britons were seduced into alluring vices: to the portico, the baths, the well-appointed dinner table. The simple natives called all this 'culture', when it was really a facet of their enslavement. (*Agricola* 21)

In the religious sphere, Romanization was not a matter of the direct export of Roman ritual; the traditional religious festivals – such as the *Lupercalia* or the *Fordicidia* – belonged to the city of Rome, and to Rome only. Romanization of religion is normally seen in terms of the so-called 'interpretatio Romana' – the process by which literally thousands of native deities became assimilated to their supposed Graeco-Roman 'equivalents', often taking a double name (such as Sul Minerva) which combined the Graeco-Roman and native elements. Again, this is a process most difficult to interpret. We cannot know, for example, which deity or what cultural associations were uppermost in the mind of a worshipper of Sul Minerva; it presumably differed from individual to individual. But, as Gordon argues in this chapter, the long-term effect was far from innocent. It led ultimately to the obliteration of native religious traditions by the traditions of the dominant Roman power – Minerva, that is, eventually obliterated Sul.

This final chapter is concerned precisely with the Romans' attempt to impose on the varied communities of the Empire their own type of priesthood and religious organization. It shows how far a religion, originally associated with a single city-state, managed to insinuate or impose its norms throughout a huge Empire; and it asks why, where and with what consequences, opposition or alternatives to the dominant religious system arose.

Religion in the Roman Empire: the civic compromise and its limits

Richard Gordon

The Romanization of the Mediterranean world meant the extension of the dominant Roman model of priesthood and the spread of the 'civic compromise' – that close nexus between sacrifice, benefaction and domination by the élite. This paper explores further the nature and consequences of that extension. How far was the 'civic compromise' spread? With what justification? And within what limits? How serious a threat to the system were competing models of priesthood and religious authority found in the so-called 'oriental' religions? Where should we place images of ascetic world rejection? And how did the élites understand the character of these threats? This paper argues that some of these types of religious authority did indeed challenge the traditional norms, but that most representations of deviant behaviour acted to confirm the efficacy and 'naturalness' of those norms.

Humanitas and superstitio: the 'theodicy of good fortune'

We know, and can know, very little indeed about the attitude of the mass of the population of the Roman Empire towards the sacrificial system maintained by the élites. The great majority of rural populations can have known little of the system anyway; but the populations of cities were ready enough, no doubt, to repay the euergetism of the élites with the return – gratitude, honour and respect – which they required to naturalize their domination.

Moreover the élites took care not to know much about the masses, their real values or concerns. It was better to believe in progress, the progress represented by the imperialism of Rome. Two ideas were of particular value here. The first was the notion that true civilization was now spread from Rome; and its keyword was *humanitas*. It has been aptly remarked that *humanitas* 'is a word which eludes definition', but very roughly we can say that during the first century BC *humanitas*, a translation of the Greek *philanthrôpia*, was appropriated by the Republican aristocracy to connote a range of desirable qualities of civilized individuals, *benevolentia* (goodwill), *observantia* (scrupulousness), *mansuetudo* (kindliness), *facilitas* (affability),

among others.[1] It came to convey a complex class ideal of
enlightenment and urbanity: 'The educative demand (implied in
humanitas) was formed not as a general human demand, in spite of its
grounding in the concept of (common) humanity, but as an estate
demand, which of course bestowed a lofty inner superiority upon the
aristocrat; the content of the demand set at least as much store by
external appearance and amiability as it did upon strength of
character and ethical principles; the idea of humanity was still (in the
late Republic) relatively seldom connected with the word.'[2] It is this
sense which the word has in relation to the *princeps*, whose *humanitas*
became a commonplace in panegyric. Characteristic is the rhetorical
question asked by Pliny the Younger: 'Do we customarily celebrate the
divinity of our Princeps or his *humanitas*, his restraint, his ease of
manner?'[3] This sense is a flattened but flattering reference to the late
Republican ideal largely formed, so far as we know, by Cicero. In the
Principate, the *topos* marks the emperor's membership of a cultural
élite.

But the ambiguity and fluidity of the concept meant that it might
always contain a contrast with *inhumanitas*, and so with 'barbarism'.[4]
Some barbarians might indeed be *humaniores* than others, but that
generally meant that they provided a useful example in the criticism of
non-*humanus* behaviour within the Graeco-Roman world.[5] But these
distinctions were by no means static under the Empire: Rome's
conquering mission brought *humanitas* in its wake – which meant both
the opposite of barbarous and the truly elevated élite ideal of gracious
conduct. We find this sense already in Caesar's Gallic Wars, when he
constrasts the *humanitas* of 'our' province (i.e. Narbonensis, the
southern province of Gaul) with the rudeness of Belgica, and in several
expansive passages of Vitruvius, written during the Principate of
Augustus.[6] Tacitus acidly comments on the confusion in the minds of
the British between *humanitas* and servitude.[7] But the most explicit
passage is Pliny the Elder's praise of Italy: 'a land which is the
nursling and mother of all other lands, chosen by the providence of the
gods to make heaven itself more glorious, to unite empires, to temper
manners, to draw together in mutual comprehension by community of

[1] For this group of related words and concepts, see R. Rieks, *Homo, humanus, humanitas* (Munich, 1967); E.S. Ramage, *Urbanitas; ancient sophistication and refinement* (Norman, Oklahoma, 1973), quote from p. 56; W. Schadewalt, 'Humanitas Romana', *ANRW* I, 4, 43-62.
[2] I. Heinemann, *PW* supp. 5, s.v. 'humanitas', col. 304.
[3] *Pan.* 2, 7 (note also Pliny, *Ep.* 6, 31, 14; 10, 106).
[4] See, for example, Cicero, *Div.* 2, 38, 80; also *Cael.* 11, 26; *Deiot.* 12 32.
[5] For example, Caesar, *BGall.* 4, 3, 3; cf. the ironic inversion of this trope in Tacitus, *Agr.* 21, 2.
[6] Caesar, *BGall.* 1, 1, 3; Vitruvius 2, 1, 6.
[7] *Agr.* 21, 2.

language the jarring and uncouth tongues of so many nations, to give mankind *humanitas* and in a word to become throughout the world the single fatherland of all peoples.'[8] Here the violence and appropriation necessarily involved in Rome's expansion is entirely suppressed in favour of a vision of civilized conduct uniting all the inhabitants of the Empire – a splendid example of the cultural imperialism of the Graeco-Roman élites. *Humanitas* was a useful notion because it suggested that what Rome offered was uniquely beneficent and positive; and among the benefits perceived by Pliny is precisely the 'softening' of foreign manners under the kindly influence of the Graeco-Roman civilization, including its religious assumptions. We may be reminded of Dionysius of Halicarnassus' praise of the superiority of the Romans' religious system over that of the Greeks, saddled as the latter was with ecstatic cults and immoral religious myths.[9]

The second idea which helped to legitimate the spread of the Graeco-Roman sacrificial system was *superstitio*. In the late Republic and early Empire *superstitio* (which originally seems to have meant prophetic ability[10]) generally referred in a contemptuous way to the beliefs and practices of popular religion, especially the popular religion of the countryside.[11] The type of the 'superstitious' person was an old woman living in ignorant poverty far from the city.[12] Now what is of interest in the present connection about the concept of *superstitio*, is that, like *humanitas*, it is based on an implied distinction of value between the centre and the periphery. In the first case, we have seen that *humanitas* was supposed to emanate gradually out from the centre, socially from the *princeps* and the Roman élite, geographically from Italy. The centre-periphery distinction implicit in *superstitio* is slightly different. In this instance, the ideological function of the concept is to represent the implied centre, the religious practices of the élite (the sacrificial system), as rational, appropriate, coherent and effective. We know of course that in another context and under the pressure of Greek radical philosophical doubt individuals within the Roman élite were capable of being scathing about aspects of the religious inheritance of the state.[13] *Superstitio* serves to push that

---

[8] *HN* 3, 5, 39 (tr. Rackham, with changes). I have translated 'ritus' as 'manners'. I would have liked 'ritus' here to mean 'religious habits', but unfortunately 'ritus molles/mollire' is something of a Plinian cliché (e.g. *HN* 2, 80, 190; 6, 14, 35).

[9] Dionysius of Halicarnassus, *Ant. Rom.* 2, 18-23.

[10] See the analysis of E. Benveniste, 'Religion et superstition', in *Le vocabulaire des institutions indo-européennes* (Paris, 1969), 2, 273-9.

[11] The best discussion is by D. Grodzynski, 'Superstitio'.

[12] Cicero, so conscious of his 'humanitas', is the most prominent exponent of this scathing view, especially when he represents men having intelligent conversations at ease in their villas: *Tusc.* 1, 2, 48; *Nat.D.* 2, 2, 5; *Div.* 2, 60, 125.

[13] See p. 192, n. 38, with North, pp. 57-8.

particular ambiguity away. Practices not admitted by the state authorities (the *princeps* and/or the Senate advised or not by the pontiffs and the *XVviri s.f.*) are depreciated by being represented as the property of those who are a double distance from the centre: rustic and uneducated on the one hand, old and female on the other. Superstitious practices do not work; and they are the product of ignorance.

Humanitas and *superstitio* are ideological instruments developed to contain possible threats to the basic assumption of the Graeco-Roman sacrificial system, that those who were at any moment in control deserved to be where they were. It is this view, supported by a religious conception of the world, which Max Weber memorably termed a theodicy of good fortune.[14] The desirability and propriety of extending *humanitas* (who could possibly object to such an ideal?) legitimated the condemnation of 'undesirable' religious practices, such as human sacrifice or the castration of human beings voluntarily or not.[15] *Superstitio* relegated alternative views of the relation between this world and the other world to the limbo of peasant silliness. But it is obvious that a theodicy of good fortune is likely to be of limited interest and value to those who happen not to be blessed by good fortune. If we take the dominant tone of this theodicy to be the relative suppression of the other world in favour of this one, on the assumption (marvellously, and ironically, represented by Pentheus in Euripides' *Bacchae*) that 'we know what the gods are like and how best to deal with them', the opposite tone is likely to be consciousness of cultivation of the 'irrational', awareness of divine irruption into this world (whether the natural world or the social world), and encouragement of mental states alternative to the dominant common sense of the social-political world. It is precisely those manifestations of religion that existed 'out there' or 'down there' from the point of view of the Graeco-Roman élite. The existence of a theodicy of good fortune itself ensured the production of its opposite in the social world excluded from good fortune; and confirmed the objectivity and reasonableness of the category *superstitio*.

There do exist a few traces in the culture of the élite of 'magical'

[14] See, for example, H.H. Gerth and C. Wright Mills, *From Max Weber: essays in sociology* (London, 1948), 271.

[15] For the attempted suppression of human sacrifice by emperors, continuing a Republican precedent, see still F. Schwenn, *Die Menschenopfer bei den Griechen und Römern* (RGVV 15. 3, Giessen, 1915), 185-7. Theophrastus argued that human sacrifice was 'naturally' outmoded, because historically animal sacrifice was its substitute (from Porphyry, *Abst.* 2, 27, 1-2). For castration, see Dio 67, 2, 3; 68, 2, 4; *Dig.* 48, 8, 4, 2; 48, 8, 6. Cf. E. Maas, 'Eunuchos und Verwandtes', *RhM* 74 (1925), 432-76 (with a useful 'Index castratorius') and G.M. Sanders, s.v. 'Gallos', *RAC* 8 (1972), cols. 1003-6; we await the *RAC* entry *Kastration with eagerness.

priesthood, beliefs which served to distinguish priesthood from other civic offices. At Rome, for example, we find the miracle of the shield which fell from heaven and so founded the priesthood of the Salii; or the story of Attus Navius, the archetypal augur, whose miraculous divining of the truth was dependent on natural, innate, magical skill, merely supplemented by formal training with the Etruscan specialists.[16] But these stories belonged to a fabulous past and by the Principate had ceased to represent anything but a world long gone: Livy's treatment is telling – though he emphasises many of the 'original' features of Roman religion, those which could become part of the Augustan revival, it is precisely these 'magical' features which he ignores.[17]

But 'magical' intervention is still found, even in relation to civic priesthood, in the Eastern Empire. Several examples may be adduced here. The first is frankly mythical; it is taken from an epic poem of the fifth century AD – Nonnus' flamboyantly unreadable *Dionysiaca*. Once upon a time, when Typhon, the monstrous earth-born giant, was running amok, he was stopped in his tracks by two words uttered by the local priest, of Zeus Lydios. 'His mouth was his lance, his word a sword, his voice a shield', and he cried 'Stop, wretch!' – which was enough to turn Typhon to jelly. But, as Nonnus later remarks, 'all this was done in time gone by'.[18] The second example concerns a miracle sent by Zeus Panamaros on account of the piety of the priest Diomedes. Diomedes was honoured by his city partly because 'the god sent a most palpable miracle in the form of the bull that was being led up – which coming for the very first time into the city in the procession as it wound its way, carried the priest into the council chamber and after the sacrifice immediately disappeared'.[19] A third example concerns the oracle at Patara in Lycia, which seems to have begun once again to give oracles, after a period of silence, because of the piety of the grand euergete, Opramoas. In other words Opramoas' role as benefactor and priest led to the miraculous reappearance of oracular activity.[20]

It is essential however to underline the subdued character of these miraculous events connected with civic priesthood. The consequence of the intervention is in each case exactly what the sacrificial system

[16] Salii: Dionysius of Halicarnassus, *Rom. Ant.* 2, 70-1; Ovid, *Fast.* 3, 259-392. Navius: Cicero, *Div.* 2, 38, 80; *Leg.* 2, 13, 33; Dionysius of Halicarnassus, *Rom. Ant.* 3, 70-2, 3; Livy 1, 36, 3-6; Plutarch, *Num.* 13, 1-3. On these stories, see M. Beard, 'Acca Larentia gains a son' *Festschrift J. Reynolds* (forthcoming).

[17] Ogilvie, *Commentary*, 90; J.H.W.G. Liebeschuetz, 'The religious position of Livy's history', *JRS* 57 (1967), 45-55; G. Stibler, *Die Religiosität des Livius* (Stuttgart, 1941, repr. Amsterdam, 1964), 3-43.

[18] Nonnus, *Dion.* 13, 483; 498.

[19] G. Cousin, *BCH* 28 (1904) 20-2, no. 1B, 15-22 = *I. Stratonikeia* 1, no. 266, 15-22.

[20] *TAM* II, 905, xiv, 45-52 and xvii, 65-8 = *IGR* III, 739, xiv, 45-52 and xvii, 65-8, with the remarks of L. Robert, *Hellenica* 11-12 (1960), 453, n. 6.

operated by the élite is intended to produce – stability, prosperity, wealth. The gods turn out, through their miraculous interventions, to be just what they are supposed to be. The miracles are 'conservative' miracles; the piety of the priests merely exemplary of the piety of their class as a whole.

Much more disquieting is the appearance of gods to ordinary people. From Didyma, for example, we have an interesting fragment of oracular responses on this subject, responses given to a priestess of Demeter, who had consulted the deity after she had been approached by ordinary people claiming to have had visions of the gods in various guises.[21] This is not of course evidence of religious 'crisis'; it is rather rare evidence of the value of the 'irrational' in preserving among those outside the pale of the theodicy of good fortune a different notion of the location of the boundary between here and there, between this world and the hypothetical other world posited by the religious system. The rapid spread of the cult of Asclepius, especially in Asia Minor during the Principate, the appearance of a rash of healing heroes at hot springs in the same area (the hot springs had of course always been there), the proliferation of minor oracles and small-scale private mysteries, the work of itinerant wonder-workers and 'divine men' such as Apollonius of Tyana – all of these phenomena are so much evidence of the limits upon the acceptance by the mass of the population of the sacrificial model imposed by the civic élites.[22] The category of 'superstition' meant however that such phenomena could easily be dismissed and held to have nothing to do with the validity of the sacrificial system.

The Romanization of religion

The validity of the sacrificial system could also be shored up by extending it in space. Throughout the Roman Empire we can see the conquerors either eradicating competing religious alternatives or implanting their own model of priesthood and religious authority. This process sometimes worked consciously, perhaps more often as the unintended consequence of actions undertaken for different motives. In Asia Minor, for example, with the advent of Roman rule, we observe a shift towards a Graeco-Roman kind of religious organization. Traditionally in the temple-estates or principalities of Asia Minor, as in the Near Eastern kingdoms from which they originated, the high priest had been the chief personage 'after the king' – often in fact a

[21] *I. Didyma* 496A. See Robert, ibid., 544-55; M. Guardicci, *Epigrafia greca*, 4 (Rome, 1978), 97-8; H.W. Parke, *The Oracles of Apollo in Asia Minor* (London, 1985), 82-3. I am glad to have been able to discuss this text with Juan Rodriguez Solomos.

[22] Debord, *Aspects*, 27-40; S.C. Barton and G.H.R. Horsley, 'A Hellenistic cult group and the New Testament churches', *JbAC* 24 (1981), pp. 7-41.

close relative or member of his court.[23] The invasion of Alexander, and even more the development of the hellenistic monarchies, reduced their power and wealth. But even in Strabo's day (our main source on these institutions, writing around the beginning of the Christian era) the most well-preserved (and easterly) of them were controlled by life-long priestly tenure, usually hereditary. This high priest in effect owned, with the restriction that he could not sell, the manpower of the estate, the *hierodouloi*.[24] The response of Rome to this situation varied depending upon the conditions under which the temple-estate came into their possession or notice. Very generally, we may say that the high priests were understood to be dynasts to be rewarded or punished as they served the interests of Rome, and all eventually turned into magistrates of the usual Graeco-Roman kind: high priesthoods became annual and were opened to the local aristocracy; city formation on the estates was encouraged. The dependent *hierodouloi* were given statuses very similar to the *paroikoi* or *incoli* of the older Greek cities of Asia Minor.[25] A variety of motives operated behind Roman actions here, the most important probably being the desire to raise taxes free from interference from an indigenous priesthood which might be the focus for resistance beginning with the issue of taxation. But the 'unintended' solution was to extend the model of the Graeco-Roman sacrificial system.

Egypt presents a slightly different case. Here most sacred land was confiscated by the Roman state when Augustus seized the kingdom in 31 BC; the priests were at once forced to depend upon a government subvention, the *syntaxis* – at a blow their historical privileges were radically weakened. All temple personnel, property and families were registered, the first known registration occurring in 4 BC; by Nero's reign, the property of individual priests was being registered. From this administrative process developed the *graphai hieron*, the annual reports on temple and priestly affairs made to higher officials.[26] Finally, probably in Hadrian's reign, a special high priest was appointed to take over the religious administration from the Prefect: this was purely administrative function. His most commonly attested task was to consider requests to circumcise candidates for the priesthood. Tight control was maintained by the Roman authorities

[23] Strabo 11, 4, 7. See, in general, D. Magie, *Roman Rule in Asia Minor* (Princeton, 1960),128; 140-2; 181-2; 269; 576; 988; 1019-20 etc.; Debord, *Aspects*, 53-61. Note also A. Kuhrt, Chapter 5 above.

[24] Broughton, 'Roman Asia Minor', 636-8; 641-3; P. Briant, 'Rémarques sur les laoi et les esclaves en Asie Mineure hellénistique', *Actes du Colloque de Besançon 1971 sur l'esclavage* (Paris, 1972), 93-133.

[25] Broughton 'Roman Asia Minor', 641-6; 676-84; Debord, *Aspects*, 76-100; 127-84.

[26] For registration of property in Egypt, see J.E.G. Whitehorn, 'P. Lond. II, 359 and Tuscus' list of temple perquisites', *CE* 53 (1978), 321-8; for the *graphai*, O. Montevecchi, '*Graphai hieron*', *Aegyptus* 12 (1932), 317-28.

over circumcision (which they considered to be the same as castration): only Egyptian priests, carefully vetted, and Jews were permitted to practise it.[27] Overall in Egypt we find a traditional and highly non-euergetic priesthood used to considerable latitude and privilege finding its rights gradually eroded by the occupying power, a power indifferent or even downright hostile to their activities.[28] It should, however, be stressed that a Graeco-Roman euergetic priesthood never did develop in Egypt, precisely because of the refusal by the emperors to encourage the building of cities, which was the necessary context for priesthood on the Graeco-Roman model.

In the West, the extent to which any sort of indigenous priesthood survived the Roman conquest is problematic. The most obvious point to make is that made by András Mócsy on Roman Pannonia: 'In Pannonia itself cults made their appearance which, although they may be taken to represent real Pannonian cults, do not show truly local non-Roman traits. Possibly the most essential trait of these cults was that everything about them – the name of the deity, appearance, iconography – was Roman, or at least, they did not show any local traits not elsewhere attested in the empire.'[29] Some fragmentary evidence does exist: cult ornaments dating from the third century AD of a sun and moon priestess from Pannonia;[30] some curious metal crowns, identified as priestly regalia for hardly any good reason, have been found in Southern England;[31] and some sacrificial utensils discovered in an indigenous grave at Mactar in North Africa.[32] But to

[27] On the whole question, see M. Stead, 'The high priest of Alexandria and all Egypt', R.S. Bagnall *et al.* (eds.), *Proceedings XVI Int. Congress Papyrology 1980* (Ann Arbor, 1981), 411-18. For circumcision in Egypt, U. Wilcken, 'Die ägyptische Beschneidungsurkunden', *APF* 2 (1903), 4-13; E.M. Smallwood, 'The legislation of Hadrian and Antoninus Pius against circumcision', *Latomus* 18 (1959), 334-47; 20 (1961), 93-6.

[28] In the Roman period, the priests generally enjoyed exemption from liturgies (see, for example, P. Aberd. 16 – *c.* AD 134; *OGI* 664 – first century AD; S.L. Wallace, *Taxation in Egypt from Augustus to Diocletian* (Princeton, 1936), 145-63) but were in certain circumstances evidently liable to pay taxes on property. On Graeco-Roman prejudice against Egyptian religion, see now K.A.D. Smelik and E.M. Hemelrijk, 'Who knows not what monsters demented Egypt worships? Opinions on Egyptian animal worship in Antiquity as part of the ancient conception of Egypt', *ANRW* II, 17, 3, 1852-2000, esp. 1955-77.

[29] *Pannonia* (London, 1978), 250. See also E. Thomas, 'Religion', in A. Lengyel and C.T.B. Radan (eds.), *The Archaeology of Roman Pannonia* (Lexington-Budapest, 1980), 177-206; G. Alföldy, 'Zur keltische Religion in Pannonien', *Germania* 42 (1964), 54-9.

[30] E. Thomas 'Ornat und Kultgeräte einer Sol und Luna Priesterin aus Pannonien', *AAntHung* 11 (1963), 49-80, esp. 57-9. These finds are in no sense 'primitive', since many of the objects were imported from Italy.

[31] Green, *Corpus of Religious Material*, 177-8 (Woodeaton); 179 (Stony Stratford); 212-16 (Hockwold – 6 crowns of diadems each with adjustable headband). See also M. Henig, *Religion in Roman Britain* (London, 1983), 136-41.

[32] J. Baradez, 'Survivances du culte de Baal et Tanit au 1er siècle de l'ère Chrétienne I: tombe d'un sacrificateur', *Libyca* 5 (1957), 221-75; but see M.H. Fantar, 'Récentes découvertes dans les domaines de l'archéologie et de l'épigraphie punique', *BCTH* NS 5 (1971), 241-64, esp. 257, n. 33.

all intents and purposes such indigenous priestly organization as had existed prior to Roman conquest in the western provinces (which may not have been very extensive) was destroyed by Roman rule: the suppression of the Druids and the German prophetesses are only the most visible instances of a much more widespread, if less violent, phenomenon.[33] Where such roles did not disappear with the spread of Roman social organization, they became assimilated into similar Roman roles: we happen to know of the title *gutuater* at Augustodunum among the Aedui, and among the Vellavi;[34] and of the title *manisnavius* at Verona.[35] In general it seems likely that at least some of the Latin priestly titles, such as *flamines* or *sacerdotes* in Western and African municipalities, reflect the continuance of what were once native priestly roles dating from before the conquest: indeed we know this to be the case in Lepcis Magna, where the native title *addir 'azerim* or *addir kohanim* was transformed into *praefectus sacrorum*.[36] This was in practice a process of obliteration – for we cannot assume that the process of *interpretatio romana* was at all innocent, or that 'ancestral custom' was capable of maintaining traditional roles indefinitely in the changed climate of subjection to Roman power and the extension of municipal status. But it can rarely have been a question of specific acts or specific decisions by emperors or governors.[37] Rather the cultural prestige of Roman forms for the emergent élite together with the institutionalization of the imperial cult after a period of direct military rule ensured the rapid development of a 'normal' sacrificial system. As P.-A. Février has observed of the situation in North Africa: 'The Graeco-Roman divinities were really in the African situation the divinities of a class which, in the city, in the provincial assemblies, and in relation to the

---

[33] Druids: Pliny, *HN* 30, 4, 13; Suetonius, *Claud.* 25, 5; Tacitus, *Hist.* 4, 54, 2 (AD 70) shows that the attempt to suppress them had by then not been entirely successful. On the other hand, there is very little real evidence to support the contention that the Druids became a powerful force again in the late Empire: E. Bachelier, 'Les druides en Gaule romaine', *Ogam* 11 (1959), 46-55; 173-84; 295-304; 12 (1960), 91-100, has much evidence of Druids, but not of Romanized Celtic religion. Human sacrifice almost certainly continued in Britain: 6 cases of decapitated and bound middle-aged women are known from the area of Durotriges (Green, *Corpus of Religious Material*, 73-4).

[34] Aedui: *CIL* XIII, 11225; 11226; 2585; Vellavi: XIII.

[35] *CIL* V, 3931-2; cf. C.B. Pascal, *The Cults of Cisalpine Gaul* (Coll. Lat., 75, Brussels, 1963), 65.

[36] *IRT* 80, no. 27, 30, 32 – compared with 319, 321-23, 347 (AD 192).

[37] See, especially, on the effective, but 'unintended' Romanization of Gallic religion, M. Clavel-Lévêque, 'Le syncretisme gallo-romaine, structures et finalités', in F. Sartori (ed.), *Praelectiones patavinae* (Univ. Padova, Pubbl. Ist. di Storia antica, 9, Rome, 1972), 51-134; cf. R. Carré, 'Cultes et idéologie religieuse en Gaule méridionale', *MHA* 5 (1981), 131-42 (on Narbonensis).

governor, possessed the power.'[38]

The relationship between traditional Roman forms and Judaism seems different again. But the conflicts between the Roman authorities and the Jews in Judaea are only a particularly well-known and complex example of the much more widespread conflict between models of priesthood. This was essentially a conflict between an 'oriental' model according to which priests had extensive social and economic authority as priests and as members of privileged religious foundations originally set up by kings, and the Graeco-Roman model, of euergetistic sacrificial status ambiguously differentiated from magistracy, itself undergoing considerable change in the Hellenistic and imperial periods. Much of the conflict between Palestinian Jews and the Roman authorities centred around the appointment of the high priest, in a context made almost incomprehensibly complicated by three fundamental factors. First, the Maccabean revolt against the Syrian kings had created a justification and precedent for violence, martyrdom and conflict against intrusive outsiders.[39] Secondly, the Romans had offered the Jews protection and privileges during the late Republican and triumviral period which it later became inconvenient to honour.[40] Thirdly, Judaea was riven with unresolvable internal conflicts, which repeatedly led one group or other to attempt to win by 'unfair' means. For example, the attempt by the Pharisees in *c*. 64 BC to split the role of ethnarch from that of the high priest under Hyrcanus I led directly to Gabinius' murderous attack on Aristoboulus and his party (supported by the Temple priests) and the subsequent defilement by the curious Pompey of the Holy of Holies.[41] But essentially the Romans attempted to treat the Jews much as they treated, with more success, the temple kingdoms in Asia Minor (which the Jewish state resembled). After AD 6 the political character of the high priest was made clear by causing him to be appointed by the governor of Judaea or the legate of Syria.[42] From this point it was agreed that the high priesthood should become an annual office on the Graeco-Roman

[38] 'Religion et domination dans l'Afrique romaine', *DHA* 2 (1976), 305-63 (quote p. 326). Février well emphasises the diversity of possible religious structures in the Empire, though he exaggerates the role of religion as political ideology. It is too much to claim that religion played a *determining* role in Rome's political and cultural domination; Graeco-Roman religious structures simply could not be mobilized in that way.

[39] For an excellent example, see Josephus, *Ap.* 1, 42-3; cf. W.H.C. Frend, *Martyrdom and Persecution in the Early Church* (Oxford, 1965), 33-59.

[40] Josephus, *AJ* 14, 185-267; 1302-23. See now T. Rajak, 'Was there a Roman charter for the Jews?' *JRS* 74 (1984), 107-23, attacking the legalism of traditional conceptions of the award of these privileges.

[41] Josephus, *AJ* 13, 288-99; cf. B. Lifshitz, 'Jérusalem sous la domination romaine: histoire de la ville depuis la conquête de Pompée, *ANRW* II, 8, 444-89, esp. 444-5.

[42] Josephus, *AJ* 20, 251; E.M. Smallwood, *The Jews under Roman Rule* (Leiden, 1976), 148.

model, even if a compromise was in practice reached, and regular re-appointment became normal: Joseph Caiaphas was high priest for nearly twenty years, and was replaced in AD 37 by his brother-in-law.[43] Under these informal rules – 'autonomy' for Jewish religion, as an ancestral religion, Jewish control over the priestly vestments but Roman control over the high priesthood – the inherent problems of Roman rule over Judaea were shelved until 65-66. After the defeat of the Jewish revolt in 70, which of course involved the destruction of the Temple, the Sanhedrin was replaced as the supreme Jewish religious body by a body of rabbis (who were not priests), whose head, the Nasi, replaced the high priest in Roman eyes (hereditary priests of course continued to exist). The rabbis at Jamnia took over the organization of the religious calendar and the regulation of festivals.[44] Thus the Jewish situation remained somewhat anomalous, even though they had been defeated.

In general, however, we should conclude that the Roman authorities ended by encouraging the formation of civic élites, and therefore extending the civic compromise, in relation to priesthood, widely over the Empire. The areas most difficult to incorporate into the model were the areas with traditional systems markedly incompatible with it. But even here some characteristic changes were made in the direction of the civic compromise. The subordination of the religious system to the political was one hallmark of 'Romanization'. But even while the Empire abroad was being tamed in this way, in Italy itself the so-called oriental religions constituted a possible threat to the civic compromise. But were they in fact a threat?

'Oriental' religions

It seems likely that the dominant sacrificial model imposed itself to a considerable extent upon the structure of the so-called 'oriental' religions in the Principate, especially in the western provinces. The most important consideration here is the fact that the *XVviri s.f.* in Rome had the authority to certify any cult which wished to set up in public: we know of several occasions on which such permission was granted, even in the third century AD.[45] Although in theory pontifical rules did not apply outside Italy, it was always open to emperor and

[43] Smallwood, ibid. 172-3.

[44] J. Neusner, 'The formation of Rabbinic Judaism: Yavneh (Jamnia) from AD 70-100', *ANRW* II, 19.2, 3-42, stresses the continuity between Rabbinism and Pharisaism, in particular. On the Nasi, L.I. Levine, 'The Jewish patriarch in third-century Palestine', *ANRW* II, 19. 2, 649-88; J.R. Brown, *Temple and Sacrifice in Rabbinic Judaism* (Evanston, 1973). On the question of vestments, Josephus, *AJ* 20, 11-14, 260-2.

[45] For example, *CIL* X, 3698 (AD 289); 3699 (AD 251); XII, 1567 (AD 245); esp. XIII, 1751. Strictly speaking, such evidence is available only for the cult of Magna Mater (and of Ceres, closely associated: X, 129).

Senate to impose what rules they thought fit to impose.[46] Although the 'oriental cults' began in most places as purely private cults, they were not immune to that widespread pattern in the ancient world whereby 'ancestral tradition' gradually enlarged itself to include originally private cults. This was the basic way in which civic cults succeeded in not becoming fossilized despite the proclaimed commitment to tradition. Individual private cults were absorbed by cities, and their priesthoods entered the roll of civic priesthoods. This occurred both in the case of the Mater Magna (Cybele) and in that of Isis. Surveys of the social status of officials of these cults in the Principate suggests that many of them were relatively wealthy; and the inscriptions frequently record that dedications were made to those gods on land given by the local council. Moreover there is every indication that in the West at least these were typically cults of freedmen, of the upwardly socially mobile (both in terms of wealth and status).[47] As this group in the late Republic and early Principate ascended the foothills of the local aristocracies, so the social profile of the membership of their cults gradually rose. The significant ceremonies in these cults were of course processions, and they could therefore be very easily absorbed, at least in part, into the pattern of municipal religious life.[48]

But in one respect they were very different: they offered numerous positions for the faithful in rituals and sacred buildings, and in their collegiate organization. Sometimes, as in the cult of Isis, these were filled mostly by foreigners; but increasingly we find local recruitment as the Principate wore on and these cults became routinized and institutionalized in the local context.[49] In effect, they offered a compromise between the 'oriental model' of priesthood, or rather of religious service, and the Graeco-Roman model of sacrificial euergetism. Certainly it is difficult to fit the well-known image (Fig. 31) of L. Lartius Anthus, the priest of Ma-Bellona in the Capitoline Museum in Rome, with his ecstatic dancing, his long hair and rolling eyes, his whip and two double-axes for self-flagellation, into any familiar kind of Graeco-Roman religious practice. And this is an

[46] The rule is stated by Trajan (Pliny, *Ep.* 10, 69; cf. 10, 49; 70-71) in relation to graves, which were in Roman law *religiosa*. It is clear, however, that Pliny was unsure whether pontifical law did or did not operate outside Italy, and the lawyers were equally vague – see Gaius, *Inst.* 2, 7.

[47] The Egyptian evidence is usefully summarized by Dunand, 'Cultes égyptiens', esp. 74-82. The example of Jupiter Dolichenus has been studied by P. Merlat, *Juppiter Dolichenus: essai d'interprétation de synthèse* (Paris, 1960).

[48] M.P. Nilsson, 'Die Prozessionstypen im griechischen Kult', in *Opuscula Selecta* 1 (Lund, 1951), 166-88; cf. R. MacMullen, *Paganism in the Roman Empire* (New Haven and London, 1981), 18-34. There is too much evidence for processions in the cults of Isis, Mater Deum, Jupiter Dolichenus and other Syrian deities to list here.

[49] *CIL* VI, 2233 = *ILS* 482; Museo Capitolino, inv. 2022. See E. Strong, 'A sepulchral relief of a priest of Bellona', *PBSR* 9 (1920), 205-13. Date: probably early third century AD.

Fig. 31. Relief from the Capitoline Museum, Rome, showing a priest of Ma-Bellona in Rome. The goddess was created by the conflation of the Ma of Cappadocia (in Asia Minor) with the Roman war-goddess Bellona. The inscription below identifies the priest as L. Lartius Anthus.

expensive memorial set up by a private individual: it is impossible to write it off as emanating from the lower orders. Despite the effort to domesticate them, the oriental cults did constitute a permanent reminder of the oddity of the Graeco-Roman political form of priesthood.

This presentation of an alternative (I do not of course claim that *all* priesthood in the Graeco-Roman world was euergetic: Pausanias has plenty of examples of an older simpler model, including temple-guardianship[50]) to the Graeco-Roman model must be in some way connected with the relative success of these cults, especially those of

[50] For example, 1, 22 3; 26, 5; 2, 27, 4; 3, 16, 1; 16, 10; 4, 9, 4-8 etc.

Cybele and Isis. Shaving one's head, dancing, ecstasy, fasting, self-flagellation and even castration, the familiar means of working on the body in order to gain spiritual goods which we find mocked in Graeco-Roman sources as 'barbaric', all of these were options within the context of the oriental cults. They all mark goals quite different from those enshrined in the theodicy of good fortune, whose religious system had reduced even Dionysus to mere jollity.[51] For ecstasy involves the loss of that dignity so carefully projected by the honorific statues which enshrine so much of the civic élite behavioural ideal.

The older oriental cults thus constituted one form of theoretical boundary to the validity of the model of civic religion. Although to some extent, due to socio-economic factors, their priesthoods became acceptable within the civic model – and to that extent routinized, as systems of belief and action they were basically orientated toward religious goals quite different from those enshrined in civic religion. Another way of expressing this point is to say that they were organized, specialized religious sub-systems of popular culture. Though they were, in fact, cultural borrowings (the mechanism of transfer is not here important), they provided specialized institutions for the expression of popular conceptions of religious goals quite different from those of the élite. They should therefore be understood as implicitly opposed to élite culture; and were duly, if vainly, attacked by the élite in the late Republic, as by successive emperors in the first century AD. The attacks were based on moral grounds; but the point lay in the unstated premise that 'real' Romans only do and want certain kinds of things. To the extent that the older oriental cults provided specialized institutions for the expression of popular cultural religious goals, they can properly be seen as forms of resistance to dominant élite goals. But there were other forms of resistance too.

'Intellectual' resistance: asceticism and the mysteries of Mithras

The most familiar to us of these forms of resistance are images produced by intellectuals, who may have been leisured but who were also to some degree free from the dominant norms of the élite. These texts all describe communities of ascetic holy men (and sometimes women), who separate themselves from the world by deliberate act of will, frequently reinforced by oaths. The basis of their life is rejection of the ordinary world, above all rejection of the family and private property, the two institutions at the centre of the Graeco-Roman sacrificial system. This rejection is at the same time an implicit claim

---

[51] cf. Plutarch's complaint that in his day the cult of Dionysus was being celebrated with excessive splendour (*De Cupiditate Divitiarum* 8, 527d); cf. H. Jeanmaire, *Dionysus* (Paris, 1951), 424-5; 434-6.

about the location of the boundary between this and the other world: the individual is seen as the meeting-point between flesh, understood to be in some degree evil, and the spirit, understood as pure, at least in principle; the other world is presented as in some sense individually present within the self.[52]

Individual asceticism is an obviously universal possibility, and duly occurs in Graeco-Roman religious history. But all our texts on the ascetics, except those concerning the Pythagoreans (which are third century AD even if based on earlier material), place their communities in the world outside Graeco-Roman civic space, in Egypt, Judaea and India. Philo and Josephus (Jewish writers of the early Principate) both note the communal atmosphere of harmony, simplicity and serious concern for learning; Philo emphasises the difference between the Graeco-Roman banquet, marked by various kinds of sexual and other excess, and the chaste, simple meals of the community of Therapeutae; Josephus stresses the Essenes' philosophical or religious theories of corruption of the flesh and immortality of the soul, and the consequent rules for bodily purity.[53]

In our present context, however, the most relevant text is Chaeremon's account, preserved in Porphyry's *De Abstinentia* (*On Abstinence*), of the life of the Egyptian priests who chose the temples as the place to philosophize.[54] They were treated more or less as sacred animals, like crocodiles and the Apis bull, or the sacred lions, and were forced to mingle with the people only at festivals. They neither worked nor received rents, but concentrated upon holiness. 'Through this vision they procured for themselves honour, security and piety.' They trained their bodies in stillness and self-control, even striving not to blink despite the desire to do so, and refraining from laughter out loud. There were numerous regular and special rules concerning diet, based upon theories about the animal and plant worlds. And there were particular rules to be observed before festivals: 'Then they spent a number of days in preparation, some forty-two, others more, others less, but never less than seven days. And during this time they abstained from all animal food, from all vegetables and pulses, but above all from sexual intercourse with women, for (needless to say) they never at any time had intercourse with males. They washed

---

[52] For various different groups, see, for example, Philo, *De Vita Contemplativa* 21-47; 64-90 (on the Therapeutae); Philo, *Quod Omnis Probus Liber Sit* 75-88; Pliny *HN* 5, 17; Josephus, *BJ* 2, 119-161; *AJ* 18, 1, 18-21 (all on Essenes); Philo, *VA* 3, 10-50 (on Brahmins); Iamblichus, *De Vita Pythagori* 74.

[53] Simplicity: Philo, *De Vita Contemplativa* 24; 27-8; 34; *Quod Omnis Probus Liber Sit* 76-7; Philostratus, *VA* 3, 15; 6, 10; symposia: Philo, *De Vita Contemplativa* 40-82; purity: Josephus, *BJ* 2, 154-8; Philo, *Quod Omnis Probus Liber Sit* 84; Iamblichus, *De Vita Pythagori* 74.

[54] *Abst.* 4, 6-8. See now the excellent edition by P.W. Van der Horst, *Chaeremon, Egyptian priest and Stoic philosopher* (EPRO 101, Leiden, 1984), fr. 10.

themselves three times a day with cold water, that is, when they rose from bed, before lunch and before going to sleep. But when they happened to have an ejaculation during their sleep, they immediately purified the body in a bath. In other daily matters they also used cold water, but not so very much' (tr. Van der Horst). Long hours at other times were devoted to learning, astronomy and mathematics. 'Their limitless and incessant labour bears witness to the endurance of these men, the absence of desire to their self-control.'[55] Many of these facts can be corroborated from Herodotus' account of the priestly traditions in Egypt,[56] but it is obvious that for Chaeremon, a Stoic philosopher as well as an Egyptian priest (and tutor to the emperor Nero), the main purpose of rehearsing them is their implicit critique of the Graeco-Roman model of civic priesthood.

If we move from representation to reality, the same appeal, to learning and asceticism, and the same implicit critique, may be found in numerous secret religions of the Empire. We may take as an example the mysteries of Mithras, which developed in the Roman world from the late first century AD. The major objective of this cult lay in the provision of religious truth through asceticism and through knowledge of the heavens understood as a veil or screen of truth. The precise significance of the central icon of this cult – the killing of the bull by Mithras – is unclear; but it is evident that it in some sense refers to the rules for Graeco-Roman civic animal sacrifice, and rejects them.[57] Having no public processions, it seems to have been virtually immune, in the Latin-speaking West, to the civic takeover so frequent in the case of cults of the Mater Magna and Isis. And its conception of priesthood, quite different from traditional Graeco-Roman civic priesthood, certainly demanded religious commitment and progress.

The nature of priesthood and priestly authority in the cult of Mithras is well illustrated by the numerous wall paintings of the early third century AD in the temple of Mithras surviving beneath the church of Santa Prisca on the Aventine in Rome.[58] One of these shows a private, ideal procession of the seven Mithraic grades, each of which

[55] *Abst.* 4, 7 = Van der Horst, ibid. 18-20.

[56] Herodotus 2, 37-47, with A.B. Lloyd, Herodotus Book II, commentary 1-98 (EPRO 48, Leiden, 1976), 164-89.

[57] R. Turcan, 'Le sacrifice mithraique: innovations de sens et de modalités' in *Le sacrifice dans l'antiquité* (Entretiens Fondation Hardt 27, 1980 – Vandoeuvres, 1981), 341-72, esp. 352-64, though I have serious doubts about his interpretation of these iconographic differences; cf. R.L. Gordon and J.R. Hinnells, 'Some new photographs of well-known Mithraic monuments', *JMS* 2 (1978), 199-223. See now R. Beck, 'Mithraism since Franz Cumont', *ANRW* II, 17. 4, 2002-15, esp. 2079-83.

[58] C.C. Van Essen and M.J. Vermaseren, *The Excavations in the Mithraeum of the Church of Santa Prisca in Rome* (Leiden, 1965), 98-109; E. Paparatti, 'I dipinti del mitreo di S. Prisca, stato attuale', in U. Bianchi (ed.), *Mysteria Mithrae* (EPRO 79, Leiden, 1979), 887-913, esp. 903-3.

is represented as a young man, beardless and grave. Six men file past, facing a seated person who wears a red robe and a 'Phrygian cap'. This figure undoubtedly represents, schematically like the other paintings, a *Pater*, Father, the highest of the grades, associated, as the painted text above him makes clear, with the highest and most distant of the seven planets, Saturn.[59] Part of the significance of this procession lies in the ambiguity of this figure of the Father. Inasmuch as he emblematizes a ritual position attainable by human beings, he belongs to the world occupied by the members of the procession of grades which approach him. But insofar as his clothes are the clothes of the god Mithras, he is not merely a man, he is not fully part of this sublunary world.

Moreover, the Mithraic grade-system is patterned upon the order of nature, in that each grade is under the protection of the appropriate planet in the heavens. The basis of the Mysteries' organization was not then history nor convention but nature, and the most visibly divine part of nature at that. Because the authority of priesthood in non-traditional cults such as the Mysteries of Mithras could not be sustained by the usual appeals, new, more specifically religious and more pointedly evocative claims had to be made for them. And a new, 'scientific' conception of the order of the universe, which could be validated independently of appeal to religious revelation, was one of the most powerful foundations that could be conceived for such a novel authority.

This second type of limitation upon the validity of the civic model of priesthood depended upon an entirely different conception of important religious goals. They were essentially world-denying religious traditions and they therefore developed forms of authority, fictional or real, which corresponded to those different goals. The justification for the authority of ascetic priests lay properly in personal purity and religious learning, which together formed a revalued conception of piety; and their authority was conceived as a private matter, without public implications. But these alternative models for religious goals existed only in literary traditions and in secret, illegitimate (not illicit) cults about which virtually nothing was known generally: for example, we only know anything at all about the doctrines of the mysteries of Mithras because they were useful to the neo-Pythagoreans in the Principate searching for intriguing examples of esoteric doctrines. The same point surely applies to early Christianity, whose world-denying features are well known.

But it was only Christianity which refused sacrifice, which meant in practice advocating a meatless diet. Otherwise vegetarianism was

---

[59] See R.L. Gordon 'The sacred geography of a *mithraeum*: the example of Sette Sfere', *JMS* I (1976), 119-65.

either merely ideal, as in the literary ascetic tradition, or was the practice of small numbers of philosophers (Seneca tried it as a young man, for example), perhaps too of the highest grade of Mithraists. The refusal of sacrifice was, in fact, the most uncompromising possible rejection of the civic model, and it marks off Christianity from all other organized sects of the empire, as the only one to take this stand.

Magicians and night-witches: the threat of disorder

The élites of the empire did not see things in quite this way. *Their* principal enemies were ones *we* think of as mere phantoms. To end this discussion of the extent and limits of the validity of the civic model, then, we should return to the realm of representations. We should ask, whom did the élites of the Empire conceive as their major symbolic enemies? What religious authority was understood to be most hostile to the 'civic compromise'? What was the ideological boundary of greatest importance to them?

In order to set these question in perspective, two preliminary points should be made. First, there is no reason to believe that the dominant model of the relation between the other world and the social order could have been seriously eroded, given the social and cultural power of the élite, while a theodicy of good fortune remained plausible. But the third-century crisis, like the late-Republican civil wars, undoubtedly brought a degree of disconfirmation, and so made alternative models at least temporarily more attractive. Sacrificial euergetism could be an effective religious mode as long as the political system of the Empire was stable enough to permit the constant accumulation of symbolic capital by the élite.

Secondly, the civic model succeeded ultimately because it was able to naturalize itself. By appropriating sacrifice, the élite announced its protection of the social rules implicit in sacrifice – sex roles, family structure, rules for food, in short, 'our way of life'. We are all familiar with the attacks made by the dominant culture upon those who failed to conform to the religious norms: they were branded as sexual perverts, consumers of forbidden food – especially human flesh – and as murderers and destroyers of the family.[60] A report by Dio Cassius of the activities of the Cyrenaic Jews during the revolt of AD 115 is characteristic: 'They would eat flesh of their victims, make belts of their entrails, anoint themselves with their blood and wear their skins for clothing.'[61] These are the standard accusations against small sects,

---

[60] The logical relationship between these accusations and the 'normal' sacrificial system will be clear to readers of J.-P. Vernant and M. Detienne, *La Cuisine du sacrifice en pays grec* (Paris, 1979) and M. Rosellini and S. Saïd, 'Usages des femmes et autres nomoi chez les "sauvages" d'Hérodote: essai de lecture structurale', *ASNP* 8. 3 (1978), 949-1005.

[61] Dio 68, 32, 1-2.

most notoriously the Bacchanals of 186 BC, fully described by Livy, but also the followers of Isis, or the adherents of Ma-Bellona, against Gnostics and Christians.[62] The accusations emphasise the extent to which civic animal sacrifice operated as a nodal motif in the Graeco-Roman world, a shorthand for acceptable adherence, whatever one's social position to the rules of the social order. Moreover there occurred a gradual shift in the meaning of *superstitio* during the first and second centuries of the Principate, from the sense of peasant religion to the sense of 'dangerous foreign religion, the religion of those who refuse to belong properly to our civilization'; and the imagery associated with this sense comes to be that of contagion and of disease.[63]

Now it is not Christianity which first impelled the development of this sense of *superstitio*, despite its radical rejection of the entire sacrificial system and its invention of names for those in authority in the new Church entirely different from the words in the pagan society around them.[64] The Christians were thought of as small fry, an obscure sect. No new ideas were developed against them. Rather the fundamental enemies of the Graeco-Roman sacrificial system supported by the pious order of the Principate were 'atheists' and 'magicians'.[65] Atheists were those who, refusing to believe in gods, refused to sacrifice. Magicians were those who perverted the sacrifical code for their own evil ends. Of the two, magicians were the more dangerous. Why should the religious systems of the Empire have represented magic, and especially necromancy, as its most horrific enemy?

I suggest that just as the emperor fulfilled the central role of paradigmatic sacrificer and euergete, offering himself as the ideal model not only to the élites of the Empire but to any for whom the theodicy of good fortune seemed appropriate, so the magician fulfilled the inverse function: the perfect illustration of what it was not to

[62] R.M. Grant, 'Charges of "immorality" against various religious groups in antiquity', in R. van den Broek and M.J. Vermaseren (eds.), *Mélanges G. Quispel* (EPRO 91, Leiden, 1981), 161-70; cf. A. Henrichs, 'Pagan ritual and the alleged crimes of the early Christians', in P. Granfield and J.A. Jungmann (eds.), *Kyriakon: Mélanges J. Quasten* (Münster, 1970), 1, 18-35; J. North, 'Religious toleration in Republican Rome', *PCPhS* 25 (1979), 88-92; 94.

[63] Grodzynski, 'Superstitio', 47-8, who dates this process to the early second century AD; in fact it occurs as early as Pliny the Elder's sections on the history of magic – *HN* 30, 2, 7-8. Contagion: Pliny, *Ep.* 10, 96, 9; Tacitus, *Ann.* 15, 44, 5.

[64] In effect *hierus* and *sacerdos* do not become part of Christian vocabulary until the fourth century AD; H. von Campenhausen, 'Die Anfänge der Priesterbegriffs in der alten Kirche', *Svensk exegetisk Arsbok* 4 (1939), 86-101: M. Jourjon, 'Rémarques sur la vocabulaire sacerdotal dans la 1ᵃ Clementis', in J. Fontaine and Ch. Kannengiesser (eds.), *Epektasis; Mélanges J. Daniélou* (Paris, 1972), 107-10.

[65] A.D. Simpson, 'Epicureans, Christians and atheists in the second century', *TAPhA* 72 (1941), 372-81; N. Brox, 'Zum Vorwurf der Atheismus gegen die alte Kirche', *TThZ* 75 (1966), 274-82.

Richard Gordon

belong, of an anti-social being who refused all co-operation with others, all social intercourse, all human meaning, all proper hierarchy. The emperor could afford to register his role in precious metals, in paint and in stone, and thereby provide an iconography of sacrificial orthodoxy, widely copied all over the Empire by other, private, sacrificants on provincial monuments and altars, on which the rows of sacrificial instruments declare as loudly as any actions conformity to the social norms. But the magician, a creature of fantasy, has no such imagery.

Nevertheless the magician or rather a special form of magician, the night-witch, is an indispensable element in the naturalization of the sacrificial system in this particular social order.[66] The night-witch emblematizes the chaos which would ensue without the emperor in his religious role, the social disorder which is dispelled by the politico-religious order he maintains. As one might expect, the fullest image of this demonic power occurs in poetry, in Lucan's accounts in Book 6 of the *Pharsalia* of the Thessalian witch Erichtho.[67]

Erichtho stands for access to forbidden power. She appears on the stage of history from nowhere in a double sense: she is Thessalian and she is female. She operates by means of incantation, the opposite form of utterance to the public, articulate speech of the forum, law-court, panegyric or public sacrifice. She performs a crazy sort of cooking, which refuses both normal female roles and the produce of the fields.[68] She works in the dark, filthy, pallid, childless; she disturbs the natural order of nature, drawing down the moon, reversing the course of the stars and summoning storms. She has foreknowledge through raising the dead, through necromancy, a reversal of the proper procedures of funerals.[69] She refuses proper sacrifices, using revolting dead animals for her sacrificial rites.[70] And finally she is a cannibal, sucking the putrid flesh of corpses as though she were a vulture or a dog: 'When the dead are coffined in stone (i.e. in a sarcophagus), which drains off the internal moisture, absorbs the corruption of the marrow, and makes

[66] The term 'night-witch', which corresponds to various terms in indigenous languages, is a term used by L. Mair, *Witchcraft* (London, 1968), ch. 3, to distinguish the normal, or 'everyday' witch, who can be identified and accused, from the witch who can never be known, who simply destroys without motivation, from sheer malice, and especially attacks the social and emotional bases of common life. Night-witches may be either male or female.

[67] Lucan 6, 413-830. On the episode in general, W. Fauth, 'Die Bedeutung der Nekromantie-szene in Lukans Pharsalia', *RhM* 118 (1975), 325-44 is to my mind the best discussion. See also M. Paratore, 'Seneca e Lucano, Medea und Erichtho', *Hispania Romana* (Rome, 1974), 169-79.

[68] Incantation (refusal or prayer): 523-6; as odd speech: 685-93; inverted cooking: 670-84; child murderer: 557-8.

[69] Reversal of nature, storms: 461-84; darkness etc: 515-20; 642-51; reversal of funerals: 529-37.

[70] No proper sacrifice: 524-5; parts of dead animals to create *venenum*: 670-84.

the corpse rigid – then she vents her rage eagerly on all the limbs, thrusting fingers into the eyes, gleefully scooping out the stiffened eyeballs, and gnawing the yellow nails on the withered hand' (6. 538-43, tr. Duff with changes).[71]

Erichtho is a solitary parodic sacrificant, an anti-emperor, a vision of ultimate disorder, a nightmare in flesh. By contrast, the world maintained by the dominant order is rational, purposive and coherent. The elaboration of a fantasy of the night-witch or 'nightmare magician' should be seen in relation to the successful extension in the principate of a model of normal sacrifice and the social world it subtends. Magical power is conceived as breaking the most fundamental social norms, those enshrined in the practice of civic sacrifice. The magician's purposes are entirely anti-social; he destroys decency, custom and law; he offends the gods; but most of all he threatens the hierarchy of the politico-social order. Literally, magical power may kill anyone, even princes or emperors (we have only to think of the death of the prince Germanicus in AD 19, the victim of sorcery). More insidiously magic offers an escape from 'fate'. It introduces an irrational element into the hierarchy of wealth and power. It creates disorder and confusion in personal relations. It gives women power over men. All these subversions of social order are summarized in the practice of necromantic 'sacrifice', in the images of puppies offered to Hekate, of nameless parts of bodies, of cannibalistic necrophagy. By comparison with the 'nightmare magician', the Christians and other 'atheists' were an insignificant danger to the political order, however much they were despised and even hated by their neighbours.

The political order of the Empire chose its moral enemies well. Being merely structural products, they functioned not as threats to the dominant order, but rather as its allies in its constant task of naturalization, of being taken for granted. One might even say that the moral enemies of the Roman order, from perverts to cannibals, from Christians to witches, were among its most effective friends, making their own contribution to weaving the veil of imperial enchantment. The Roman order attempted to dehistoricize sacrifice. Part of its strategy was to invent 'natural' social diseases which lurked, like germs, in dark cracks, waiting to pounce. In alliance with the civic gods, the emperors, like Vim, kept the sink sparkling.

---

[71] The familiarity of Lucan with techniques of learned magic has been well established since the work of L. Bourgery; see recently L. Baldini Moscadi, 'Osservazioni sull'episodio magico del VI libro della Farsaglia', *SIFC* 48 (1976), 140-99, esp. 142-50; J. Volpilhac, 'Lucian et l'Egypte dans la scène de nécromantie de la *Pharsale* (VI, 413-830) à la lumière des papyri grecs magiques', *REL* 56 (1978), 272-88, though she vastly overestimates the importance of Egypt – Lucan is concerned not so much with learned magic, as with evil power.

Bibliography

This bibliography contains full references to those works cited in the notes by abbreviated title only. The exact form of the short title is given in parentheses after the full reference where it seems helpful.

Adams, R. McC., *The Evolution of Urban Society: early Mesopotamia and prehispanic Mexico* (Chicago, 1966). (*Evolution*)
———, 'Factors influencing the rise of civilization in the alluvium: illustrated by Mesopotamia', in C.H. Kraeling and R. McC. Adams (eds.), *City Invincible: a symposium on urbanization and cultural development in the Ancient Near East* (Chicago, 1960), 24-34. ('Factors')
Beard, M., 'The sexual status of Vestal Virgins', *JRS* 70 (1980), 12-27. ('Vestal Virgins')
———, 'Cicero and divination: the formation of a Latin discourse', *JRS* 76 (1986), 33-46. ('Cicero and Divination')
Beard, M., and Crawford, M., *Rome in the Late Republic* (London, 1985).
Berger, P.-R., *Die neubabylonischen Königsinschriften: Königsinschriften des ausgehenden babylonischen Reiches (626-539 a. Chr.)* (AOAT 4/1, Neukirchen-Vluyn, 1973).
Black, J.A., 'The New Year ceremonies in ancient Babylon: "Taking Bel by the hand" and a cultic picnic', *Religion* 11 (1981), 39-59.
Bleicken, J., 'Oberpontifex und Pontifikalkollegium: eine Studie zur Römischen Sakralverfassung', *Hermes* 85 (1957), 345-66.
———, 'Kollisionen zwischen Sacrum und Publicum', *Hermes* 85 (1957), 446-80.
Bloch, R., *Les prodiges dans l'antiquité classique* (Paris, 1963).
Boels, N., 'Le statut religieux de la flaminica Dialis', *REL* 51 (1973), 77-100. ('Flaminica Dialis')
Bömer, F. (ed.), *P. Ovidius Naso. Die Fasten* (Heidelberg, 1957-58). (*Fasten*)
Bouché Leclercq, A., *Les pontifes de l'ancienne Rome* (Paris, 1871).
Bourdieu, P., *Outline of a Theory of Practice* (Cambridge, 1977).
Boyce, M., *A History of Zoroastrianism II: under the Achaemenians* (Handbuch der Orientalistik, Leiden, 1982). (*History*)
Brendel, O., 'Immolatio boum', *RhM* 45 (1930), 196-226.
Briant, P., *Etat et pasteurs au Moyen Orient antique* (Cambridge, 1982).
Brinkman, J.A., 'Babylonia under the Assyrian Empire, 745-627 BC' in M.T. Larsen (ed.), *Power and Propaganda: a symposium on ancient empires* (Mesopotamia 7, Copenhagen, 1979), 223-50. ('Babylonia')
Broughton, T.R.S., 'Roman Asia Minor', in T. Frank (ed.), *Economic and Social History of Ancient Rome* 4 (Baltimore, 1938), 505-916.
Cardauns, B. (ed.), *M. Terentius Varro Antiquitates Rerum Divinarum* (Wiesbaden, 1976). (*Varros Antiquitates RD*)
Clinton, K., 'The sacred officials of the Eleusinian Mysteries', *TAPhS* n.s. 64

257

(1974), part 3.

Conquerillat, D., *Palmeraies et cultures de l'Eanna d'Uruk (559-520)* (ADFU 8, Berlin, 1968).

Crawford, D.J., 'Ptolemy, Ptah and Apis in Hellenistic Memphis', *Studia Hellenistica* 24 (1980), 1-42.

Dandamaev, M., 'Der Tempelzehnte in Babylonien während des 6-4 Jh. v.u.Z.', *Beiträge zur Alten Geschichte und deren Nachleben, Festschrift für F. Altheim* (Berlin, 1969), 82-90. ('Tempelzehnte')

————, 'State and temple in Babylonia in the first millennium BC', in E. Lipínski (ed.), *State and Temple Economy in the Ancient Near East* (Orientalia Lovaniensia Analecta 6, Leuven, 1979) 2, 589-96. ('State and temple')

————, 'The Neo-Babylonian citizens', *Klio* 63 (1981), 45-9. ('Citizens')

Davies, J.K., *Athenian Propertied Families, 600-300 BC* (Oxford, 1971). (*APF*)

Debord, P., *Aspects sociaux et économiques de la vie religieuse dans l'Anatolie gréco-romaine* (EPRO 88, Leiden, 1982). (*Aspects*)

De Fidio, P., *I dosmoi pilii a Poseidon* (Rome, 1977).

Deimel, A., *Sumerische Tempelwirtschaft zur Zeit Urukaginas und seiner Vorgänger* (An. Or. 2, Rome, 1931). (*Tempelwirtschaft*)

Diakonoff, I.M., *Structure of Society and State in Early Dynastic Sumer* (MANE 1/3. Los Angeles, 1974). (*Society and State*)

Diels, H., *Sibyllinische Blätter* (Berlin, 1890).

Doty, T.L., *Cuneiform Archives from Hellenistic Uruk* (Diss. Yale, 1977). (*Archives*)

Dougherty, R.P., *Nabonidus and Belshazzar: a study of the closing events of the New Babylonian empire* (YOSR 15, New Haven, 1929). (*Nabonidus*)

Dumézil, G., *Archaic Roman Religion* (Chicago, 1970).

Dunand, F., 'Cultes égyptiens hors d'Egypte', in *Religions, pouvoirs, rapports sociaux* (Annales Litt. Univ. Besançon 237, Paris, 1980), 69-148.

Falkenstein, A., *Archaische Texte aus Uruk* (ADFU 2, Berlin & Leipzig, 1936). (*Texte*)

Feaver, D.D., 'Historical development in the priesthoods of Athens', *YClS* 15 (1957), 123-58. ('Priesthoods')

Gadd, J., 'The Harran inscriptions of Nabonidus', *AS* 8 (1958), 35-92. ('Inscriptions')

Gagé, J., *Apollon romain: essai sur le culte d'Apollon et le développement du 'ritus Graecus' à Rome des origines à Auguste* (Paris, 1935).

Garelli, P., s.v. 'Nabonide', *Dictionnaire de la Bible* (Paris, 1961), cols. 269-86. ('Nabonide')

————, *Le Proche Orient Asiatique: les empires mésopotamiens* (Paris, 1974). (*Empires*)

Garland, R., 'Religious authority in Archaic and Classical Greece', *ABSA* 77 (1982), 125-76.

Gelb, I.J., 'On the alleged temple and state economies in ancient Mesopotamia', *Studi in Onore di Eduardo Volterra* 6 (Rome, 1969), 137-54. ('Economies')

Gellner, E., 'Is belief really necessary?', in I.C. Jarvie and J. Agassi (eds.), *The Devil in Modern Philosophy* (London, 1974), 52-63.

Goody, J. *The Domestication of the Savage Mind* (Cambridge, 1978).

Grayson, A.K., 'Chronicles and the Akitu Festival', in A. Finet (ed.), *Actes de la XVIIe Rencontre Assyriologique* (Ham-sur-Heure, 1970), 160-70. ('Akitu Festival')

————, *Assyrian and Babylonian Chronicles* (TCS 5, Locust Valley, NY,

1975). (*Chronicles*)

Green, M., *A Corpus of Religious Material from the Civilian Areas of Roman Britain* (BAR 24, Oxford, 1976).

Grodzynski, D., 'Superstitio', *REA* 76 (1974), 36-60.

Gros, P., *Aurea Templa: recherches sur l'architecture religieuse à l'époque d'Auguste* (BEFAR 231, Rome, 1976).

Güterbock, H.G., 'Die historische Tradition und ihre literarische Gestaltung bei Babyloniern und Hethitern bis 1200', *ZA* 42 (1934), 1-91. ('Tradition')

Guittard, Ch. (ed.), *La divination dans le monde etrusco-italique* 2 (Caesarodunum supp. 54, Univ. de Tours, 1986). (*Divination*)

Guizzi, F., *Il sacerdozio di Vesta. Aspetti giuridici dei culti romani* (Naples, 1962).

Hoffmann Lewis, M.W., *The Official Priests of Rome under the Julio-Claudians: a study of the nobility from 44 BC to 68 AD* (Papers and Mon. of the American Ac. in Rome 16, Rome, 1955). (*Official Priests*)

Hooke, S.H., *Babylonian and Assyrian Religion* (London, 1953). (*Religion*)

Jacobsen, T., 'Early political development in Mesopotamia', in W.L. Moran (ed.), *Toward the Image of Tammuz and other Essays on Mesopotamian History by Thorkild Jacobsen* (Harvard Semitic Series 21, Cambridge, Mass., 1970), 132-56.)

Jacoby, F., *Atthis: the local chronicles of Ancient Athens* (Oxford, 1949).

Kümmel, H.M., *Familie, Beruf und Amt in spätbabylonischen Uruk: Prosopographische Untersuchungen zu Berufsgruppen des 6. Jahrhunderts v. Chr. in Uruk* (ADOG 20, Berlin, 1979). (*Familie*).

Kuhrt, A., 'Assyrian and Babylonian traditions in classical authors: a critical synthesis', in H.-G. Nissen and J. Renger (eds.), *Mesopotamien und seine Nachbarn: politische und kulturelle Wechselbeziehungen im alten Vorderasien vom 4. bis 1. Jahrtausend* (Berliner Beiträge zum Vorderen Orient 1, Berlin, 1982), 539-53. ('Synthesis')

————, 'The Cyrus Cylinder and Achaemenid imperial policy', *JSOT* 25 (1983) 83-97. ('Cyrus Cylinder')

————, 'Conquest, usurpation and ceremonial: from Babylon to Persia', in D. Cannadine and S. Price (eds.), *Royal Rituals* (Cambridge, 1987), 20-55. ('Conquest')

————, 'Babylonia from Cyrus to Xerxes', *CAH* 4 (Cambridge, 1988). ('Babylonia')

Labat, R., *Le caractère religieux de la royauté assyro-babylonienne* (Paris, 1939). ('Caractère religieux')

————, 'Assyrien und seine Nachbarländer (Babylonien, Elam, Iran) von 1000 bis 617 v. Chr.', in E. Cassin, J. Bottéro and J. Vercoutter (eds.), *Die Altorientalischen Reiche III: Die erste Hälfte des 1. Jahrtausends* (Frankfurt-am-Main, 1967), 9-111. ('Assyrien')

Langdon, S., *Die neubabylonischen Königsinschriften* (VAB 4, Leipzig, 1912). (*Königsinschriften*)

————, 'New inscriptions of Nabonidus', *AJSL* 32 (1915), 102-17. ('Inscriptions')

Latte, K., *Römische Religionsgeschichte* (Munich, 1960). (*RRG*)

Liebeschuetz, J.H.W.G., *Continuity and Change in Roman Religion* (Oxford, 1979).

Linderski, J., 'The augural law', *ANRW* II, 16. 3, 2146-312.

MacBain, B., *Prodigy and Expiation: a study in religion and politics in Republican Rome* (Coll. Lat. 177, Brussels, 1982). (*Prodigy*)

Martha, J., *Les sacerdoces athéniens* (Paris, 1882).

Merquior, J.G., *The Veil and the Mask: essays on culture and ideology* (London, 1979).

Momigliano, A.D., 'The theological efforts of the Roman upper classes in the first century BC', *CPh* 79 (1984), 199-211.

Mommsen, Th., *Römisches Staatsrecht* (3rd ed., Leipzig, 1887). (*Staatsrecht³*)

Oates, J., *Babylon* (London, 1979, rev. ed. 1985).

Oelsner, J., 'Erwägungen zum Gesellschaftsaufbau Babyloniens von der neubabylonischen bis zur achämenideschen Zeit (7.4. Jh. v.u.Z., *AOF* 4 (1976), 131-49.

Ogilvie, R.M., *A Commentary on Livy Books I-V* (Oxford, 1965). (*Commentary*)

Oliver, J.H., *The Athenian Expounders of the Sacred and Ancestral Law* (Baltimore, 1950).

Oppenheim, A.L., *Ancient Mesopotamia: portrait of a dead civilization* (Chicago, 1964). (*Mesopotamia*)

Parker, R.A. and Dubberstein, W.H., *Babylonian Chronology 626 BC – AD 75* (Brown University Studies 19, Providence, R.I., 1956). (*Chronology*)

Parpola, S., *Letters from Assyrian Scholars to Kings Esarhaddon and Assurbanipal*, part 2: commentary and appendices (AOAT 5/II, Neukirchen-Vluyn, 1983)

Pötscher, W., 'Flamen Dialis', *Mnemosyne* s. 4, 21 (1961), 215-39.

Postgate, J.N., 'The role of the temple in the Mesopotamian secular community', in P.J. Ucko, R. Tringham and G.W. Dimbleby (eds.), *Man, Settlement and Urbanism* (London, 1972), 811-25.

Price, S.R.F., *Rituals and Power: the Roman imperial cult in Asia Minor* (Cambridge, 1984).

Pritchard, J.B., *Ancient Near Eastern Texts relating to the Old Testament* (rev. ed., Princeton, 1969). (*Texts*)

Quaegebeur, J., 'The genealogy of the Memphite high priest family in the Hellenistic period', *Studia Hellenistica* 24, 43-82. (*Geneaology*)

Radke, G., s.v. 'Quindecimviri sacris faciundis', *PW* 24, 1114-48. ('Quindecimviri)

Rawson, E., *Intellectual Life in the Late Roman Republic* (London, 1985).

Redmond, E.A.E., *From the Records of a Priestly Family from Memphis* 1 (Ägyptolische Abhandlungen Band 38, Wiesbaden, 1981). (*Priestly Family*)

Rhodes, P.J., *The Athenian Boule* (Oxford, 1972)

Richard, J.-C., 'Sur quelques grands pontifes plébéiens', *Latomus* 27 (1968), 786-801.

Röllig, W., 'Erwägungen zu neuen Stelen König Nabonids', *ZA* 56 (1974), 218-60.

Ryberg, I. Scott, *Rites of the State Religion in Roman Art* (MAAR 22, Rome, 1955). (*Rites*)

San Nicoló, M. *Beiträge zu einer Prosopographie der neubabylonischen Beamten der Zivil- und Tempelverwaltung* (SBAW, Phil.-Hist. Abt. 11/2, Munich, 1941).

Scheid, J., 'Le flamine de Jupiter, les Vestales et le général triomphant: variations romaines sur le thème de la figuration des dieux', *Le temps de la réflexion* 7 (1986), 213-30.

————, *Les Frères Arvales. Recrutement et origine sociale sous les empereurs julio-claudiens* (Paris, 1975). (*Arvales*)

————, 'Le prêtre et le magistrat', in C. Nicolet (ed.), *Des ordres à Rome* (Paris, 1984). ('Prêtre')

————, 'Les prêtres officiels sous les empereurs julio-claudiens', *ANRW* II, 16. 1, 610-54. ('Prêtres')

————, *Religion et piété à Rome* (Paris, 1985).

Schilling, R., *Rites, cultes et dieux de Rome* (Paris, 1979).

Schmitt-Pantel, P., 'La festin dans le fête de la cité greque 'hellénistique', in *La fête: pratique et discours* (Centre de Recherche hist. anc. 42, Annales Litt. Univ. Besançon 262, Paris, 1981), 85-99. ('Festin')

Schumacher, L., 'Die vier hohen römischen Priesterkollegien unter den Flaviern, den Antoninen und Severen, 69-235 n. Chr.)', *ANRW* II, 16. 1, 655-819. ('Vier Kollegien')

Scullard, H.H., *Festivals and Ceremonies of the Roman Republic* (London, 1981).

Sethe, K., *Hieroglyphische Urkunden der griechischen-römischen Zeit* (Leipzig, 1904)

Simon, E., *Ara Pacis Augustae* (Greenwich, 1968).

Smith, S., *Babylonian Historical Texts Relating to the Capture and Downfall of Babylon* (London, 1924). (*Historical Texts*)

————, 'Sennacherib and Esarhadon', *CAH* 3 (Cambridge, 1925), 61-87.

————, 'Isaiah Chapters XL-LV, literary criticism and history (London 1944).

Strommenger, E. and Hirmer, M., *The Art of Mesopotamia* (London, 1964). (*Art*)

Szemler, G., *The Priests of the Roman Republic: a study of interactions between priesthoods and magistracies* (Coll. Lat. 127, Brussels, 1972).

Tadmor, H., 'The inscriptions of Nabonidus: historical arrangement', in H.G. Güterbock and T. Jacobsen (eds.), *Studies in Honor of Benno Landsberger* (AS 16, Chicago, 1965), 351-63. ('Inscriptions')

Thulin, C.D., *Die etruskische Disziplin. 1. Die Blitzlehre. 2. Die haruspizin. 3. Die Ritualbücher* (Göteborgs Högskilas Arsskrifter 11 (1905); 12 (1909)). (*Disziplin*)

Thureau-Dangin, F., *Rituels Accadiens* (Paris, 1921).

Torelli, M., *Elogia Tarquiniensia* (Studi e materiali di etruscologia e antichità italiche 15, Florence, 1975).

Voigtlander, E. von, *A Survey of Neo-Babylonian History* (Diss. Ann Arbor, 1963). (*Survey*)

Wiseman, D.J., *Chronicles of Chaldaean Kings (626-556) in the British Museum* (London, 1956).

Wissowa, G., *Religion und Kultus der Römer* (2nd ed., Munich, 1912). (*RK²*)

Wittfogel, K., *Oriental Despotism: a comparative study of total power* (New Haven, 1957). (*Despotism*)

Index